DRUMORE ECHOES,
STORIES FROM UPSTREAM

Drumore Echoes, Stories from Upstream

Tom Smith

Copyright © 2011 by Tom Smith.

Library of Congress Control Number: 2011960155
ISBN: Hardcover   978-1-4653-9273-2
              Softcover   978-1-4653-9272-5
              Ebook   978-1-4653-9274-9

All rights reserved. No part of this book may be reproduced or transmitted in any form or by any means, electronic or mechanical, including photocopying, recording, or by any information storage and retrieval system, without permission in writing from the copyright owner.

This book was printed in the United States of America.

To order additional copies of this book, contact:
Xlibris Corporation
1-888-795-4274
www.Xlibris.com
Orders@Xlibris.com
84978

CONTENTS

Introduction 11

PART ONE: THE BUCK
THE BIGGEST LITTLE TOWN IN THE USA

1. Abner Musser, The Stimulus Of The Buck 27
2. Robert Blair Risk: The Sage of the Buck 42
3. Irene Garner, The Spirit of The Buck 46
4. The Old Buck School Recalled... 51
5. Memories, by Debbie Byers Wenger 54
6. Beagles and Beaglers in The Buck 57
7. Light at the Buck By Stu Mylin... 61
8. Fond Memories of the Buck 62
9. Wrestling in The Buck... 65
10. Softball At The Buck 69
11. Growing Up Near The Buck, By Stu Mylin 74
12. Buck Company 83
13. Black And Blue In The Buck 85
14. Buck Tractor Pull 87
15. Locating The Buck Boys 89
16. Flyin' & Racin' In The Buck 91
17. Sparks in The Buck.. 95
18. Folks Remembered 100

PART TWO: EVERYWHERE
"AROUND" LIBERTY SQUARE

19. Farmhouse with a view.. 105
20. Amish Winter Olympics 108
21. Liberty Square Lions Club...112

22. Sounds From Behind The Barn 116
23. Motivating Morning Meditation 119
24. Halloween in Liberty Square 121
25. Amish Summer Olympics 124
26. Appreciating Susan Boyle 127
27. Thanksgiving 129
28. Public Farm Sales 132

PART THREE: EVERYWHERE "BUT" LIBERTY SQUARE

29. The Old Farmer Duz Stone Harbor 143
30. Mooving Along 153
31. Observations From Local Grocery Store Parking Lots 156
32. The Party Line 164
33. The Old Farmer Duz Woodstock 170

PART FOUR: BEAUTY, FORGOTTEN VOICES AND MEMORIES

34. Scalpy Hollow 179
35. The Blacks Of Fishing Creek Hollow 187
36. Fishing Creek 210

PART FIVE: STORIES "FROM" AND "ON" THE LEVEL

37. Echoes From The Past The Academy 230
38. Echoes From The Past Bats in the Belfry 232
39. Echoes From The Past Church Furniture 234
40. Echoes From The Past The Old Sunday School 236
41. Echoes From The Past Racing Results from Chestnut Level 238
42. Echoes From The Past Christmas Eve 240
43. Echoes From The Present Family Life Center 242
44. Echoes From The Present The Wedding Day—Razing 244
45. Echoes From The Present So Who's in Charge? 247

46. Echoes From The Present Stitchers in Stitches 249
47. Echoes From The Present The Dormant Stone 252
48. Echoes From The Present A Fair to Remember 255

PART SIX: PARADISE LOST

49. Thoughts and Musings 259
50. Armageddon 268

Acknowledgements 273

DEDICATION

To Ken, My closest friend during my entire life through both sunshine and storms. You are the one who continues to regularly provide inspiration and confidence to this less than ordinary life and humble word-winder. Your expertise in grammar and punctuation causes and succeeds in actually making these words readable. I'm greatly encouraged when you laugh at a silly, mind-wondering line then later compliment me on another that you describe as powerful. Because of your praise, you more than anyone should receive the fame or accept the blame for this book. Thank-You, "Ken."

Tom Smith on the left and Ken Denlinger on the right.

Introduction

Before beginning another humble attempt at rearranging and redefining the English language, I offer the following as a thank-you and tribute to all who read "Liberty Square Observed and Noted." I have said to many of you both—publicly and—privately that I am not an author but simply an old farmer who wrote a book. That is how I'm known and how I wish to be remembered. The words "Thank-You" for your overwhelming response to my words seem trivial to the way each of you have expressed a sincere appreciation of my thoughts and observations. The fact that all was written by an old farmer in the language of an old farmer turned out to be an attribute and evidently warrants no apology from me. To the nearly 100 folks who took the time to send me cards, notes, e-mails even a 5 page letter from Sue Hoffer mentioning different chapters and lines from the book—that each of you personally related to, I have saved them all and periodically reread each one. To everyone that called on the phone or thanked me personally, all of your kindness is sincerely appreciated and not forgotten. Unknowingly, each of you filled a void in a most ordinary life that I never knew existed. Consequently, each of you must share the responsibility and shoulder the blame for any further encouraged writings that emanate from the rolling hills around Liberty Square.

During the writing of this book our Church embarked on building a new Community Family Life Center that was greatly needed. It seemed only logical to us to contribute the profits from this book to that project. Therefore our church family became overwhelmingly involved in this large financial undertaking and also greatly participated in buying and selling my book. There were few Sundays following church services, within the quiet confines of the parking lot, that sales between my fellow Presbyterians and me weren't conducted. For fear of retribution I shall not name those who participated in these perhaps unethical Sunday sales but one near 90-year-old lady bought a book every Sunday for 11 weeks.

Our first 2 public book signings were held at our chicken and waffle supper and the original Christmas at the Level with both held in the old Sunday school.

They were very successful and a preview of what was ahead for this reluctant, first time author. It all began with my church family and, through Southern-end conversations, spread without the assistance of any advertisements on my part.

Some local business folks offered to sell my book, keeping nothing for themselves. Those involved were Ferguson and Hassler, Life Song, Powl's Feed, Darrenkamps, Muddy Run Park, DJ's Barbershop, Mussers and Maplecroft. As a result, at the completion of our building this book generated over $10,000.00 toward this project thanks to the generosity of these businesses and all of you. The satisfaction of writing and recording some family and community history is my reward as this was never about personal glory or money. Through word of mouth we have sold somewhere over 2000 copies, the majority of them locally. I am grateful to Jim Wolfe of the Chronicle, Lou Ann Good of Lancaster Farming, Jack Brubaker of the Lancaster Newspaper and Joanne Green of the Sunday News, all gave me great reviews and publicity.

I recall when we received our first shipment of 500 books and Ruthie and I each sitting in our garage observing them. We of course had to buy the books, pay the shipping and the tax. I wanted to only order 50 but the greater the amount ordered the lower the price per book for us so I reluctantly agreed with her to this large amount of 500. Sitting in silence, Ruthie finally looked at me and said, "Well there they are, tell me what you're thinking." I said, "I'm thinking, some day the undertaker is gonna come for me and there's gonna be 475 books under our bed."

Originally, when I began writing I strived to please everyone I wrote about. I soon realized pleasing all others was impossible and in the end, selfishly only wrote to please myself. To anyone I may have offended, I sincerely apologize.

Some of my most appreciated compliments have come from old farmers like me. I shall not list or name all those who worked the land and tended the animals for their entire lives who have contacted me in various forms of communication, commending my book. Many commented that, like the author, they have not been readers with some stating this was the first book they've ever read cover to cover. Everyone desires to be accepted and appreciated by his or her peers. Most of my peers feel more comfortable on a tractor or driving an old dusty pick-up truck with a few unrecalled, unimportant dents than any shiny new vehicle. Their hands will be calloused with a concoction of soil, grease, animal feed and oil very much at home under their fingernails. At least one of their fingers will display tape or a band-aid. A certain percentage will be minus an end or more of a finger. They shave coarse whiskers regularly but not always daily. Beards are optional but are most prevalent and visible on those who have grown tired of the daily shaving routine. Their hair is styled by sweat and an advertising cap from someone they regularly do business with. Upon removal at the end of the day a white sun withheld angel halo is visible across their forehead and completely encircles our farmer's skull. Daily showers are encouraged but not mandatory, motivated and depending on daily activity and outside temperature with 20 degrees or less the cut-off point. Working with and caring for animals 365 days a year, one can easily detect the different odors and observe the manure of the appropriate animal of choice located somewhere on our farmer and always on his footwear. Despite all of these imperfections most of my fellow corncob college fraternity members clean up very well, Thank-You, and fit nicely into even today's society, although most of us realize we are an endangered species. I find it most ironic at this point in time that a mutli-million dollar project may be squelched by a toad or rodent near extinction and a 4th generation farmer can be forced from his land with the use of eminent domain.

Reflections from the Community

Stories from residents relating to my first book continue to surface and are shuffled to me from participants. We met a gal from Quarryville whose family I knew, but not personally. This face-to-face encounter with Claire Ferguson Mastriania occurred as she arrived, sent by our in house contractor, Wayne Lefever, to paint a small downstairs bathroom. Wayne and a plumber, Adam Bilheimer, had installed a shower and new porcelain throne, refurbishing deemed necessary by my wife, Ruthie. The throne, in my own personal man-cave, hopefully a preview of future expectations, resides a full 6 inches closer to heaven than the old one.

These changes were instigated because of upcoming knee replacement for this ol' farmer and the temporary forbidden step climbing to my normal, welcoming, upstairs facilities. In ol' farmer language, I had my engine over-hauled 3 years ago with the addition of a stent in my heart and now required new runnin' gears.

During a conversation with Ruthie, Claire asked if yours truly was any relation to the guy who wrote the Liberty Square book. She seemed startled that it was me and related the following story from her parents. It seems her father, Edsel Ferguson, as he became older and suffering from diabetes not only lost his leg but also suffered from macular degeneration, becoming nearly blind. As a result Claire's mother, Novelda or "Bo," would read to her husband daily. She stated they thoroughly enjoyed my book, as her mom would read a chapter every night to her bed-ridden husband.

Claire relates that their favorite chapter was Farm Dogs and Farm Cats and the scene and vivid description of me unknowingly sitting on a cat in my old truck during total darkness. Claire had arrived unannounced that particular evening. As she cautiously approached her dad's bedroom, and hearing unfamiliar sounds emanating from his bed, she noticed her mom seated closely with book in hand as tears flowed down her cheeks. Totally in shock, expecting the worst, she approached cautiously to discover both were laughing uncontrollably at the vivid description of me and the oxygen-starved puddy cat firmly attached to one another.

I recall Edsel Ferguson from years earlier and remember he thoroughly enjoyed being a soloist or an active vocal participant in a choir of laughter. The fact that my simple, factual account of this trivial event brought brief bursts of amused emotions and enjoyment to this man near the conclusion of his life is the most appreciated, inspiring and gratifying compliment one could ever receive.

Doris Fite, wife of the late cattle dealer Glen, whom I knew well, offered a similar experience to me during his final, bed-fast days. She also read to her husband from my book—and he evidently related to having known many of the characters from these lines of locals. One particular chapter describing my 30-year association with my hired man, Bob Lefever, proved especially amusing to Glen. In that particular chapter I mentioned that Lefever had names for many southern-enders that he knew that possibly, he believed, described them. A few were Ken Probst-"ol' money bags," over weight women-"Tankers," God-"ol boy upstairs" and Glen Fite-"Sly Dog." This eventually became the primary subject of any subsequent conversation between Doris and me, as even she would humorously refer to her late husband as "Sly Dog."

Vera Herr, who retains even a couple more years into the category of senior citizenship than this ol' farmer, was one of the first and most vocal to express her sincere appreciation and enjoyment of my humble words and thoughts. Following a few recent face-to-face confrontations, she expressed her determined desire to read another book containing my local observations. This last conversation between us ended with her stating emphatically, "You know I'm not getting any younger!" Peer pressure promotes and prods the unmotivated. Thank-you, Vera, this one's for you!

Shortly after my first book was published and distributed locally, Loraine Hess Herr, phoned her sincere, appreciated enjoyment. Her friend, Dottie Freese, at a student performance at Solanco High School singled me out following the program. She wished to have her picture taken with me. Unbelievable is what I was thinking when we posed together as spectators gathered, stared, whispered and wondered with very few recognizing either similin' participant as the camera flashed. I recall glancing at Dottie, who seemed pleased, grateful and happy. As for this simple ol' farmer, unknown to all but a handful of the entire crowd that evening, for those brief 2 minutes of stardom extracted from a much less than ordinary existence, I became "Elvis."

I received this most appreciated comment early on from my old, intelligent schoolmate, Glenn Wenger. "I was very impressed with your story telling abilities. The book is very interesting, funny and at points hilarious. Particularly important are the profound, and valuable nuggets of wisdom and insight that you sprinkled in descriptions of everyday relationships between people. I would be quite proud if I would have been able to create such an interesting, insightful and entertaining piece of writing."

During conversations with my late father, near the end of a well-lived life, he uttered these never to be forgotten words to me. These were also the final lines spoken by Rev. Dr. Michael Wilson, our Pastor, at pop's funeral service. "If anyone asks where I'm going, tell them to look in the Bible, it's all there. If anyone asks where I've been, tell them to look in Tom's book, it's also all there." My father died October 1, 2010, stating he had no regrets. No father has ever given a son a more profound, grateful compliment.

As a result of this book friends and distant relatives known and unknown from Seattle to New Jersey and from Germany to Costa Rica have contacted me. A few copies went north to Alaska and one in particular was photographed in the hands of Mitch Huber lounging on a tropical beach. I've been told a copy went along with Mechanic Grove Church of the Brethren on a European cruise and a chapter was read aloud every evening. I've been reacquainted with old friends from Drumore Elementary and Solanco High School, plus a few teachers from each that I hadn't seen or heard from in nearly 50 years. A former pupil supposedly asked one of my favorite teachers, whom I will not embarrass, if he ever thought any of his students were capable of or would ever write a book? He replied that he thought several were competent for that task but that Tom Smith wasn't one he had in mind when making that prediction. To him I offer this rebuttal-No one was more shocked than I that this was accomplished.

During conversations with my 2 daughters, Chris and Jen, they each light an occasional warning flare reminding me that not everyone "gets me" and my distorted sense of humor. This is beneficial in keeping my unfamiliar, unwarranted success in check and my hat size from increasing.

Very few of us ever achieve immortality, although many of us may desire to be remembered after death. Those of us fortunate enough to have children and grandchildren will hopefully be recalled by them, but by few others. It is my hope that any who have read or will read my humble words in the future may learn something about me, my thoughts, observations and what and who I encountered passing through my local rural world. Perhaps, concealed, hidden and well camouflaged within these lines you may also discover me.

I do not bare my soul, just what rattles around between my ears beneath the vanishing grasses that are slowly receding from a barren, approaching desert. For those of you familiar with agriculture chemicals, my cranium is the poster plot for atrizine carry-over. My grandmother Shoemaker once tried to console my imminent baldness with this comforting phrase, "You can't have both hair and brains." I sure hope there's another component in her words of wisdom because as of now I'm 0 for 2. While recently surveying a few early baby pictures of myself and the absence of very little scalp covered fuzz I am resigned to the fact that I will surely leave this world exactly as I entered it, baffled, broke and bald. A hairline that once resided next door to my eyebrows and observed everything and everyone approaching me now only witnesses all those behind me that are constantly gaining on and eventually passing me. This family hair loss trait is shared by my son Roger and many other blood relatives, including Rick & Rob Powl, and I'm sure inspires and is greatly anticipated by our future generations.

The first book has transported Ruthie and me well outside our familiar circle of Liberty Square. Meeting new folks and becoming acquainted with their different, unfamiliar lives has been a wonderful experience that without the book would not have occurred. We participated in a book review at Oxford Library to a signing at our local library in Quarryville to a presentation at a senior's luncheon at the Church of the Good Shepard near Lancaster. We thoroughly enjoyed meeting and conversing with several folks at "First Friday" in Lancaster and other similar functions. This book also evidently lit the fire for a distant relative, Laura England, to compose her wonderful historical memoir of her family and mine.

Paul and Kathy Adams Weaver, formerly of Lancaster and presently residents of New Canaan, Connecticut, arranged the highlight of our book-signing marathon. They hosted a wonderful weekend reception at their home inviting many of their friends, relatives and neighbors plus several of the former Liberty Square Gibsons.

We were graciously received by all of these folks who seemed genuinely interested in the book and our rural lives. During on going conversations I kept thinking, most of these people who obviously live a completely different life style from the visiting author will not purchase any books. We sold 75 that evening and both of us were overwhelmed by this out-of-our-element success. Kathy Weaver is the daughter of our neighbors, John and the late Loretta Adams, who owned Shady, the most famous dog in Drumore written about in my book. I would describe New Cannan, Connecticut, home of the Weavers, as a place of new money. Most of those we met were our age and treated us cordially. Driving into New York City regularly, as we would to Lancaster, shopping and attending Broadway shows and dining at exclusive eating establishments were evidently the norm for most. I suppose this could be compared to those of us who shop at Goods, meet one another at the salad bar at Lapps, continue to Maplehofe for an ice cream cone then stop at Mussers for gas. While listening to their small talk, I realized most had other homes somewhere else, where they escaped to over the cold Connecticut winters. The line that kept playing over and over inside the head of this old farmer was: where in the world does all the money come from? But in retrospect I'm constantly reminded that I've envied a lot of folks during my lifetime but none for more than 15 minutes. Most seemed genuinely concerned about their food and its organic source. A few seemed to be considering growing their own food rather than trusting the reliability of what they buy in local stores. One lady mentioned she was expecting a delivery of 2-dozen chicks she was going to raise. When I inquired about her 6 weeks absence while on vacation as to the tending of her flock she assumed the roosters and hens could go to the kennel along with their dogs and cats. Men of Spanish descent were observed working in yards, flowerbeds and even removing storm windows and replacing screens.

We also spent one night at the home of former Drumore resident John Gibson and his wife June in Greenwich Conn. Ruthie had worked for John's late wife Sally for over 30 years and thoroughly enjoyed reminiscing for a couple hours with John. She cooked and they had eaten literally hundreds of meals together during those 3 decades of employment. I would describe Greenwich as old money with old stately homes located at the end of long private driveways. We both remarked about how similar their home and its location was to John's home in Drumore. Occasionally, on a large wooded lot a new house was being constructed and being built to appear old as the others in this area. One particular new home under construction, we were told, would have over 90 people working on it and the adjoining grounds on any given day. The lady having this multi-million dollar castle built, we were also told, was a TV personality known as Judge Judy.

Echoes from Drumore, Stories from Upstream

I have been approached by folks living in and around the Buck to write of this place. The older ones may wish to be remembered along with those from years past and businesses that are no more. The underlying current that is driving this not to be forgotten place is the fact that a giant Wal-Mart may one day appear at this rural crossroads and change this immediate area forever. Change is inevitable and for the most part acceptable if it occurs gradually. If this happens, this would not be a prolonged alteration and could affect all remaining businesses and folks living at this place.

As with any small community, the folks that have lived in The Buck past and present are what makes this tiny village noteworthy and unique. These folks of whom I write, each one different from the other yet living in close proximity to one another, make up the heart and soul of this present and past close-knit community. Each knew the others' strengths and weakness, their good qualities and their flaws and for the most part accepted one another for what they were with each realizing their own imperfections.

It would also appear that most but not all local residents are against this huge shopping complex being built in The Buck. This evidently is true for those who have recently moved and built or purchased homes in this area during the last 4 decades but also for those whose families have been here for generations. I find it ironic that many of those that have relocated to this rural paradise complain the loudest when in actuality they are the most important factor in attracting that which they now oppose. A giant complex similar to a Wal-Mart does not locate in a sparsely populated area, then hope multitudes will patronize it. Those of us who have been a witness to developments and the influx of transplants locally knew very well what would eventually follow: Crowded schools, higher taxes, clogged highways, and big-box stores.

I suppose this is to be regarded as progress and should be accepted and welcomed. Please allow this old farmer to release all thoughts of a time when this productive farm to be developed at The Buck produced an abundance of crops and livestock nurtured for generations by thrifty farm families. When corn, hay, wheat, tomatoes and tobacco were grown and harvested on our local golf courses surrounded by large wooded areas that have since sprouted densely sown homes. When during the 1950s I sat upon a sorrel, gaited mare and rode through acres of undeveloped, native woodland that now contains 50 or 60 houses. Where houses also line the roads on fertile land that I once farmed but unfortunately didn't own. The end of an era, my friends, is occurring in Southern Lancaster County and with the influx of the Amish reminds me more and more of the region just east of Lancaster. I suppose the words that may condense my thoughts are Bird-In-Hand gained, Paradise lost.

In writing of the Amish that are arriving and thankfully acquiring most available farms in our area I submit this short poem, It was written by my fellow Drumore neighbor, harness and saddle maker, Eli Beiler. In it he voices the concerns of his Amish community and that of many local residents. These lines were concocted a few years ago when news of an impending large, big box shopping center at The Buck first appeared and surfaced locally. These lines were published in our local Lancaster Newspaper. Supposedly the construction of this giant complex will begin in 2012.

New Business at The Buck

In a quiet nook in this big nation,
Where horses and cows are the biggest population,
They tell us the way to succeed:
With a new shopping center they must proceed.
Eight acres under roof on the dear sod,
Where for years, horses and plows have trod.
"Traffic," they say, "friend,
With each of us, we will have to contend."
Our dear little town in its valley—
Is this time for residents to rally?
Our little fishing creek, so sparkling and clear,
To each of us holds something dear.
In the meadow of this site starts this creek
What is the destination it will meet?
The Buck as we know it, my friend—
Will the rural atmosphere soon come to an end?
The native Indians in the area did gather,
A shopping center, for them, never did matter,
Their needs were few—off the land they did live;
They took from the land, and back they did give,
What is the answer, we all do ask?
Just take a look in the looking glass.

I write respectfully of Robert Risk, who a century past was known as Lancaster County's first and most famous columnist and one of the first in the nation. I believe most folks living in The Buck today do not know of him and his influence nationally or realize he sprang from and was a resident of this tiny village. He should be remembered as The Buck's most famous and well-known citizen.

Abner Musser,Sr. was the sparkplug and stimulus of The Buck beginning in 1925. He probably had more to do with the businesses located in The Buck during these last 75-80 years than any other individual. A testament to his diligent work, forward thinking and planning is that Musser's Market remains to this day located in The Buck operated by his great grandsons. DON'T PASS THE BUCK!

Irene Garner, the spirit of The Buck, was truly one of a kind. To me she was a throw-back to an era when this area was first settled, offering a tiny glimpse into our past. She was the epitome of our pioneer women who lived and settled this area 2 centuries ago.

Come ride with me in my old farm truck down Scalpy Hollow on the scenic trail along the twists and turns of Fishing Creek. I shall describe places, some old, some new along the way. We will then turn onto Fishing Creek Road, an unpaved byway first used by those migrating up the Susquehanna River before heading north and east. This early road crosses the waterway of Fishing Creek 3 times and runs along some of the former black settlement written about later. It ends at the Susquehanna River in the tiny village of Fishing Creek that once was the home of a boat marina and storage, a general store and post office that are all now completely gone and only a fleeting memory in my mind of by-gone days.

There are also stories of rafting on the Susquehanna extracted from words written by Cookman Dunkle, who owned a neighboring farm that lies under the deep water that makes up Muddy Run Lake. This story will answer any questions as to why so many hotels and places serving alcohol were located along the river during that era.

Several folks approached me and sparked my interest concerning the black settlement in Fishing Creek Hollow years ago. Growing up I had observed a few of these folks but knew only a couple personally. The very last one, Jim Wilson, had died in 1992 at age 82. I began thinking; this era was now officially over and sadly would be forgotten forever without some form of documentation. My last book on Liberty Square was 95 percent inside my head and was written through memories mostly mine. I knew from the start, a book documenting these Fishing Creek folks from years past would involve much research and stories from others. Joe Sinclair has been invaluable in relating these stories to me from a lifetime of living beside and among these families. I have no idea how this local story will be received but I firmly believe it should be documented and remembered and probably would have been dismissed had it not been for Joe. His son-in-law, my high school classmate, Denny Hess, has provided old photos that only tend to stimulate my interest and will greatly add to this project.

Jim Wilson once told my father while they were seated together on a bench at Musser's store that a man never becomes anything more than what's expected of him. Sadly, little was expected of these black folks of Fishing Creek after the Civil War and in the following years. Although Joe provided several humorous accounts of their lives in this place that may coax a smile or 2, having reread what I've written, in the final analysis their story is basically a sad one.

Near the end of this book are a few articles I wrote for our church's monthly newsletter that illustrates a few historical facts concerning Chestnut Level Church. It was during this time of writing these stories that I met Diane Risk Stern, daughter of our friends and fellow church members, Paul and Shirley Risk. Diane was dealing with a brain tumor that left this intelligent, young former Miss Solanco, who held a doctorate in Pathology with mental lapses.

Having only met her once or twice at church I again, during the latter stages of her illness saw her at Donna Long Yarnell's barbershop. I spoke to her as she cautiously walked toward me intently surveying my face. I could see in her eyes that she was struggling to make the connection as she caressed my cheek with her warm, soft hand. As I thought I should tell her my name I paused and remained silent, as she appeared to look and search deeply into my very soul with penetrating, investigating eyes. Just as I began to speak, her sad eyes lit up and sparkled as she blurted out joyfully, "I know you, you're the old farmer my parents talk about that wrote the book." She hugged me as a long lost friend, not because we were but because she was relieved and grateful that she had searched her mind and actually found who I was. In remembrance of her and that brief, intimate moment we shared I have since signed all of my writings "The Old Farmer." Diane lived with her husband and 3 children in Rockford, Illinois. All occasional, correspondence we sent her was read aloud by her parents who stayed with her to the end. I'm not sure if all our words were completely comprehended by her but both Paul and Shirley indicated they observed a change in her demeanor when they read the signature on the card-The Old Farmer.

Diane, born in 1956, died in 2008. A moving, full church memorial service was held for her in Chestnut Level Church and she was laid to rest in the adjoining cemetery. I visualize her attractive face every time I write and her aroused voice still echoes within the imaginary hills and valleys inside my mind exclaiming joyfully, "I know you, you're the old farmer."

As with my first book I write what I see and feel in my local, rural world that regretfully is changing. I point out a few local landmarks that may interest a few today and perhaps tomorrow. Occasionally, my mind wanders resulting in stories that have absolutely no relation or similarity to my Drumore home. Titles and stories included are the Old Farmer Duz Stone Harbor, Sounds From Behind The Barn, The Party Line, Flyin' and Racin' in the Buck, and Observations From Local Grocery Parking Lots. During these writings lapses my primary goal is somehow, someway to coax a sincere smile. If you read this book without laughing out loud or quietly chuckling to yourself then as an author I feel I have failed and you should probably request a refund from this word-winder. I can be reached at 1-800-Mr. Obama and be sure to specify and ask for the struggling author's slush-fund to receive your newly printed $20.00 bill.

I wrote Armageddon one evening feeling old and pessimistic. I have observed this trait in older folks as they contemplate their own demise and on this particular evening, I sadly realized for a couple of hours I have joined them. As a 50-year plus church member and presently serving as an elder in the Presbyterian Church, I gave much thought as to putting into print my unrestrained thoughts. I reluctantly submitted to a voice inside me that said, "Give them something to think about and contemplate."

There are those who truly believe the best of times in our country have passed. I hope and pray they are wrong and that the best is yet to come for our children and grandchildren. All I ask and propose is that each of you considers what I have written at perhaps a gloomy moment and takes a stand against that which you detest and wish to change and support that which you favor.

If we sit idly by our freedoms may be slowly but methodically removed from our lives without ever realizing it. Our God may be ushered out of our churches through time in such a fashion we won't notice or even miss the one we have worshipped for centuries as the church walls eventually crumble in rubble. Change is a necessary component in our lives, our government, our churches and our world if we're to survive, but surely some of our values we've held dear in this nation since its birth are worth preserving for future generations. I believe change blended with our ancient values have been a welcome, rich blessing to our present church family. It can work!

I suppose before concluding this introduction I should explain the title and cover. "Drumore Echoes, Stories from Upstream." The "Echoes" originated from words written for our monthly church newsletter. These stories were mostly of earlier church history as this congregation approached our 300th anniversary in 2011. My memories and that of other locals also drive this book, as the Liberty Square one. Dear old "Drumore" is what I know and therefore what I write. It is my hope and desire that those of you unfamiliar with this once rural but now changing area can visualize this place from the past and the present through these words. For those who have resided in downtown Drumore for most of your life or for generations I hope to renew your appreciation of your home and perhaps that of your ancestors.

I had approached a relative, John Powl, whose grandmother was a Smith, for ideas pertaining to a cover for this book. All I told him was I wanted something different and something relevant to Drumore that might coax a smile. You recall I mentioned earlier that if a smile or laughter never surfaced in your demeanor while reading my words I believe I have completely failed you and myself. Well, hopefully I may achieve this aspiration of mine before you even open this book and we will both have this desire realized and behind us.

I knew from viewing John's earlier photos he is known for, (sorry for the pun) off the wall pictures. He had called later and said, "Meet me at Drumore Park wearing old shoes, jeans, a shirt and tie and a sport jacket. Bring a table, chair, writing material, a pen or 2 and a typewriter if you have one." I realized this guy is an eccentric photographer but as we drove the 2 miles to the park I retained genuine visions of past unreal occurrences in life of being up the creek without a paddle. This turned out to be dejavu all over again and not an imaginary experience.

The spring fed water of Fishing Creek was cold-and halfway into the photo shoot my feet went completely numb. I was told by John to pretend I was writing or typing, as he was never the same place twice when I looked up. He disappeared behind those large boulders in the background, then reappeared on their crest. He stood on the creek's shore, then was completely submerged in the water with only head, hand and camera visible to my unbelieving eyes. It was his idea to crumple-up that yellow writing paper, throw it up-stream and allow it to flow to me. Hence, "stories from upstream."

As the photo shoot concluded I developed a whole new admiration for anyone who models for a living. This occurred before upcoming knee replacement for me. So now I had to somehow get ashore with unfeeling, unconscious feet, a knee frozen in time while negotiating numerous rocks and stones that I had somehow easily navigated earlier. My photographer cordially removed all my props handing them to my nervous photo assistant on shore, Ruthie. It was then I realized I had nothing to hold onto in the rushing water, and for a second or so I thought this is not going to end well. John, realizing my difficulty scrambled back to save me, as would an attentive, concerned lifeguard. No telling what could have happened, as the water, considered deep by me, was a full 6 inches above my ankles. Had I fallen, all the stories from this book would have originated and surfaced downstream instead of up.

PART ONE: THE BUCK

THE BIGGEST LITTLE TOWN IN THE USA

Abner Musser, The Stimulus Of The Buck

The answer as to how The Buck got its name seems to raise more questions, particularly ones relating to a long-ago 19th century tavern and the town's shadowy Irish beginnings. The settlement that became The Buck first appears on a map of the area dated 1776 (though it was labeled as the village of Tunes). Settled predominately by Presbyterian immigrants from Northern Ireland, the village would have considered itself very much in the heart of Drumore Township for more than a century. East Drumore split from Drumore in 1883, with the boundary between the townships being the road that would later become Route 272. Answers about why the village was called Tunes have been lost.

The Buck Hotel–established in 1824.

Local lore tells of a 19th century inn and tavern that stood on the triangle of land that today is on the West side of Route 272, across from the Turkey Hill mini-market. If standing today the The Buck Hotel would reside in the lower corner of this triangle adjacent to 272 and facing the parking area of Buck Beverage. Called The Buck Hotel, this tavern featured a metal sign of a buck deer head. This barroom and inn was one of the few landmarks that folks could use in the 17 and 18 hundreds, back when Southern Lancaster County consisted of only a few poorly marked dirt roads. We are talking about a time when freight was being transported by horse-drawn wagons. Over time "The Buck," (tavern) became such a landmark, (meet you at The Buck) that the name was eventually applied to the entire area.

The Buck, similar to other small villages that sprang-up in this wilderness nearly 3 centuries past, lives on. Although established by stout-hearted men who crossed the vast Atlantic Ocean in search of a better life and religious freedom, I find it most ironic that establishments similar to The Buck Hotel played such an important part in these new settlements in most early villages. Churches and schools were, of course, also built and important in these rural communities. But lest we forget the hotels and liquid refreshment they served evidently were nearly as numerous in our area as houses of worship during the establishment of early America.

The stories this long-ago Buck Hotel could relate, from the birth of our nation and Lafayette having a meal at this inn to this place serving as the residence of Dave and Marie Banzhof and their large family, would be many. Both Ruthie and I attended local schools, and knew several of the Banzhof children personally. As for Lafayette, a Frenchman, born 1757 and died 1834, he served as a General in the American Revolutionary War under George Washington. The tavern, reportedly in operation since 1824 and listed in 1899 county records as being owned by H. S. Lynes, was raided as a speakeasy during prohibition. Supposedly, financial mismanagement was the final nail in the Hotel's coffin. The property was subdivided into apartments and then torn down when Route 272 was widened in the 1950s. The Buck Hotel was located at a strategic place in both locality and time in the early history of Southern Lancaster County.

Original Buck store, barn and Blacksmith shop with stack.
Right, The Buck Hotel and Livery Stable—1871.

Other buildings and businesses located early in The Buck included a store built by Abram Reese and Henry Richardson for Harry Marsh in 1871. A blacksmith shop with a barn, a creamery, a livery stable and a post office established here in 1830

Founded in 1925 by 2-transplants from Ohio, Abner and Esther Musser, Musser's Market, may have had the most to do with preserving "The" in The Buck. Beginning in the early 1950s, the store began posting Route 272 with an ad campaign harkening back to President Truman that read, "Don't Pass The Buck, Stop at Musser's." Abner Musser Sr. had most recently lived in York and worked as a Fuller Brush man before relocating to The Buck. He had previously lived and worked on a farm in Kirkwood. Abner Jr. related to me his father could have become many things in his life, but recognized early on that a farmer was not one of them. During his vast Fuller Brush travels he heard of a store for sale at The Buck. He traveled to this unfamiliar area, ended up at Bethesda asking directions, then back tracked to The Buck. Supposedly, this is why a later posted sign originated at Musser's store reading, "Don't Pass The Buck" as Abner evidently had earlier. I've been told he borrowed the money from his aunt, and then purchased the store.

Ab Musser Jr. gave me this store-operating lineage given to him by his mother, Esther Musser. He later added the next 2-generations of Mussers for this list, with more Mussers certainly to be added in the future. The legacy of Abner Sr. and Esther Musser continues to this day and well into the future:

1. Harry Marsh
2. Ambrose Singleton
3. Mr. Yerkes
4. Harry Myers
5. David Kiehl
6. Ephraim Seldomridge
7. Philip Schmidt
8. Stauffer & Fritz
9. David Eshbach
10. Abner G. Musser, Sr.
11. Abner Jr. & John Musser
12. Mike, Abner III, & Scott Musser
13. Eric, Brian, Brent, Greg, Michael, Gray, & Matt Musser

Ab recalls that 50-years ago "people came to our store in buggies or spring wagons. For many years after the auto took over, there were no horse and buggy customers at our store. Recently, we have acquired some Amish neighbors. Now we are seeing them again. The spring wagon always intrigued me. I consider it the forerunner of the pick-up truck of the motor age."

The Mussers had 4 children: John, Abner Jr., Ruth and Ben. Mussers was a typical country store—shelf and floor space devoted more to dry goods and hardware than to groceries. Mussers handled bulk crackers, but not in a barrel, cartwheel cheese, molasses in a barrel, sugar in 100-pound quantities, dry fruit, etc. and a whole showcase of penny candy-to the delight of all the children. The store soon became the meeting place for local farmers and hired hands. In addition to running his business, Musser served as the village Justice of the Peace for many years. He presided at about 50 trials a year, most of them traffic cases, and a wedding or 2. He was busiest at the beginning of the hunting and fishing seasons, for he issued the licenses.

Abner Musser's store in The Buck–1930s.

Musser had always been the municipal spark plug. He and 2 or 3 local citizens had built a pond following a lack of water when Morris Lowe's house burnt. This house of Morris Lowe's was located across Route 372 from this present pond and during much of my lifetime was owned by John Lefever. Hot coals dropped on the floor by children tendin' the stove evidently caused this fire. Pete Frey now owns this place. This pond remains today just west of The Buck along Route 372. Locals used this body of water for swimming, ice-skating and it was stocked with bass and blue gills.

Musser was responsible for much of the early businesses located in The Buck. In 1930, Sam Wenger worked for H.H. Wiggins as an auto mechanic in Quarryville. In 1935, he was offered and remodeled Musser's chicken house near the store at The Buck to begin his own auto repair business. He married Pearl Moore in 1937 and they later had 4 children: Dave, Nancy, Dick and Dan. In 1941, Sam constructed the present garage and then added a showroom 2 years later when he took on the Pontiac Agency. The GMC truck franchise was added in 1948.

Sam's son, Dick, worked in this shop from childhood and later formed a partnership with his father in 1974. Early in this present century, Dick retired and sold the very successful dealership. He remains living in this area near The Buck and on a warm, clear day both he and his wife, Kelly, will be found on one of our local golf courses. The Wenger car dealership in The Buck has ended and perhaps because of this General Motors no longer makes Pontiacs!

Ralph DuBree, concerning the construction of Sam Wenger's garage, related the following story to me. It seems several local men were involved with installing the roof on this large building. One day during this roof construction a military plane began circling the area around The Buck. This occurred when WWII was raging and startled those "Piddlers on the Roof."

Without warning, this plane slowly descended toward The Buck proper, heading directly towards Sam Wenger's unfinished garage. The workmen, thinking this out of control flying machine was about to crash on or near them dropped face-down on the unfinished roof. The plane cleared them by a few feet, but as it banked in the west, evidently returning for another pass, all workers either jumped or quickly slid down unfastened lumber to the ground below. Once again this plane made another near-miss pass above the roof top. Some of the workmen involved thought Germans had hijacked a military plane and were invading The Buck. Following one final fly-by, with the pilot waving to those below, the plane disappeared on the horizon. Days later, a local man in uniform appeared in The Buck as those carpenters were completing the construction of Wenger's garage. It was a local man, named Gerald Hake, who accepted the blame and responsibility for this scary, fly-by scenario. It should be noted Hake also had 5 brothers in the military at this time—Glenn, William, Wilbur, Robert and James. Farther down the road in Chestnut Level the Henry family had 4 children in the service—Richard, Dave, Robert and Mary.

Hake had lived in the house along Route 272 between Oregon Hollow and Osceola Roads. I believe he had a sister, Mary Lou, who married Ralph Herman. These buildings that stood facing one another on either side of 272 are no longer standing. I have been entertained by young men who are no longer youthful that during the late 1940s would race their cars in this particular section of 272 in the middle of a deserted night, one being Oliver Sheaffer. This speedy, inclined, straight away was referred to as Hake's Hill.

Leroy Wenger began his machinery business in 1941 in the same old barn where his brother Sam began in 1935. He first got a franchise for Buch Wheelbarrows. Leroy's wife, Naomi once sold a wheelbarrow during the depression years that was their only income for that week. Leroy and Naomi's children, Marion, Dot, Clarence and Ben, all grew up working in the family business. The shop gradually expanded from wheelbarrows to plumbing and heating installation and supplies to new and used farm machinery.

Leroy constructed the new shop in 1945 and added a John Deere franchise. From the mid-50s through the 1980s, I would bet more machinery was sold at Wenger Implement than any other similar establishment in Southern Lancaster County. Leroy Wenger died suddenly in his early 60s with the business continued by his son, Ben. As I think back the 1970s were finally a profitable time down on the farm and Wenger Implement flourished accordingly. Several local mechanics were hired as the needed work force was increased to meet the demand. Wenger also offered at one time new appliances.

Park Moore farm, 1950s–home still standing, other buildings razed and presently occupied by Turkey Hill Mini Market.

As the influx of Amish greatly increased in the late 80s, the farming practices of the locals changed dramatically and the products and service provided by Wengers diminished. Consequently, Ben Wenger sold his business and Art Yost now owns and operates the facility as a hardware, lawn and garden center. Ben Wenger remains in The Buck working as a mechanic at his used car facility. Agriculture change had arrived in The Buck with the decrease of English farmers and the increase of suburban sprawl. But I fondly recall a time when I could buy a new or used car or truck then simply walk directly across Route 272 and purchase a new John Deere tractor or any accompanying machinery. All this could be accomplished in the tiny village that bordered either side of Route 272 for less than a quarter-mile. It was a good time for The Buck community and the surrounding area with these businesses all close to home.

Abner Musser Sr. and Esther Musser at opening
of new air-conditioned supermarket–1956.

Musser's 3 sons began coming of age when WW II began and, as they came home from the armed forces, he immediately got them established in businesses of their own. Abner Jr. got out of the Air Corps after the war and took over Musser's general store, and later in 1956, a new air-conditioned supermarket. This supermarket was the first of its kind to be fully air-conditioned in the entire local area. This was the first time I recall hearing the word supermarket. Ben got out of the Air Force in 1949, and Musser built a food locker to get him started. Ben then set up his own slaughterhouse. John got out of the Navy in 1950 and Musser built him a feed mill. If the father hadn't run out of sons, his neighbors say, The Buck would have been as big as Pittsburgh in another 10 years.

It was during that period of expansion that Musser, his imagination fired by the possibilities of The Buck, erected a metal sign stating: "This is The Buck The Biggest Little Town in the U.S.A." At the same time, Musser conceived the idea of getting silver dollars from the bank and passing them out as change at the store. Practically every citizen in The Buck during that era carried a silver buck as a pocket piece.

Abner Musser proudly displays his famous sign,
Buck Hotel on left, Park Moore barn on right–1950.

My wife Ruthie reveals that when she was a little girl, she and her parents lived in the old Buck Hotel from 1945 till the spring of 1952. Her mother worked for Mrs. Musser, with Monday morning always wash day. The washing was done in the morning, then hung out to dry. Ruthie recalls Mrs. Musser always made her own soap. When the clothes were dry, they were brought home by her mom and ironed. Ruthie remembers Mrs. Musser had an electric toaster and relished the taste of a piece of this toast she made her every Monday topped with homemade jelly. Toast at Ruthie's home, at this time, was made by holding a slice of bread over hot coals in a cook stove and had a completely different taste.

Ruthie's mom also cleaned for Mrs. Musser and Ruthie, tagging along, remembers thinking of Mr. Musser as a very important man. She recalls Abner Sr. as always wearing a starched white shirt and necktie and, when working in the store, an ironed, pristine white apron. When working in the store continuously he would change his shoes 2 or 3 times daily to alleviate stress on his legs and feet. Ruthie's mom, who also cleaned for Ab Jr. and his wife, Ellen, also relates that Ab Jr. regularly changed his shoes and also polished them, setting them by a heater to dry. Ruthie, remembers Mr. Musser occasionally seated at a large desk inside 3 bay windows as he served as the local Justice of the Peace. She recalls being frightened when State Police periodically arrived and went to Mr. Musser's desk.

Although Mrs. Musser worked side by side in the store with her husband, she would, as the children got older, take an occasional trip with other ladies, usually bringing Ruthie a souvenir. A couple young boys remembered as working in Musser's original store were Dick Wenger and Glen Groff.

Later, when the new store was built behind the old original one, several folks from the community found employment at Mussers. Those recalled working in the butcher shop were, Lloyd Rohrer, Pete Byers, Dutch Feiler, Bill Ambler, Ken Waltman and Ike Hershey. Then later, Mike Duffy, Paulie Stokes, Carrol Herr, Don Dearoff, Deb Peters and Scott & Skip Musser also worked in the butcher shop, while Mike worked in the store. Frances and Millie Reedy, Ruthie Campbell and Dot Richardson wrapped the meat. Martha Mendenhall and Kenny Miles worked with meat in the cold storage lockers.

Within the butcher shop steers, cull cows, pigs, and, during the first half of December, deer were butchered to the specifications for the owners. Mussers also bought and butchered steers and pigs raised locally, then sold the meat to the public. This developed into quite a business, with the meat from all local farms and all the processing done in their butcher shop. Because of this operation, much of this meat ended up outside our local community. During this period Musser's meat was considered the freshest and the best in the area.

This also was before home freezers were familiar in homes as Musser's established cold storage lockers for their use and the community. Stainless steel pull-out bins in stacks of 3 or 4 were rented, with individual keys for each hung on the wall before entering this frigid area. The handiest bins near the floor cost a little more then ones near the top that required a stepladder to deposit or remove food. This was most folk's first experience with central air as the thermostat for the entire locker room was set below freezing. It was a great place to visit during an August heat wave as one's perspiration would freeze and form an icy glaze on over-heated farm boys. Folks today speak of getting caught in a dysfunctional elevator. 60-years ago it crossed my mind of spending eternity behind locked doors in Mussers Frozen Food Locker.

My mother also worked for Abner Musser Sr. in the new store. She related he prided himself in cordially greeting the customers and in his personal appearance. He expected no less of his employees, especially the ones who came face to face with customers. Mom worked at the checkout with Mary Jane Rineer, Marian Neff, Alice Lehman, Dot Shenk, and Charlotte Miller. Upon arriving at work, Mr. Musser gave all a measured glance assuring a perfectly manicured physical appearance. Others who worked at Mussers store during that era were, Reba & Jack Carter, Mrs. Jake Groff, and Ben Doulin. Four generations of Carters worked over the years at Mussers.

Lauren Herr Musser, wife of Scott, recalls going with her dad, Mart Herr, and her 2 little sisters to Musser's store as small children. Ab Musser Jr. always greeted these 3 lasses with these same words. He would say, "Hi, how are you boys today?" the girls would always sternly state, "We are girls, not boys." And Ab would laugh. Who would have thought that years later Lauren Herr would become Scott's wife and Ab and Ellen's daughter-in-law. Another reflective memory from The Buck.

Ruthie recalls Ab Jr. and her always greeted one another with these same words: Ab would ask her how she was doin', she answered, "Just fine." When she posed the same question to Ab saying, "How are you Junior?" Ab always answered, "Pretty and Good." This is the opening conversation between them today as it has been for over 50 years. Over the years I have conversed with more than 1 grandmother who as a teenager recalls purchasing her first pair of nylons at Musser's store. This evidently occurred well before tanning beds, piercings, panty hose and Madonna in the areas surrounding The Buck, the fashion hub of Southern Lancaster County. During this time Ellen Musser, wife of Ab Jr. moved her hair salon from their home to the basement of the store. This shop was later relinquished to Jesse Crotti. Paul Riggs also operated a barber shop at his present home.

Those recalled who worked for John Musser at the feed mill, which opened in 1952, were, John Carter, Bob Althouse, Jim Moss, Wilbur Pollock, Bob Alexander, Weldon Reedy and Wayne Lefever. Pete Howard later ran the Mill, as Red Rose Feeds owned it, and also Carl Lapp. I believe Lee and Sue Haldeman were the last to own the Mill at The Buck that has been vacant for several years and during this writing was razed.

Abner Musser Sr. and his wife, Esther, were members of Chestnut Level Presbyterian Church for many years, both participating and playing an active role during their years in The Buck in the life of this church. I believe Abner Musser Sr. died suddenly at home of an apparent heart attack at the age of 75. Earlier in these writings, Robert Blair Risk was described as the "Sage" of The Buck, meaning having profound wisdom. I suppose Abner Musser Sr. could be remembered as the "Stimulus" of The Buck, meaning he was aroused with energy to activity. During his lifetime, he did more than any other to contribute to the success and growth of this tiny, road-hugging community. Mrs. Musser stood by her husband and also deserves credit for their business, community and family success. Following a lengthy well-lived life she died at the Long Home in Lancaster, at the age of 100. Their legacy continues into a 4th generation of Mussers that operate the present store at The Buck, which opened in Feb of 2003. Phoebe Musser Shaubach, Becky Musser Hambleton and Pat Musser Neff also began working in this new store when it opened.

I wish to contribute a brief tribute to John Musser, son of Abner Sr. & Esther and brother of Ab, that certainly belongs with The Buck-Musser chapter.

Unbeknownst to him, John played a part and was an important contributing factor for this old farmer to begin writing down thoughts and stories from the past. I thoroughly enjoyed reading and remembering his accounts etched within his 4 wonderful pamphlets entitled, "USETA" both shortly after each was written and before this humble publication was composed. I thought his well-written, yet simple USETA remembrances touched the lives of all who lived during that early era of Mussers in The Buck. I believe he has left a legacy of historical importance to this area that increases in value daily. When reading his anecdotes, I believe he has also revealed a tiny clue of himself, his thoughts, sense of humor and what he truly was about. I believe he more than anyone else would have enjoyed and smiled at my words of observation. I have thought of him daily while writing this book. Sadly for all who knew him, he died suddenly and unexpectedly in 1989 at the age of 70. A few of his USETA's follow as a tribute and remembrance of a full-well-lived life.

The Buck-Back Then

The rural school keeps popping into my memories. The rural schoolteacher was not only teacher but also janitor, school nurse, physical education instructor, advisor and disciplinarian.
One job that was most always done by first graders was to clean the erasers. They would take all the black board erasers out on the porch and bang them together until most of the dust was gone with the wind. This was a fun job for beginners.
The older boys were volunteer water boys. Two would go to the nearest adjoining farm to get water in a bucket. A broomstick made it an easy chore for 2 boys to carry a pail of water. The water was then dumped into a crock cooler. It was not always cold but it was wet enough to quench most thirsts.

Written in 1985

The needs of most folks can be met by a visit to The Buck. You can buy a mammoth tractor, or a box of tooth picks; buy an automobile or a bag of pet food; buy a pound of nails or a mobile home; buy a pizza or get a permanent wave; get a loan to buy a car or get a tin cup welded; buy self-service gasoline or have a roller skating party; buy a farm or used auto part; see a tractor pull or get livestock feed ground; go to church or buy a building lot; have an auto radiator repaired or get a beef butchered; buy a new kitchen appliance or a loaf of fresh baked bread; buy paint or livestock spray;—you name it and we've probably got it. We are in search of a doctor to settle here to help keep us all healthy (we now have a doctor!) In any event we look forward to seeing "you" at The Buck.

I remember an occasion, when I was a lad, on which a young couple stopped in front of our store. My dad, Mr. Millard Kilby and I were on the store porch. Mr. Kilby was a man from the south. A hard working farmer and so honest he couldn't hammer a crooked nail.

The young man got out of the car and in a PA. Dutch accent asked the way to Elkton MD. which was, at that time, the "The Marrying Capital" of our area. A couple could drive to Elkton and get married—no waiting, no fuss and no age limit. Of course Mr. Kilby and dad had to tease the young man a little about getting married. They gave him directions to Elkton. When he turned to go, my dad said, "Now don't do anything I wouldn't do!" To this the young fellow turned and said, "Ach, I already did that!!!"

WOW! I thought Mr. Kilby would break his leg the way he slapped it and laughed. That was a "Knee Slapper" for him and me and dad.

One mode of earning money when we were lads was to deliver magazines. Instead of a paper route, we sold Colliers, Saturday Evening Post, and Country Gentleman. I don't remember we "stuck" very long at this project but at least we worked at it for a while. All three magazines later quit being published. Saturday Evening Post and Country Gentleman are back in circulation. Selling seeds was another money-making project. In many cases premiums were the pay off in the seed business. John Jamison tells me that he earned a Hamilton 22 rifle by this method of selling. Whether magazines, papers, seeds or what have you, it was a great experience. My sister, Ruth, reminded me of this bit of yesteryear experience.

Musser's are really pleased to carry the reputation as the store that sells excellent beef and pork. We would like to share that reputation with the folks who produce the livestock. This week we are selling beef produced by Bill Weiler of Drumore Township and pork from Clair DeLong of East Drumore Township. These men produce top quality livestock and deserve our vote of appreciation and thanks for helping us all be well fed Americans.

Finally, I conclude this chapter with a poem from one of the 4 John Musser "USETA" publications. I'm sure this verse that he found in an old newspaper tickled him. Titled: "The Mule," it relates a vivid description of this beast that was being fazed-out at my first cries. My deceased father, a friend of John, talked of working as a lad with mules saying they were the reason he learned to cuss. Although unfamiliar to most who will read this, perhaps these descriptive, rhyming lines will be appreciated by my Amish friends.

THE MULE

The mule, he is a funny sight,
He's made of ears and dynamite.
His heels is full of bricks and springs,
Tornadoes, batterin rams and things.
He's fat as any poisoned pup;
It's just his meanness swells him up,
He's always scheming round to do
The things you most don't want him to.

The mule, he lives on anything;
He's got a lovely voice to sing,
And when he lets it loose at noon,
It sounds like buzz saws out of tune.
He stands around with sleepy eye
And looks as if he'd like to die.
But when there's any dying done,
It ain't the mule, I'll bet a bun.

Some folks don't treat mules with respect.
They say they ain't got intellect;
That may be so, but if you've got
To go to heaven on the spot,
And want a way that doesn't fail,
Just pull the tassel on his tail.
The mule, he tends to his own biz;
He don't look loaded, but he is.

There remains several of John Musser's "USETA" books scattered throughout our local area. They occasionally appear at public sales. Whether you've lived locally for a lifetime or are a recent transplant, you will not be disappointed if you obtain one or all four. Perhaps you may also recall things you useta do, places you useta go, folks you useta know and the good times you useta have? It would be pleasing to the memory of John Musser if you listed a few 'USETAS" from your own life. "DON'T PASS THE BUCK—STOP AT MUSSERS!

The Buck village, as all rural villages, are recalled not only for the businesses that evolved and developed providing services for this once predominantly agriculture area but mostly for the folks who lived out their lives within this community. Each individual was special and all contributed something along their journey. I hope those of you reading this Musser-Buck story will reminisce and remember with me and, hopefully through a smile or moistened eyes, recall these folks who made this place unique.

Years from now there may be another Buck tale written as new generations emerge and other folks relocate to this place. But for now this is Ruthie's and my story and the one we cherish.

Robert Blair Risk: The Sage of the Buck

Robert Blair Risk, seated in his office at his farm in
The Buck known as "Four Pines"–1920s.

Robert Blair Risk was born February 20, 1848 on a small farm in East Drumore Township. He died at Lancaster General Hospital on March 20, 1926. His funeral was from Chestnut Level Church and he was buried in Chestnut Level Cemetery. He was laid away in an oak casket made from trees grown in Lancaster County. There was no outer case, so that he might "return to mother earth from which he sprung" as quickly as possible. His tombstone reads, "a man not fit to die is not fit to live."

Risk was a newspaperman of the old school and, as editor of the Lancaster Examier that became the New Era, wielded a very considerable influence in local affairs for many years. Poor health compelled his retirement from active newspaper work, but he kept in touch with the "game" through weekly articles, which mixed facts, opinions and philosophy in entertaining, enlightening fashion. He lived quietly on his farm now owned by Dave Byers but never lost interest in his fellow man and is remembered as the "Sage of the Buck."

At age 11 he left the old log schoolhouse at the Buck for academies at Williamsburg, Chestnut Level, and Parkesburg, later returning to teach in the Buck school for 2 years. He later attended law school and became an attorney practicing in Lancaster. The practice of law never filled his taste and he was drawn to what clearly seemed his calling: Newspapering. He was well known far beyond the borders of Lancaster County for his weekly column "Observed and Noted." He is entitled to be known as Lancaster County's most famous and perhaps its first columnist, and among the earliest in the nation.

Mr. Risk's left leg became troublesome and in, 1922, had to be amputated above the knee. He suffered the loss philosophically saying, "It never was much good any way." Risk had purchased the farm at the Buck before 1900 and named it Four Pines. It was here that he set up an office and continued to write his pungent articles. John Todd, mentioned in Risk's articles as "Farmer John," farmed this farm for over 33 years. Todd was a former pupil of Risk's when he taught at the old Buck school.

Being a founding member, Risk entertained his fellow Slumbering Groundhogs at his farm annually for a summer picnic and also a group of men of a unique and fanatic organization known as the Continental Congress. They met at Four Pines every year on July 4th. I'm not sure of their endeavors, but in a photo of this Congressional get together they are all carrying guns! Robert Risk had one brother, James, who was described as a great character. Quite different from writer Robert, James thought of himself as an orator who spoke just "words" and was the jest of much fun. In reality he was a cattle dealer who supposedly sold the same old cow 50 times.

Robert Risk writes magically of spring, "Last Sunday I sat upon a moss-covered bank of a stream I fished in boyhood. It came dashing down a little gorge with springtime merriment. Around me and about me crept modest, unobtrusive but beautiful arbutus, hugging close dear old mother earth, and sending out from its pale pink petals the first incense of spring, swayed by no unfeeling, perfunctory, flabby human hand, but by nature's own immortal breezes toward the altar of the infinite and eternal." Risk continues, "Another thing which gives me comfort and pleasure is to sit in a big rocking chair on the front porch and look at somebody else working during the first few warm days of spring.

"When I was a farm lad it fell to my lot to work the oxen. I rather liked the big calm-eyed patient brutes. It is true the Buck was the center of the lower end cattle trade at one time. I believe John A. Brown who farmed between Chestnut Level and Fairfield used the last pair of oxen for farming this area." (A note from this writer—I believe the Bill Weiler family owned this Brown farm during much of my lifetime.) Another quote from Risk 100 years ago, "one-fourth the population of Lancaster never see the sun rise, the other three-fourths must, as their bread-winning occupations require it. As a rule I go to bed and get up the same day. It was the fourth of July at the Buck and quiet reigned. Store, shop and dwelling house were closed, the babies were in the backyard, and the dogs chained in the stable. But one patriotic sound, at the stated intervals, reminded one it was the way we celebrate-a blast of powder from the old anvil at the Buck blacksmith shop."

Another opinion of Risks that encourages, stimulates and relays a connection to this old 5th generation farmer is the following. The tenderest sentiment one can form is a love for the home of his sires, and the noblest satisfaction one can have is an honorable ancestry. Many a time I have heard the story of Lafayette's welcome and meal taken in the Buck from the old folks. Tales of revolution from grandmother received from her mother who remembered Indian savagery. From this writer, I believe it was 1825 when Lafayette took a meal in the Buck Hotel run by Harry Harnish. During this era Lafayette also supposedly stayed in a frame house across the street to the south of Chestnut Level Church. This fact was relayed to me by Charlotte Garner Musser whose mother, Irene Garner uncovered this fact when removing old wall paper while living in this house early in the 20th century. The words written on the bare wall were, Lafayette stayed here in 1825.

These words of wisdom from Robert Risk seem even more appropriate today than when they were composed over 120 years ago.

There is such a thing as being killed by kindness. I hate to be forced to eat, or have reflections passed upon my health because I cannot devour half a chicken, swallow 5 kinds of pickles, 10 kinds of preserves along with an over abundant meal, and top off with half a pie embalmed in crust 3/4 of a inch thick. Now what does common sense say? A physician thus explains how one may live long: Take an hour of exercise on every pound of food. We are not nourished by what we eat, but by what we digest. Every hour you steal from digestion will be reclaimed by indigestion. Beware of the wrath of a patient stomach! The oftener you eat the oftener you will repent it. Abstinence from all drugs is easier than temperance from food. Sleep is sweeter after a fast-day than after a feast-day. For every meal you lose you gain a better. The human stomach is a long-suffering organ, but when it turns upon its possessor it is capable of mischief as dire as is the much abused "heart," though, of course, it is not as likely to become prominent in mortuary reports. "Heart failure" has a more aristocratic sound than "stomach failure" and the feelings of the survivors must be spared.

Finally, Robert Risk's thoughts on death. "To a philosopher, death is not so terrible. The mystery of earth is birth; the aim of man should be right living. Death is inevitable and takes care of itself. It is a submission to conditions. Whether young or old, if our physical make-up cannot longer resist our environment or contend against temptation, occupation, greed and all the vices, and even virtues, overdone, then the silver cord is cut and the golden bowl broken. My brother, natural affection sheds a tear over those near and dear, but reason gives the comfort that right living robs death of its terrors. If you have a soul worth saving, it will benefit you to give the world evidence of the fact before you die. Live nobly think the best, and all will be well. Death does not end all-it begins every thing."

Irene Garner, The Spirit of The Buck

Irene Garner takes a rare break while working in her garden.

Irene Rice Garner was born April 29, 1898 in Safe Harbor. During her childhood she lived with her parents, James and Phoebe Snyder Rice, and her brother, John, on a small farm near Liberty Square, now submerged under water along the eastern edge of Muddy Run Lake. Her father's occupation is listed in an old Drumore Township assessment book as farmer, trapper, hunter and fisherman.

Irene later married Charles "Gussie" Garner and they had 2 daughters, Dot, married to the late John Jamison, and Charlotte, married to the late John Musser. The Garners lived locally at different locations, including Chestnut Level, then moved to The Buck in 1937. They lived and owned a small farm at the famous Buck crossroads at the northeast corner of this, notorious for deadly accidents, intersection. The frame house that she lived in for 50 years still stands and is owned and occupied by Irene (known by many as Ma) Garner's great-grandson, Steve Shaubach. The Garners were only the 3rd family to own this nearly 200-year-old house. Numerous building lots have over the years been sold off Garner's farm. Irene remembered fondly The Buck Hotel, the blacksmith shop and the creamery from years past. At this farm they kept chickens, pigs and 2 mules named Cappy and Old Petey.

While living at The Buck Hotel, as a little girl with her parents, my wife, Ruthie, recalls Gussie Garner often walking the short distance to Abner Musser Sr's. store. He would visit with Musser and other acquaintances, purchase a couple of necessary items then return past The Buck Hotel. Ruthie observed his walk-by and would sit on the porch awaiting his return. He would always stop and give her a piece of candy and with a smile refer to her as "Dolly Dimples." Gussie Garner, as many others of that era would on occasion, sample available alcohol. Supposedly if Ma would observe her husband coming up the walk late at night, enthralled with an over-abundance of joy and happiness, she locked the door, went to bed and Gus welcomed slumber curled up in the barn. Gussie Garner died in 1952.

Irene Garner is remembered as a jack-of-all trades. Among a few of her talents were carpentry, wallpaper hanging, house painting, farming, sewing, cooking, canning and baking. Her home always had a professional look inside and out with painting and papering regularly done by her. Her yearly-planted large garden was her pride and joy as she raised, harvested and preserved everything grown. She shared her over-abundance of food with family, friends, and neighbors. Year-round, inside her windows with panes that would shine, were numerous African Violets of all colors that flourished with Ma's constant attention.

During her lifetime, she worked as a waitress, ran 7 automatic sewing machines at once at Singing Needles in Leola, as a practical nurse at Quarryville Presbyterian Home and during W.W.II at Armstrong, making components for bombs. I thought it most ironic that this woman, known to be impulsive, full of fire, excitable and wired was working with bombs!

I believe Irene owned and operated a 1961 Chevy the last 25-years she drove. Speaking of the local highway (Route 272) running south of Lancaster to

The Buck, she stated, "you may pass me on the flats south of Lancaster but I'll catch and go around you on the Smithville hills." She also stated, "I've never had any trouble with my car and I wouldn't take 3 times of what I paid for it." Ruthie recalls riding with Ma Garner in her Chevy nearly 50 years ago to Ma's granddaughter Phoebe's college graduation in Delaware. She describes Ma's driving in the following manner. Her speed seemed to remain constant, uphill, downhill and around corners. On curves she would lean into them as if riding a motorcycle. Granddaughters Phoebe and Becky recall as children riding with their grandmother to the shore in Wildwood, New Jersey, where according to them she took enough food along to feed the entire block where they stayed. Let's just say she drove as she lived her life-full speed ahead, never slowing down or, heaven forbid, "coasting," always pushing forward with the pedal to the metal, her nose to the grindstone, her hands never idle and her tongue constantly expressing her thoughts!

Irene Garner was a more than 50-year member of Chestnut Level Church. Her colorful peonies, grown in her yard adorned and beautified the stage in the old Sunday School at Chestnut Level during many Children's Day exercises. Her needlework was unmatched and a prized possession for those who've acquired it. Her baking of homemade bread, raised homemade doughnuts, cherry pies and apple dumplings in the fall were enjoyed by many who knew her. She once stated, "One day my son-in-law and I picked 5 huge buckets full of cherries by 10:30 a. m. and by the 10:30 p.m. they were all canned."

"Most people don't cook from scratch anymore. 'They don't take the time the way we usta do. Now it's from the freezer to the table. Not me, I like my food fresh; even my chicken I raise or buy alive and dress them at home. I don't go for foods just because they're convenient." Ruthie's son, Kenneth, mowed Ma Garners yard several summers when he was a boy. He stated he did it not for the money but for the delicious home-cooked meals she served him.

Ma Garner was described to me by former friends and neighbors as one of the kindest ladies to ever reside in The Buck. Ruthie recalls that when her dad was sick and subsequently died in the hospital there was cake, salad, soup and various other food items weekly delivered to her home by Ma Garner. I'm sure this thoughtful gesture was repeated numerous times to others she knew.

There were those who referred to Ma Garner as a saint. But this saint, when riled, could out-cuss a drunken sailor. Those who should know stated that she slept with a loaded shotgun under her bed. If she heard a ruckus outside her house in the middle of the night she raised her bedroom window, shot once and then opened fire with an arsenal of tongue-lashing words that may have stung worse than the gunpowder charged, shot gun pellets. During her lifetime at The Buck, the traffic and the numerous out of the area folks passing through and sometimes lingering increased dramatically. By the end of Ma Garner's life this once rural crossroads may have been the busiest, most dangerous corner in Southern Lancaster County. But it was well understood that in The Buck nobody messed with Ma Garner.

During a senior citizen interview when she was 87, she revealed she recently painted her porches and mixed and poured the cement for her walkways. "Too many people nowadays give up and sit in rocking chairs; you have to have ambition and determination to keep on the go."

Robert Risk was referred to as the "Sage of The Buck." I thought of Abner Musser Sr. as the "stimulus" or "spark plug" of The Buck and thus I have concluded that Irene Garner, during her half-century of living at this place, should be remembered as the "Spirit of The Buck." A few words that define spirit are fire, energy, enthusiasm, liveliness and readiness to assert one's energy. Ask any who remember Irene Garner and I think they will be in agreement of my assessment and assumption of this remembered, special woman.

When reminiscing and contemplating the lives of early settlers and pioneers of these area I immediately think of the brave, rugged, stout-hearted men that cleared and farmed this land. But what of the women? How did they survive all the hardships and heartaches they encountered almost daily? Could the men and, more importantly, the women of this 21st century survive what our ancestors endured? Perhaps the Amish. But even for them it would have been a dramatic change in their lifestyle and every day habits.

But as I remember Irene Garner she could have survived 200-years-ago in this area and flourished as those gone before. For me she was a throw-back to an era when this area was first settled offering a tiny, realistic glimpse into our past. She was a survivor who could do most anything she put her mind and body to that appeared before her. She could live off the land, butcher a hog, chicken, duck or turkey and if necessary shoot dead an attacking Indian outside her window! She could have totally prepared the first Thanksgiving dinner for the Pilgrims. She was the epitome of our pioneer women who lived and settled this surrounding, rolling, wilderness forest. Perhaps you may recall a woman from your past that exemplified this pioneer spirit. However for this old farmer-author it was Irene Garner. You missed something in your full, rich life if you missed her.

During a recent conversation with Jack Stoner, a son who continues his father's welding business in The Buck, he related this descriptive Ma Garner anecdote. Ma lived directly across the road from our one and only bank in The Buck. The bank contacted Jack to have it's mailbox taken down and replaced. This mailbox was located near Ma Garners, and Jack, with torch in hand, mistakenly cut off Ma's mailbox and returned the one-quarter mile to his shop. Jack said he head his phone ringing in the shop even before departing his truck. It continued ringing several more times till, breathlessly toting the mailbox, Jack answered. Relating to me this was a one-way conversation with Ma Garner at the other end asking this simple question, as only Ma Garner could. "Jack, why in the hell did you just cut off my blankity-blank mailbox?" It was then that Jack realized his mistake, thinking to himself, anybody but Irene Garner! Tears of laughter rolled down Jack's cheeks when relating this story to me. I'm sure when this incident occurred neither Jack nor Irene was laughing. Needless to say, Jack rectified his mistake immediately, apology included. Another justification for the premise everyone locally understood, "Don't mess with Irene Garner."

The John and Luella Byers family raised and butchered chickens, ducks, and turkeys regularly at holidays. Most were sold locally to regular customers. Ruthie, her mom and Ma Garner helped with this fowl slaughter and subsequent cleaning or dressing as it was referred to. This endeavor was not for the squeamish, feeble or faint-hearted. It involved a strong arm and hand to remove feathers and innards and an even stronger constitution to block the foul, fowl odor permeating throughout Luella's kitchen. Being no stranger to these last 3 descriptive lines, Ma Garner was in her glory. Accordingly and predictably, a few of Ma's jokes and stories that occasionally surfaced may have been as off color as the buckets of discarded innards of the appropriate fowl. However, her laughter seemed to greatly diminish this smelly situation and eventually eliminate it altogether. Everyone had a different description of Irene Garner but I believe Debbie Byers Wenger offered the shortest and most accurate of all. "Absolutely no subject was off-limits within Ma Garner's conversations." Finally Ruthie relates, "All of us enjoyed working together but Ma Garner relished it. She was one of a kind and deserves to be remembered in this Buck story." Irene (Ma) Garner died December 21, 1989 at the age of 91 following a rich, full, life, fully applying her many capabilities within her life and into the lives of others.

The Old Buck School Recalled

An account of the Buck school by Robert B. Risk taken from the Quarryville Sun of about December 1923:

"The first school was built before 1823 opposite the entrance to the present Byers farm. It was a rough, log structure with crude benches and desks for the pupils and as primitive in all regards as the homes and way of our early ancestors.

"In the course of time that old building became worm-eaten, moldy and unsafe. More than that, the increase in population rendered this first schoolhouse unfit to accommodate the young barbarians of the day. With strict views of economy the directors thought the cheapest spot the best for school purposes. So they purchased a site at the foot of Harry Good's meadow, mostly swamp, near a little spring and its tiny, sluggish rivilet. This was surrounded by an old-fashioned worm fence on 3 sides and a post fence in front with a gate painted green for entrance. As the ground was generally very wet and muddy there was practically no playground. This building was of stone and considerably larger than its log predecessor. In the summer time it had quite a picturesque look with its moss-covered, shingle roof, the worm fence hidden by rich growths of clustering plants and vines, and its swampy surroundings richly green with luxuriant beds of calamus. But it soon got a name that, like all nicknames, cling to it all its days—"Tadpole" or "Frog Swamp Academy."

"This was the first school I went to only a few hundred yards from my home. My first teacher was a Miss. Smith pronounced a good one by the parents of the neighborhood. A few of her successors were Frank Jenkins, Edwin Shoemaker, George Lamborn and Westley Lefever. The latter one whipped 2 of the Deaver boys the first day and thus broke a precedent, as it was unusual to begin thrashing on opening day. About 1859, when I was 11, a new building was erected on the site of the present one. It was a proud day when Miss Walker and her flock of scholars marched from swamp academy to new quarters, located on high ground. This building was a substantial structure and why it was later torn down to make a place for the present brick one I never found out except on the theory of Mark Twain who said, "It is true the Lord made idiots. He did it by way of experiment. Then he invented school boards.

"The school of 1860 was a large one. Pupils came in crowds of all sizes, styles of beauty and freckles and variety of dress. This school was later demolished and the present brick one erected in its place in 1908. It is doubtful if our youth today are taught the principles of citizenship, good manners, respect for age and observance of law and order as were the lads of a former age in the original log schoolhouse of the Buck or its successor "Tadpole Academy."

"The ideal of the present schoolboy seems to be to get away from the land or farm as soon as possible, be able to run an automobile and play basketball. His sister's ideal is the same, almost, to get into the city factory and attend movies. There must be something wrong in the spirit and scope of our educational system that makes our school boys hate to learn a trade and despise the plow and our girls to prefer the whiz of a factory spindle to the homely duties of the housewife."

A few final thoughts from this present day writer. The last Buck school, I believe closed in 1937. During much of my lifetime it was owned and turned into a residence by Mr. & Mrs Francis Wenger. An Amish family presently owns it.

The Buck School–1925: L to R, Martin Byers, Robert Morrison, Everett Schneider, Kathryn Todd, Nora Schneider, Ruth Byers, Warren Reinhart, Clyde Sider and Bill Schneider. Second row: L to R, John Musser, John Byers, Ruth Todd, Isabelle Byers, Hazel Byers, Verna Schneider, Helen Woerner, Helen Schneider, David Kochel, and Robert Good. Bottom row: L to R, Charles Kochel, Abner Musser Jr., David Shenery, Frank Woerner, Harry Woerner, Chester Todd, David Vehenery and Hess Byers.

Memories, by Debbie Byers Wenger

I grew up at the Buck on a farm called "Four Pines," because of the four large pine trees in front of the house. The businesses in The Buck at that time were Wenger Pontiac, sold Pontiac vehicles, Wenger Implement sold John Deere equipment, Wayne Byers plumber and electrician, John Stoner welding, Musser's grocery store and butcher shop, and Eshleman Feed Store sold animal feed and all these stores were closed on Sunday. The closest thing we had to a convenience store was Mel Marron's about 1 & ½ miles south of The Buck along 272 which was open on Sunday because that's where you went to get the Sunday paper and they also had 2 gas pumps, where Valero is now. Between The Buck and Marron's was Shudy's Rainbow Park. I remember it was a small diner with a couple of pinball machines.

My father, John T. Byers, Harry Keene & Ralph Byers all helped each other when it came time to planting and harvesting crops. Each had a hired hand, the ones I remember were, Harry's was Jim Mullen, Ralph's was Dick Lefever and ours was Clair Linkey. In the summer I helped plant tobacco, hoe it and try to see how many tobacco worms we could find and toss at each other. I laid the tobacco lathe in the rows and handed the speared tobacco up to who ever was on the wagon. I didn't top the tobacco, but I did try cutting it but I wasn't as fast as most of the others. I wasn't allowed to spear it on the lathe; my dad probably figured I would run the spear through my hand, which I probably would have. This was always supposed to be done before school started so there would be plenty of help. I drove tractor for other chores around the farm and helped with the milking. When I went back to school I had a "natural" tan, not like some girls who put iodine and baby oil on their skin to get a tan.

We always planted sweet corn for the whole Byers family. When it was ready to pick my dad and Clair would go out after the morning milking and pick carts full and my aunts and grandparents would come to help. We always husked and silked it out in the front yard, that kept the mess outside and at that time we had a wood stove we cooked on so it got pretty hot in the kitchen on a summer day. After it was cooked and bagged for freezing everyone took home what they needed for the year.

For several summers "bums," we didn't have to be politically correct back then and call them "homeless," would come through The Buck. We weren't along 272 so they must've looked down the road and saw our farm and thought that would be a place to get a meal. He would knock on the door and ask for a meal, mother would get one ready and he ate it out on the porch and when he was done would knock on the door and return the plate back and always said, "thank-you."

When I went to school all the grades rode the same bus and got dropped off at different one-room schools through out East Drumore Township. Children west of 272 south went to Drumore schools so if you lived in The Buck and had friends across the road you went to 2 different schools. The bus driver I had the longest was Stanley, "Stiff," Stauffer. Back then we didn't have too many discipline problems either at school or on the bus because if you got spanked at school you got spanked at home. On the bus the older kids looked out for the younger ones. I remember one winter when I went to Ashland School, which only had grades 1 & 2 Mrs. Shenk was the teacher and we had a snow storm while we were at school and for some reason the bus couldn't come get us so they sent the hearse. At that time it was a black panel van, so they put benches down each side. The older girls held us younger ones on their laps and some one was up front to tell the driver where to stop. When I got home it was dark and the snow was high for a first grader to walk through. Our family didn't have a phone so my parents were surprised when I walked through the door. When I was older the Byers kids and the Dombach kids and occasionally the Lefever kids, at Ralph Byers' would go sledding at night on the road, which is now the intersection of Four Pines Road and Deaver Road. We would sled for 2 to 3 hours and in that time maybe 2 vehicles would come through.

My father went to Buck School, which was where the Francis Wenger family lived when I was growing up. The alumni of that school got together at our home for several summers. I went to one room schools till I got to middle school then I went to what was the old Quarryville High School, which is now the Administration building. When I went to high school I joined the staff of the school newspaper, the Quill. I had to ride the activity bus home, which would let me off at Musser's Store, which at that time was where Buck Beverage is now. I would go get a soda or a snack and walk home. Mr. & Mrs. Park Moore lived at the corner of our road with the house on one side and barn on the other. If she saw me and had supper almost ready she would come out and talk for a bit.

At Halloween my parents would pick up some of the neighborhood kids and pile into our Pontiac, not a station wagon, and go trick or treating to the neighbors. One evening in the fall Wenger Implement would have John Deere days. Families in the community would turn out to see the new equipment, have snacks and see a movie, Abbott and Costello or other comedy.

Later my parents started raising turkeys for Thanksgiving and Christmas. Some of the neighbors would come help. The two helped more often were Ralph Byers, and Irene, "Mom" Garner. "Mom" was the oldest resident of The Buck. She lived on the corner of 272 and Buck Road. She had a laugh, more like a cackle, she never beat around the bush she always asked you straight out and you never knew what she was going to say, nothing was off limits. You always saw her with a dress and apron. She had chickens fenced in her yard.

Beagles and Beaglers in The Buck

Owners and dogs L to R, Robert Reinhart and "Reinhart's Spot;" E. H. Duffy with "Beggar Row Gizmo;" Clayton Root and "Gephart's Pleasant Place Smoky;" William Little and "Little's Boots;" Oscar Barefoot and "Eberle's Tru-Boy;" and Vance Reinhart with "Peach Bottom Doll." Judges James Cook, Nelson Glackin and Clark Eckman, Field Marshall.

The Lanco Beagle club began in The Buck in 1951. It originally consisted of approximately 50 members. 60 years ago Beagle popularity had risen to the point that more beagles were registered than any other breed of dogs. The field trials for these rabbit chasers that pursued bunnies by scent and smell, not sight or sound, was held on the 250 acres of reserve land owned by Bobby Reinhart. This land was located on the north side of Route 372 in the general area around and behind the present-day building owned by Cedar

Crest Equipment. This sport was totally about the chase with no harm done to bugs and his buddies.

This property was originally 2 farms, with the main farm and buildings located east of Cedar Crest. During the 1950s, Ralph and Edith Reinhart lived in this farmhouse. Bobby Reinhart during this time lived on the back farm but, later this house burnt completely down. A mobile home was placed near the original house that served him his remaining years.

The Beaglers constructed a clubhouse halfway in the lane leading to the still—standing, main farmhouse. This homemade building seated over 75 and also had a kitchen, with wives of members serving meals. Living directly across 372 as a child, Ruthie recalls neighbors being invited and attending an occasional breakfast held in this clubhouse. I'm sure the homemade food was delicious, the facilities adequate and fortunately, for the members, those who nowadays do health and food inspections for the state were not yet born. I'm told of an occasional fish fry held at the club. I'm thinking a member, Ward Ressel, who worked for Park Zook, our local fish man during this era, may have supplied the fish. Park Zook, I believe, was the grandfather of Dick McMinn, current President of Buck Iron Company. I've also heard through the years that a groundhog feast was held at this place, with the hogs for this "Whistle Pig Roast" supplied by Fred and Ward Ressel.

Ken Granbois, brother-in-law to Bobby Rinehart, later purchased all this land. For several years George and Lucy Warfel, who lived in the main house and operated a dairy, farmed this land. Later this farm passed to Mike Granbois, Ken and Margaret's son. I believe the farmhouse is presently rented and the land farmed by a local farmer, Ronnie Metzler. This old farm that was once thriving vigorously with howling hounds, tails and tales and tobacco using, beagle bragging folks that loved nothing more than a good rabbit chase, today appears forlorn. There are few left that remember the glorious days 60 years ago spent here with good dogs, numerous tail bobbin rabbits and appreciated friends.

A few locals I recall as beaglers in The Buck were Keel Hambleton, Harry O'Donnell, Park Eckman, Frank Cassidy, John Glass, Lloyd Witmer, Harry Able, Risser Strickler, Haines Duffy, Vance Reinhart, Frank Reese, Bobby Reinhart, George Harnish, Fred and Ward Ressel, Nelson Glackin, Guy Lefever, Oscar Barefoot, Jim Cook, John Eidemiller, John Cochran, Clayton Root, Charles Murray, Clayton Rutt and Giles Hambleton. During this time in Buck history Giles Hambleton owned a farm just over the hill from the Beagle Club where bunnies, beaglers and beagles were also known to regularly traverse, travel and train these sniffing, short-legged humble hounds. Southern Lancaster County Farmer Sportsman Association presently owns this land.

I shall attempt to briefly explain the function and activity of this Beagle Club from years ago. The idea is to train the dogs so they work in pairs with unfamiliar partners. I suppose those of you younger than I may equate this to the TV show "Dancing with the Stars." Drawing for braces or "partners" was accomplished by putting numbered balls inside a rotating wire cage. Each participating dog was also assigned a number corresponding to those being mixed together. Following the combining of the numbered balls in the rotated—by—hand circular container, 2 are allowed to exit together. The beagles with corresponding numbers are then paired together as are the others in this fashion for this particular field trial. Any resemblance of this manner of selecting pairs of dogs to our present day lottery is strictly coincidental.

The dogs are measured from the top of their front shoulder to the ground, resulting in 15 inch, 13 inch and 12 inch classes. The dogs are taken to the field and, when a rabbit is seen, someone hollers "Tally-Ho" and these 2 dogs are released together. Judges intently observe the dogs on their trailing ability and working with one another. There is a whole lot more to this procedure of which I know very little. John Allen Hambleton, son of the late Keel, could educate you on much of this.

Sometime during the late 50s the Beagle Club purchased 200 acres of land and moved to Mt. Nebo. They acquired this land at a sheriff's sale through Clayton Rutt for $8500.00. Over the years rabbits have been trapped locally and transported to and released at this site of the present club. Members provide feed during and following snowstorms to ensure their survival and propagation for later field trials. However, the recent abundance of hawks, foxes and coyotes in this area has greatly diminished the population of burr rabbit. The hawks that are now protected have flourished and when they find an area filled with bunnies they set up housekeeping and remain there as long as the smorgasbord remains well stocked and open. Owls that hatch their young mid-winter also will feed themselves and their chicks on the timid hare in the open fields. As a farmer I have witnessed this annihilation of the rabbit population during my lifetime.

My son and daughter-in-law, Roger and Shirl Smith, live on Hillcrest Avenue in Quarryville. During visits to their home I observe more rabbits around their house than on the 3 farms locally that I farm. Perhaps predators as solicitors are not welcome in downtown Quarryville or maybe as folks move from urban areas to the country the wildlife moves to town. This causes me to predict both beagles and beaglers will one day conduct their sport on the streets and lawns of this, named for a hole in the ground, town of Quarryville.

I envision the hare trailed by the hounds streaking from the back yard of Frank Reese, crossing the parking lot of Good's store, and then heading for the

Presbyterian home. I'm not sure how the scent of the bunny or the smell of the hound may be affected by asphalt and concrete. I hope the borough council erects a few signs reading: Please brake for Beagles and Bunnies!

Although membership has somewhat diminished from years ago, field trials are still held at Mt. Nebo and as far away as New York and Virginia. I'm sure those participating are every bit as enthused with the chase of bunnies by beagles as the original, founding members of the Lanco Beagle Club 60 years ago in The Buck. TALLY-HO!

Light at the Buck By Stu Mylin

My father moved to our family farm in 1932 and from our farmhouse, if you look towards the east, you could see the Buck. Obviously this is easier to do in the winter since the view isn't obstructed by crops, tree leaves or what have you.

There was no electric service back our road in the early thirties, so the farm relied in part on generators, and the one we had was in the tobacco stripping room. Father ran it during the night so he could see to milk and perform the necessities of farm life before bed time.

One cold winter night a young sailor arrived at the farm long after anyone "respectful" would be traveling. Visitors were always welcome at our place, but Dad was a little puzzled at this fellow, especially at such an hour.

As it turns out, the young man was looking for his girlfriend, who was supposed to be staying at the hotel at the Buck. The girlfriend said, "Come to the Buck. Musser's store is there and Abner Musser keeps his porch light on all the time (an extravagance.) It's the only light at night in the Buck! I'm in the hotel across the road."

The sailor went on to say that when he got into the Buck that night the only light he saw was the one to the west on top of the hill. He obviously thought the Buck boundaries were very large. So, like the shepherds of yore on that snowy eve long ago, he followed the light to the inn (hotel).

Well, Dad mused at the fact that his power plant was now a beacon of romance. Apparently Abner's light had burnt out.

My father explained what happened and told the traveler that he should stay the night and in the morning after breakfast he could return to the hotel and meet the girl. He did, and as far as we know, romance blossomed from there.

Today, 67 years later, I find this story amusing in that I can still see the Buck from my house on the farm. However, along with the many other changes to take place there, the idea of 24-hour lighting, started by Abner Musser long ago, has been taken up and elaborated. Now, we have become quite illuminated. I don't think anyone could give directions simply by saying, "There's only one light after dark . . . and I'm right across the road."

Fond Memories of the Buck

One of my unexpected joys of writing has come by way of folks from my past resurfacing and rekindling a long ago friendship. J. Elvin (Shorty) Herr and his wife, Elizabeth, lived at the top of the hill south of the Buck during my childhood and teenage years until 1962. The locals always referred to this location as, Shorty Herr's Hill. The Herrs had 7 children, Henry, Carl, Pete, Ruth, Lydia Ann, Mary Grace and Betty.

The Herrs, through e-mail and personal contact, recall the wonderful view of the Buck from their home, which remains to this day imbedded in their fond, reflective memories. They more than any other family of that era experienced and enjoyed daily the premier, panoramic view before them. The busy 272 highway that ran parallel to their home intersected the Buck and all road hugging businesses.

The tree-lined hill to the north that this roadway clung to and climbed was even steeper and more elevated then the one beside their farm. The Herrs observed several tractor-trailers over the years jack-knifed on this mountainside. They also saw from a distance numerous accidents, with many fatalities, that occurred regularly and until recently at the dangerous Buck crossroads. This was rectified by road relocation and the addition of a traffic light. Their view to the east stretched halfway to Quarryville and to the west was restrained only by the forested, Rawlinsville Ridge.

A few remembrances of these Herr folks, who were once children on this farm at the Buck and who are no longer young, warms the hearts of all who grew up in that era in this area. The simple ordinary things, the happy occasions and the heartaches all residing together in the recesses of mature, contemplative minds now regularly rise to the surface as each of them recall their lives when younger.

The Herr kids, lives, as all others from that time, have been cast to the winds of change with one residing nearby and the others far away. We go wherever life leads us but our childhood home and memories always accompanies us. They recall the pond at the Buck: skating, swimming, fishing and skipping stones across the water's surface. They remember the big Drumore snows with drifts from bank to bank across the deep cuts on 272. They mention a visit from the State Police motivated by their dog, Shep, chasing vehicles on the busy highway. An older boy, with gun in hand taking Shep for his final trek to the woods, rectified this.

They write of picking stones in their fields and when blessed with boredom by their surroundings would simply, when bent over retrieving rocks, look between their legs at the landscape before them. It appeared totally different, altered and unfamiliar from this position. Only we farm kids can appreciate this attempt to adjust and improve this unpleasant chore. I've participated in this upside-down phenomenon many times in my life, one that can alter a landscape and also one's perspective on life. This is why, as we grow old, many folks become uninterested and unenthused with life. Uncooperative, arthritic limbs no longer allow we senior citizens to bend over and glance between our fibulas to view the world and life anew.

I believe Henry Herr my have helped with the construction of the ball field at the Buck, and Carl Herr mentioned playing basketball in Leroy Wenger's shop. Carl, Ruth and Mary Grace, who was in my class in school, were the only Herr children I knew personally. Pete, the youngest child, wrote of watching for the school bus tracking its daily course and hollerin' to his siblings, "The bus is coming down Wilbur Pollock's hill . . . its leavin' Dick Lefevers . . . it just went past Joe Holabeins . . . it's pullin' out of the Buck." He states that this fortuitous location of their home prevented many a missed school bus following chores, soap and water and a hasty breakfast

Tom Lefever, a neighbor, former classmate and one who also rode their school bus, has recently informed me that the Herr kids actually missed the school bus on one rare occasion. Rev. Tom now a local respected minister recalls of this happening and the Herr children, instructed by their father, to walk the approximately 4 miles to Drumore School. This never happened again!

I shall conclude this story as Mary Grace and I prepare to celebrate our 50-year class reunion from Solanco High School. Her sister, Lydia Ann Herr Mahabirsingh, now residing in Florida, confirmed this account. It seems to me that, 50 years ago, a story such as this was not nearly as uncommon as today.

She writes that in June of 1961 she was home for a week between teaching in Tampa, Florida and college classes in Virginia. Her parents were planting sweet potatoes in their garden when her mother rushed into the house for water and a pill thinking their father was having a heart attack. Lydia was instructed to call Dr. Bair, who informed them to bring Shorty to his office immediately. She relates, "With mother driving, daddy in the front seat and me in the back we raced to Quarryville. Daddy struggled for a while leaning over the back of his seat, then tuned around, sat down on his seat. His head dropped, and it was over." He was 52 and left his wife, 3 children married, 2 in college, one graduating from high school that evening and one still in high school. Obviously, Mary Grace on this tragic day, did not attend her high school graduation, but was thankful her parents had attended her baccalaureate the night before.

This Herr homestead has since been owned by Leon Kreider, Gerald and Linda Kreider and presently by Amos Fisher, who operates it as a dairy and produce farm.

Wrestling in The Buck

Wayne and Mabel Byers, along with their son, June once owned and operated a plumbing and electrical business in The Buck. Their headquarters also Wayne and Mabel's home was located in The Buck south across from the former home of John and Pauline Stoner and beside the present Buck Hardware. I believe this building currently accommodates Delta Glass and is still owned by Jim Hostetter C.P.A. whose tax and accounting business began at this place. He has since built a larger building on Friendly Drive opposite Musser's Market to expand his business.

Wayne Byers also sold stoves, refrigerators, freezers and other electrical appliances. He reportedly also owned the first TV in The Buck in the early 50s. I'm told the wooden case that held this unfamiliar marvel was huge and the small screen was round, possibly a Sylvania. Locals would gather in the evening to watch this in house wonder in the long, narrow, dark room of Wayne's world.

Wrestling from Baltimore on Tuesday nights was a crowded, crowd pleaser with late-comers accepting standing room only. Reportedly cheering, booing and cussin' were well represented by regular wrestling attendees. None of those original wrestling fans from The Buck could ever have imagined that 50 years later a professional wrestler from that era would own a business in The Buck only a couple hundred yards from where this was first observed.

I believe Bailey Goss was the ringside commentator and National Bohemian Beer was the sponsor. Although certainly not a beer connoisseur, I'm assuming both Bailey Goss and Boh Beer are now but a fleeting memory, with the head of neither rising on the TV screen or near the top of a sparkling glass on my sweeping Baltimore radar. I do recall this Boh Beer logo sporting a one-eyed, monocle-wearing figure.

I'm told most who attended these televised Baltimore bouts in The Buck were convinced of and would swear by and accept all of it as credible. Anyone thinking otherwise kept their thoughts of wrestling deception, illusion and a pre-choreographed hoax to themselves. The application of a hammerlock, headlock or chokehold by a believer on a non-believer quickly squelched and quieted any wrestling dissenters. I personally witnessed this occur in Liberty Square store, with Bill Stauffer ranting as to the fake of wrestling on TV. Hidden from Stauffer in a darkened corner was Bob Haldeman, probably the strongest man known locally and a Buck wrestling attendee. In an instant he grabbed short, stocky and befuddled Bill, twisting his arm behind his back and shoving his hand up between his shoulder blades. Stauffer's lit cigar dropped from his mouth, apparently opening from pain, and rolled across his belly-releasing sparks and smoke on its journey to the floor between his feet that appeared to be dangling. Haldeman's only comment during this brief 30 second encounter, "Does this feel fake?"

This made quite an impression on the shocked store onlookers and me. As for Willie Lump Lump his face turned scarlet, I thought his large, bulging eyes would spring from their sockets and he departed the store with his arm still behind his back. Bob Haldeman punctuated this chance meeting and wrestling discussion as he stepped on and extinguished Bill Stauffer's still smoldering cigar. To my knowledge wrestling was never again discussed in Liberty Square store. Conversation returned to talk of less intense and non-controversial subjects such as politics, religion and taxes.

This was the early 1950s when it seemed most of the local men smoked cigarettes, cigars or pipes. Ruthie, as a little girl, attended this nearby entertainment with her parents. She recalls that by the final bout on the wrestling card this tiny round light presenting these ringside rumbles at The Buck, Byer's free for view theater was completely shrouded in smoke. Some claimed the TV screen appeared as a far, distant lighthouse on a dense, foggy shore. Thinking back to 60 years ago the 1950s, are recalled as simple, less complicated times than today. Perhaps wrestling portrayed this, as there was always a good guy who wrestled by the rules and a bad opponent who disregarded and broke them all with a referee who attempted to police and keep order. Most times the good guy prevailed and won, but as in life this did not always happen.

A few wrestlers, recalled from that era that arrived weekly in The Buck via television were Antonino Rocca from Argentina. Part wrestler, part acrobat he wrestled in bare feet as he bounced around the ring delivering flying drop kicks to opponents chest or head. He also could pick-up opponents seemingly twice his size; position them on their back across his broad shoulders into a submission hold he referred to as the back-breaker. Benito Gardenea, of Spanish or Mexican descents claim to fame was his ability, when body slammed by an opponent to the canvas to somehow bounce 2 feet into the air. The very first pretty boy was proud, blond haired Gorgeous George but there have been many since. Lew Thesz as I recall was considered and billed as the World Champion wrestler. Verne Gagne's specialty was referred to as a sleeper hold when he wrapped his powerful arms around an opponent's head. When this was applied to the other one in the ring facing him this guy would begin to yawn, eventually close his eyes, drop to the canvas and feign snoring. Killer Kawalski was every bit as mean as his name.

There were those with German and Japanese names that were booed without mercy. You realize this was but a decade following WWII. Haystacks Calhoun wore bib overalls while wrestling and supposedly weighed over 600 pounds. His submission hold occurred when he simply sat on an opponent. Yukon Eric, from Alaska, paralyzed his competition by wrapping his muscular arms around their chest then squeezing. He referred to this as his bear hug. For recreation he supposedly applied his bear hug to trees then raised them from the earth! Skull Murphy knocked those he faced unconscious with a head butt. Don Eagle, an Indian, when riled would do a war dance then attack and pulverize his opponent. His local claim to fame was that a couple boys in Drumore Elementary School copied his hairstyle. This hairstyle has endured 60 years and is still visible here and around the world. The midgets, male and female also wrestled, mostly as tag teams. Two I recall were Sky Low Low and Little Beaver. Slave Girl Mula was one of the female wrestlers I remember but there were numerous others.

This wrestling in The Buck retains another close tie to this area, as Joe Gagliano and his wife were the original owners of Pappa Joes, a pizza parlor located very near the home of Wayne Byers where this entertaining sport was introduced 50 years ago. Joe Gagliano was a Pro-Wrestler during that era known as Count Gagliano. There are numerous photos of him and other wrestlers on the walls of his establishment. In researching a few of these wrestlers from the 50s the majority of them died before reaching the age of 50. Everyone now realizes that this was an entertainment show but evidently the wear and tear on the bodies of those participating shortened their lives.

Ken Denlinger, my editing cousin, relates the following anecdote to this wrestling account. The Washington Post actually published the results from Pro Wrestling matches held locally in Washington years ago. A man named Joe Holman would call the paper at 11 P.M. with the results from ringside. When the Post moved the deadline up one hour to 10 P.M. Holman would call at 10 with the results as screaming fans could be heard in the background with matches still in progress. Joe Holman evidently knew beforehand the winners of the matches, regardless of the fact that some had not yet occurred.

Ken also relates a story he heard on an airplane while returning from a Celtics-Lakers basketball game in Boston. He stated that at Lakers home games Hollywood celebrities would appear regularly. A few mentioned were Jack Nicholson, Henry Winkler (The Fonz), Angie Dickinson, Kirk Douglas and several others. I'm thinking these expensive courtside seats were purchased to see the game, cheer for the Lakers and more importantly to be seen. On this particular night the only well known who patronized the Celtics was a wrestler named Big John Studd. Flying home from Boston, Ken was seated near Big John Studd and professional boxer Sugar Ray Leonard. What Ken recalls from these pro athletes conversation was neither had a fear inside their perspective rings of wrestling or boxing. Their greatest fear occurred during the walk from their dressing room to the ring, then their return through the crowd following their matches. They were worried about objects being thrown at them and being stuck with the hatpins of little old ladies. Both claimed that was the only time they were afraid.

Personally from where I sit, wrestling is not as popular locally as it was in the past. But I'm sure, around the world it remains a multi-million dollar business driven, promoted and propelled by an entirely new cast of characters. These folks displaying steroid enhanced bodies continue to fill a good versus evil void in the lives of those who support it. But to this ol' farmer it has never again reached the level of intensity as when it first appeared 60 years ago in The Buck.

Softball At The Buck

Literally scores of young, local lads and surrounding area men have at one time or another played fast pitch softball at Sam Wenger Field located in the Buck. Named for the man who owned the land on which the ball field was located and, along with his brother Leroy, built this facility in the early 50s that became the site for numerous ball games for well over 3 decades. During their lifetime, both Sam and Leroy had the opportunity to enjoy observing this community activity they created. They surely must also have experienced a great deal of pride and satisfaction. I'm sure Sam's sons, Dave, Dick and Dan participated in the planning, building and maintaining of this field, as did Leroy's sons, Clarence and Ben. Those who played also helped with the daily maintenance of this field, as did resident fellow farmer and current Mayor of the Buck, Stan Moore.

Softball and baseball differ somewhat but the basics are similar for the hitter. 3 strikes and you're out, 4 pitches outside the strike zone and you go to first base and 3 outs made by the team hitting conclude every half inning. In baseball, the bases are 90 feet apart with the pitcher's mound 60 feet, 6 inches from home plate. In softball, the bases are 60 feet, apart with the pitcher's mound 46 feet from home plate. The softball, although larger than a baseball, is most assuredly not soft, and when hit by it the discomfort is equal.

In softball, pitching the ball to the batter underhand, as is the rule, quickly developed into the pitchers rotating their arms in a complete 360-degree circular motion referred to as windmill-style. Shorty Barr, who pitched for Little Britain, was one of the first I saw locally to develop this type of pitching motion that was soon copied by most other hurlers at the Buck. This speed and ball movement some could develop was eventually used to exploit many a hitter, allowing only a brief moment of decision to swing at or take a pitch. The close proximity of pitcher and fielders to the batter only added to the intensity and quickness of the game.

Consequently, from the hitter's view, it was all about timing. With his bat cocked in clenched hands, the batter began to swing in the split second somewhere between the rotating ball leaving the pitcher's hand and it whizzing past his naval.

The good hitters eventually could catch up with this white streak and hit it cleanly. The good hard-throwing pitchers soon developed a change-up or a pitch released similar to the one equipped with a booster rocket but arriving at the speed of a hot-air balloon. As the hitter swung franticly, completing his dislocation of air, the ball, only halfway to the plate, hung precariously in front of the wide-eyed, embarrassed batter appearing to be the size of a soccer ball. I have witnessed a few, far from professional players, actually swing twice and miss an off speed pitch.

A good hard-throwing pitcher was usually in control of most fast-pitch softball games. A few pitchers who could bring it, from the nearly half-century-ago play at the Buck were Harold Ferrar, Dick Spence, John Sellers, Jacque Huber, Ron Shaub, Jim Herr and a host of others, including Ellis Sheetz, who during his and my playing days was old enough to be my father.

Although this was church league softball, it could be downright dangerous to mock a hard-throwing pitcher who for some unknown reason could become inexplicably erratic when pitching to anyone who made fun of him.

Reminding the hitter of his farm background, this first pitch may arrive near his calf as he quickly jumps away. If in return the hitter sneers or worse laughs at this, the next pitch is rarely ever seen; the catcher snares it under the batter's chin. Later in the count this humble, church-attending pitcher delivers a white streak-of-lightning bolt that burrows into a rotating thigh just to accent the sermon he has just sternly preached and concluded. AMEN!

To avoid embarrassment, the hitter postpones acknowledging the pain of this encounter till later, and the pitcher never offers an apology. Considering those involved, I suppose any display of pain, malice and pride is diverted by the hitter and the absence of apology by the pitcher, with each drawing a few verses from the book of testosterone. The hitter, however, will recall this final pitch 2-weeks later while exiting the shower with a black and blue circle on a cheek below the belt that partially reads Spalding or Dudley, the company that produces softballs.

Lights were added in 1961 as volunteers and several fellows who worked for PP&L assisted with poles and lights, allowing 2 games to be played every evening. From the top of Shorty Herr's hill, now the Amish produce stand, these never-before-seen streams of light appeared to bring daylight to all the surrounding area west of Route 272. Walt Eberly, who owned the farm across from Papa Joes, wondered out loud if his cows could rest at night. Even spluttery John Lefever, who owned the first farm west of the Buck on Route

372, supposedly grumbled that the ball field lights eliminated half of nighttime while illuminating John and Nora's bedroom. I refuse to comment any further on this last statement other than to say John evidently appreciated the dark!

The building of a refreshment stand and restrooms was welcomed during the mid-sixties. Many who participated on the diamond came unfed directly after work to the early games and enjoyed this tasty food before, during and after playing, as did those in the stands. Each church team was responsible for running this stand for 1 week at a time. In later years, Mary Shaub, then daughter Norma assumed these appreciated responsibilities. The food was great and the restrooms eliminated a few players and spectators from occasionally visiting the shadowy confines of Sam Wenger's junkyard. When asked the reason for their untimely brief absence, players claimed they were inspecting a wrecked 56 Chevy or a 55 Pontiac minus its motor and doors. No one requested further information upon their return from darkness, but I thought most appeared relieved.

Conversations may have varied as the locals gathered on the bleachers and the playing field. However, most local chatter, as I recall, centered on the game at hand and those played by the Phillies and Orioles heard on portable radios. There was always a group of older men who critiqued the game while solving all the world's problems. Wives and mothers visited as their children played together nearby. The games were truly a family oriented outing.

To play ball in this league, it was mandatory to attend church services at least twice a month. To help defray the expense of lights and umpires, a collection was taken at every game. These donated funds were received in a box fastened to a long pole able to reach spectators at the very back benches. This giving was personalized by a small sign attached to the front of this wooden collection money box that appeared in your lap and said, "Thank-You." With the mention of umpires, a few I remember were Dick Hanks, Dick and Bob Work and Pete Scotten. An All Star game and chicken barbeque were combined and occurred mid season, around July 4th for the community. A large tent was raised where food was served in the Lancaster County tradition with John Stoner remembered as one of the many who manned the open-pit grilling of the succulent featherless fowl.

Although Church sponsored, there was rivalry between teams, with a couple evidently desiring victory at all costs. Perhaps winning equates to reserved, front row seats at the World Series played in heaven! Jack Heidelbaugh, who played several years at the Buck for Fairview Church of God and also coached a youth Church team, once offered the following: Win graciously—lose gracefully. Jack believed it was every bit as important to teach kids how to lose as how to win. I think of him today when observing winners taunting losers in many televised sporting events.

Church teams I recall that played fast pitch softball at the Buck beginning in the late 50s were Little Britain, Mt. Nebo, Calvary, Chestnut Level, Mt. Hope, Middle Octorara, Fairview, Mt. Zion, Mechanic Grove, Bethesda, Wesley, Willow Street, Wrightsdale, Quarryville and Conowingo. Young lads referred to as midgets played hardball here in the 1950s. Eventually, an electric scoreboard was paired with our patriotic flag waving proudly atop a flag pole beside the outfield fence.

Sam Wenger also had a used car lot to the east of the playing field and several old trade-ins behind his garage directly in back of home plate. It was not unusual to hear a loud thud following a towering foul ball striking the metal that adorned a car or truck. An occasional windshield was also cracked on these vehicles and also on those belonging to the abundance of spectators surrounding the infield. Those who recently bought a new car or truck chose to park it near Musser's old store and walk the 100 yards to the stadium.

Originally, home run balls to right field disappeared into a cornfield, which is why left-handed power hitters were especially feared. During tournaments, with games played continually, hit balls eventually became in short supply because of so many fouls to right. Consequently, younger spectators could receive a nickel by retrieving a softball hit out of play. Few of these kids, however, would venture into foul territory in right field, being fearful of rodents and snakes that had been observed there in daylight. Supposedly, a rat the size of a groundhog had been seen on the passenger seat of a color faded, old Dodge cattle truck and a black snake curled up in the back window of a rusty, 4-door DeSoto.

With balls needed to continue the game, the story is told of a couple fearless 10-year olds negotiating for 25 cents a ball with the umpire to encroach this dark, steel—mangled, rodent-infested area. They returned receiving enough revenue to each purchase a cheeseburger, french fries and soda at the food stand.

Although this was never mentioned, the entire playing field at the Buck was not perfectly level. Left field in particular gradually dropped off as it approached the fence over which any ball hit was ruled a home run. Standing along the first base line in foul territory, the left fielder appeared to be absent of shoes and feet to insert into them. These amputated limb extensions miraculously reappeared at the end of an inning as this particular out fielder trotted across shortstop on his way to his team's bench.

Every aspect of this sport that appeared and surfaced in the major leagues occurred nightly at Sam Wenger Field and that was the joy of it. Perhaps a pitcher's duel, a long home run, a great play in the field or a loud argument with the umpire on a close play at home may have occurred. All of this was deemed important and verbally considered on the field and in the stands.

In a span of less than 2 hours we became a part of something with others on their particular teams that transported each outside their daily struggle of work, stress and perhaps an unfulfilled life. This happened on the playing field and in the stands as for this brief time everyone escaped their daily routine. This was a brief temporary distraction from reality for some and a poor man's vacation for others.

But we all realize times change and nothing apparently remains the same forever. At this writing, Dick Wenger, the current owner of Sam Wenger Field that was once as important to the Buck as Yankee Stadium was to New York is planning to turn it into a mini mall.

I have visions of a few of us old church league softball players gathered at a fast food restaurant near the former residence of second base, pointing to the streaking Jeep turning into the gas station that now hugs first, then glancing at the loud 4-wheel drive truck sliding into the convenience store near third. Directly in front of us on the other side of a speed bump that was once the pitcher's mound, an Amish horse with a buggy behind lopes toward the bank near home plate.

Later in our conversation, one of us old timers will point out a rear window and recall a ball hit by someone we all knew personally that today would have landed on Route 372 that runs behind this expected mini mall. An argument of course will ensue following a disagreement as each old former player recalls someone from their particular team that hit a ball farther and a pitcher that threw faster than any other who played.

I'm sure all of us old geezers will enjoy our unhealthy pizza and fast food today at this location but the entire conversation, as in the past, will be of yesterday and softball played at the Buck. I could mention all who played ball at Wenger Field during this era who were much more accomplished than this old farmer, but the list would completely fill the remaining pages of this book. Even then, I surely would forget several good players. Sadly, some who have stood for the last time within the lime boundary of the batter's box at the Buck have passed on as those of us remaining wait in the on deck circle.

During the present traffic congested environment around the Buck-and I'm sure in the projected future-silence will be difficult to observe or encounter. However, if you stand quietly behind Jack Stoner's welding shop on a warm, summer, still night, I wonder if you might hear a few sounds from the past lingering in the warm breeze cautiously floating above the evening mist rising slightly from the former Sam Wenger Field. Stee-rike one, foul ball, you're out, come on ump, the crack of the bat and the cheers from the local fans may still be heard and reluctant to depart this place where young men from 16 to 60 once became immortal, if only briefly. **PLAY BALL!**

Growing Up Near The Buck, By Stu Mylin

Tom, my friend. Here are some things I remember about growing up near the Buck. They are random memories.

Of course the focal point of the Buck when I was a boy was the businesses. Since we lived on the farm, which was about a mile away, we paid attention to those shops that served our farm needs.

Musser's store for groceries, Musser's feed mill for obvious reasons, Wenger Implement and Stoner Welding.

These merchants and tradesmen were providers of goods and services that we came to rely on for everyday necessities.

Wayne Byers also had his plumbing shop at the Buck which he ran with his son, June, and when the water was off in the barn Wayne Byers and June quickly moved up the list of important businesses.

I recall Musser's original store that stood in the corner of what is now the parking lot of the Buck Beverage store. I visited the old store occasionally with my father or mother, when I was just a small boy. I recall that it was the quaint old country store, complete with a front porch and benches for old codgers to gather on. I remember Abner Musser with fondness. On one particular visit to his store, I stood in front of the sales counter while my father and Abner transacted business. I gawked at all the merchandise on display and was minding my own business as well. Mr. Musser came from behind the counter and picked me up and placed me on the counter. Then he presented me with a large box of penny candy and offered that I should have a piece or two. I felt special and thought that he must be the richest guy I ever met at that time.

I don't recall what year the "new" store was built, (the store that is now the Beverage Store) but I know I was in elementary school at the time. I recall riding by the store on the school bus coming home in the afternoon and seeing the old store gradually being demolished. For some peculiar reason, I remember that on one occasion the workman had removed the roof and some of the siding of second floor and left the attic area exposed. The steps and risers from the second floor to the attic were visible and there was a lone wooden barrel sitting on what was left of the attic floor. This intrigued me. I wondered what was in that barrel and what was going to happen to it. I was so bothered by this that I told my father about what I had seen as soon as I got home to the farm. Dad assured me that Mr. Musser would save the barrel. I still wonder though.

Somehow my older brother, Skip, was part of the crew that built the new store. I don't know exactly what he did but I remember him telling me that they had placed a silver dollar in the floor just inside the door as part of the construction. I looked for it on my first visit there and was amazed at the thing. A silver dollar!! Over the years it became worn smooth from all the shoe leather kissing its face, to the point where it was just a shiny dot in the linoleum. If I'm correct, I believe the Mussers removed the silver dollar some time ago, I hope they still have it. I was quite familiar with the new store and here are some things I vividly recollect:

Two short but efficient checkout counters near the door, tended by Mary Jane Rineer and Muriel Smith.

Abner Musser's desk in the corner, where you went to buy ammunition, dog license and hunting license. A loaded single barrel shotgun standing in the corner by the desk and that the barrel was broken off so that the shot would scatter.

I remember the butcher shop that was in the rear right hand corner of the store, and that it was always cooler back there. I remember Lloyd Rohrer and Pete Byers in particular. They always were friendly and helpful. I remember the smell of fresh cut meat and that the butchers worked out in the open. The large butcher block and the many saws and knives. Also, the freezer section, or as we called it, the "lockers." You could rent a drawer in the freezer section of the store and keep meats and vegetables in it. Our locker was number 182 and if you wanted something you would walk behind the display case and go to the key cabinet and take down your key. Then you would put on any one of the many winter coats that hung on the complimentary coat racks and go in after your frozen items. Mother always insisted that one of us kids go along with her. She was claustrophobic and terrified that she was going to be trapped in the freezer. She always kept that big heavy door ajar just in case. She didn't trust that it would unlatch.

The Musser kids, Scott, Skip, Mike and Pat, all worked in the store. They were and still are very friendly and helpful. They worked under the direction of their father, Abner Jr. I remember Scott Musser was a tremendous shot with a slingshot. One morning I stopped to talk to him while mom was shopping. Scott was stocking shelves, and he stopped when he saw a fly land on the wall about 10 feet from where we stood talking. Scott pulled his slingshot from his hip pocket, loaded it and plastered that fly to the wall!

In the early 70s, the roof of Musser's store gained the reputation as one of the best spots to go for a night of casual beer drinking.

Musser's Mill was a great place to go while mother shopped at the store. John Musser ran it and he didn't mind a kid like me nosing around for a while. I loved the smell of the feed mill, the molasses and ground grain. To me that aroma was sweeter than the scent of roses. There was a small office in the corner of the mill that had a counter at which business was accomplished. The office also served as a tiny little hardware store, where you could get nails and fencing supplies. I remember that the wooden floor inside the mill was always so smooth and shiny. It got that way from the thousands of feedbags being drug across it over the years.

The mill had a scale built into the floor and the weight was displayed on a large dial that resembled a big clock. I guess that dial was about 2 feet in diameter, and the arrow would point to the weight of the items on the scale. As I recall the scale could measure up to one thousand pounds. I have a very good friend who has struggled with his weight problem since boyhood, and when we were teenagers he went on a diet and diligently lost a lot of weight. He was quite heavy before and no regular household scale could weigh him. So for a while I would take him to the mill on Saturday mornings, and while I would distract the miller by buying a pound of nails, my friend would step on the big Howe scale and measure the progress of his diet. The guy at the mill might have wondered why I came in each Saturday for a pound of 10-penny nails, but he never said anything.

In front of the mill was Sam Wenger's, "Junkyard." It lay behind Wenger's GMC-Pontiac dealership, but in front of the mill. Sunday afternoons in the summer it was fun to nose around the wrecked and junked cars at Sam's lot. John Hambleton was a thrill seeker or dare devil, maybe both. John thought it was sport to drop a lighted match down the gas fill of the cars to see if there was any gas left. Usually there was just a burp of smoke but on one occasion a recently arrived car had a little more than he thought and the explosion rocked the vehicle and popped the tank lid open! Pretty funny stuff for a bunch of kids.

The softball diamond was a huge success and people and teams came from miles around to play and watch the game. I always thought it was very generous of Wengers to provide the softball field for the community. A bunch of us guys, Jack Stoner, Rick and Randie Rineer, Wayne Lefever, Scott Musser, me and others would gather there on Sunday afternoons and play ball. There was no regular group or time; it was whoever showed up and whenever they wanted to.

The local church leagues played week nights and Saturdays. I only ever played in one game for a church league. I am not and never will be an accomplished athlete. I struck out my only time at bat in that game. Reverend Ferrerar was the pitcher and I was so humiliated I didn't play again. Other guys in the area were really very good. Jack Stoner, John Hambleton, Mike Murry and Jerry O'Donnell come to mind.

My brother, Dean, is married to Jerry O'Donnell's sister, June, and I got to know Jerry early on. Jerry helped Dean on the farm. I guess they farmed together on some things. I was around to help as much as possible. Jerry was in high school at the time, about four or five years older than I was and I admired him a great deal. He was the strong silent type and next to my brother, Tim, I thought that the two of them could do just about anything and be cool at it.

One spring Jerry broke his right arm and had it in a cast from the elbow down to the hand. Even though he was right handed, that cast didn't slow him down a lick. Jerry, Dean, June and I planted tobacco one Saturday in May. Jerry dropped plants and worked just as hard as ever despite the cast on his arm.

That night Jerry played ball at the Buck. I was there to watch the game and eventually the bases started to fill up. Jerry O'Donnell came up to bat; there was the usual chatter from the opposing team. "Heavy Hitter!" "Back-up!" "One-armed man," stuff like that. Jerry was warned by Harry, his father, to: "Watch your arm boy!" Jerry, did better than that. He took the bat in his left hand and held it with only that hand. He turned into a stance to bat left handed and when the ball crossed the plate, he swung and connected-one-handed—and drove the ball over the outfield fence for home run! The cheers that erupted were greater than any I've ever heard at a big league game.

Another thing I recall about the Buck ball diamond is that I would sometimes go along with mother to Musser's store on Saturday mornings. As I mentioned earlier, I would wander around the Buck while she shopped. Sometimes to the feed mill, other times to Wenger Implement, where I would look at the John Deere tractors and other implements.

One Saturday morning I walked over to the ball field. This was back when soft drinks were sold in glass bottles. Wenger Implement and Wenger Pontiac each had Pepsi and Coca-Cola machines in front of their businesses. Back then the bottles were redeemable at Musser's store for 5 or 10 cents depending on the brand. This particular morning I was the only kid at the ball field and I was thrilled to see soft drink bottles strewn across the bleacher area. Those bottles were just laying there like gold nuggets, gleaming in the sun.

I did some quick math and started to gather my treasure. I had collected about twenty bottles when one of the Phipps boys rode up on his bicycle. He stopped and watched for a moment and then rode off. I went about my business and managed to find a wooden box to put my treasure in. Just as I was turning to walk towards Musser's, the Phipps kid came back with

Sam Wenger in tow. Sam always had a stern look and I was intimidated by him.

"What are you doing?" he asked and when I explained he said, "This boy has permission to gather these bottles every morning after a game." I said I didn't know. I thought they were simply discarded and were for whoever was lucky enough to find them. I set the box down and started to walk away. Sam said, "You can have them today, but he gets them from now on." Fair enough I guess. I cashed in my bottles and Abner Musser soon had the money he paid me, returned to him in exchange for candy bars.

For the longest time from a civics standpoint, I was confused about the Buck. Before I studied government I really didn't understand what "The Buck" was. There was a sign that hung in front of Musser's Store. White letters on a dark green background that read, "Buck PA. The biggest little town in the U.S.A." I didn't know who was the Mayor. I heard many people refer to Abner Musser as the man who held that title, and wasn't the Buck exclusively in Drumore Township?

I learned later that "72" (PA Rt. 272 today) actually split the Buck by serving as a boundary between Drumore and East Drumore Townships. But where did the The Buck, (by the way, it's always referred to as The Buck, by natives. Never just Buck as it appears on the map) really stop and start. What were the boundaries? The question remained without answer until one day Jack Stoner and I solved it while sitting in a senior boys home economics class in high school.

We sat down with pen and paper and took a census of The Buck and defined its borders as well. The borders were declared official, I might add, by the two of us. We became a self appointed arm of government. Kind of like a Township Department of the Interior and Department of State combined. We also certified ourselves as Registered Surveyors and used fixed landmarks as the bench marks for points of the compass. There was no bloodshed, no uprising of government, no petition to any board and no legal description beyond what we declared there should be.

Thus it was decided the The Buck was, "all that certain area on either side of '72' in Drumore and East Drumore Townships with specific properties and curtilege as may be referred to by the common knowledge of neighbors and the public of their present owners and occupants." By this description we decided that The Buck began at the crossroads of 372 the Holtwood Road & Buck Road, east/west, and 72 north and south. Northbound on 72 it stopped at Paul Riggs Barber Shop. (Jack was dating Paul's daughter, Denise, at the time and it only seemed fit that she should be considered a "hometown girl.")

Southbound, it stopped at what was Walt Eberly's farm. I don't recall if Amos Fisher was on that property or not at the time, although I guess he was. Westbound on the Holtwood Road, it stopped at John Lefever's farm and eastbound it stopped at Jay and Shelba Eberly's house. It was really very simple. Furthermore, our census showed that there were 73 people living in The Buck proper at the time of our decree. At that time, Friendly Drive didn't exist and neither did any of the homes or businesses that are built along it. The Buck was basically a crossroads community.

At the time of our survey and census there was a popular television show called, "Hee Haw," a country western variety hour. One small segment of the show was, 'Hee Haw salutes . . . " and the characters would stand up in a corn field and salute some obscure town in America and furthermore announce the town's population.

Randi Rineer and I decided the public should be made aware of this minor metropolis and took it upon ourselves to make signs that read, "Buck. Pop. 73." We constructed them one Saturday morning in Sam Rineer's garage using left over planks and some silver paint. Afterwards, we promptly drove to the telephone pole nearest each boundary mark and nailed the signs fast.

These signs raised some questions around The Buck. We heard a variety of explanations for them. The one I remember specifically was that a bunch of hippies put them up and that the signs meant that there was going to be a "pop" concert in The Buck in 1973. Kind of an Amish Woodstock, I suppose.

We took our promotion of The Buck one stop closer. A little while after that, when we learned that some of the cast from "Hee Haw" was going to appear at the "Cripple Creek" stage in Strasburg, a bunch of us Buck Boys went to see the show. During intermission, we approached Granpa Jones while he was signing autographs and asked him to announce The Buck and it's population on the "Hee Haw Show." He said he'd see what he could do. I learned sometime later that, "The Buck, PA., population 73" was indeed announced on the show, although I didn't see that episode.

Recently, The Buck received a lot of press when the controversial "Wal-Mart" shopping center was bantered about in court. I for one am strongly opposed to it. I believe it's a crime at least, if not a sin, to take such valuable productive and beautiful farmland and pave it over for the sake of selling Chinese made sundries to the masses.

That particular farm, last known as the Fisher farm, has a marvelous tract of fields. Sadly, the buildings have all been demolished by the cold, senseless mechanism of corporate greed.

That farm was beautiful in its day, and it thrived with crops and cattle. The big farmhouse with the shade trees in front, the lawn hemmed in by the limestone wall, the dairy barn with its arch roof and the tobacco shed. It was very sad to see all of those buildings flattened by the wrecking ball and the timber splintered beyond use. Of all those buildings the tobacco shed is the one that was scarred the most. That old shed sure had a history. I say that because it used to stand further back from where its final resting place was. Tim Lefever farmed that farm in the mid-to-late 50s and he said that labor day weekend of 1956-1957—during Hurricane Hazel——he came out of the house to find his tobacco shed flattened by the wind, and full of tobacco.

Tim was renting the farm at the time. The widow woman who owned it decided to rebuild it with new lumber. It was then rebuilt parallel to 72. The tobacco shed stood along the highway for a number of years, until the State decided it wanted to straighten the highway and smooth out the Buck Hill a little. The shed was dismantled and rebuilt perpendicular to the highway. It stood there until it was demolished once and for all by the present owners-developers.

I mentioned Sam Wenger earlier. He owned and operated Wenger Pontiac GMC at The Buck. When Sam retired, his son, Dick, took over the business and he and his wife, Kelly, ran it successfully for a number of years. The Wengers are all good people. The only business I ever did with them was some small notary work that Dick performed for me when I built my house 30-years ago. Pop was a Ford man so we didn't deal in automobiles with them. But lots of local folks did, and I never heard a negative work spoken of them or their business.

A lot of guys worked for Wenger Pontiac over the years and I knew some of them pretty well. I remember "Clate." He was the parts guy, short and gruff, with thick gray hair and glasses so scratched up it's a wonder he could see. Dick Irwin worked there since they laid the corner stone and he was always as neat as a pin.

Ralph DuBree worked there also but I don't know for how long. Ralph's an easy going, fun loving guy and he told the story of the tire salesman who came in one day and boasted that he had the best tires around. He claimed that the tires he sold would get terrific mileage and that they put all theirs to shame. A regular customer overheard this. I believe it was one of the McVey boys, and he said he bet he could prove the salesman wrong.

The bet was taken and a new set of tires was put on the rear rims of the customer's Pontiac and out the door he went. The customer returned to the garage sometime the next day and, much to the salesman's chagrin, the new "super" tires were worn nearly smooth. It seems the customer had quite a reputation for "cowboying" and had no trouble at all smearing the rubber from the new tires onto the macadam between The Buck and Willow Street!

The Buck has been in existence for well over 100 years. I wrote a brief history of The Buck 30-plus-years-ago as an English project when I was in high school. Solanco High School's library received a donation from someone in the district that included a very large, very old book which was the history of Lancaster County.

Edith Ankrum was the high school librarian at the time and when I explained my need for research material, she very graciously allowed me the use of this marvelous book, on the condition that I not remove it from the library or her careful supervision. God bless her, she helped me a great deal. I received an "A" on the essay, but sadly the only copy of the history I wrote has been lost long ago.

I remember from my research that The Buck got its name from, "The Buck Hotel" that stood on the corner of what is now 272 and an extension of Four Pines Road. It's that little triangle of real estate that used to be Vernie Woods Mobile Home Sales. I do remember the building and there was a stone barn behind it. The hotel had a large oak tree in the front yard that provided acres of shade in the summer time. I was never in the building but I recall that it was occupied when I was a kid. It was demolished in the mid to late 60s to make room for a sales lot.

My father told the story that back in the 30s there was a rather fetching woman who lived in the hotel who the local boys referred to as "Teat" for obvious reasons. It seems that "Teats" room was on the second floor of the hotel and on those hot sultry summer nights, Teat would bare all in an effort to stay cool. The boys soon realized that they could climb the oak tree and have a perfect view of her and all her womanly charms, after dark. The boys, and perhaps Teat, enjoyed until one of them slipped and fell to the ground making quite a commotion.

Of all things, The Buck is probably infamous for its "deadly intersection," as the newspapers have described it. I suppose there were accidents at the crossroads of 272 (72) and 372 (The Buck/Holtwood Road) for years, but it seems that they became more frequent after Park Moore sold his farm to Turkey Hill and they tore down his barn and built that annoying convenience store on it's spot, in the early 70s.

Like many people, I recall when stop signs regulated the traffic, but now there is a traffic signal. There were numerous traffic accidents there over the years, some very serious. One in particular involved 6 older women, who were killed when a railroad truck ran through the stop sign east bound and hit their car broadside in 1972. The state tried a variety of remedies to enhance safety, speed bumps, double stop signs, a flashing light, and lighting the intersection. All helped; but nothing really cured the problem.

Some folks, myself included, blamed the Turkey Hill store as a distraction to motorists and claimed that it added to the confusion of the traffic. Maybe, but ultimately, it's driver error.

I had 2 accidents at The Buck. In 1972 a van load of hippies made an illegal pass when I was southbound, driving a dump truck, and attempted to turn left and go to Quarryville. The Van rolled over on its roof and slid to a stop near Musser's parking lot. The hippies climbed out of the van, bruised but not broken. John Musser and some guys from Wenger Implement came up, and we all "righted" the van back onto its wheels. The hippies said something like, "Peace Man." They didn't want the police called. They got back on board and drove away and we all went back to work.

The second time, a woman pulled in front of me when I was northbound on a motorcycle I bought from Dave Byers. I hit her broad side and was flipped onto her car trunk. I broke my ankle. John Byers came upon the accident and told me later, "Stu, I couldn't bring myself to look at you, I was afraid you were a gonner."

The Buck sure has changed in the 50-plus years that I've lived here, or near it. I suppose Abner Musser would either smile or simply be bewildered. Wenger Implement is a hardware store. Wenger Pontiac has closed its door. The lights are extinguished at the Pontiac dealers' car lot and the ball diamond is grown up in weeds. Wayne Byers plumbing shop no longer stops leaks or thaws pipes. It was last a tax office/accounting house, and briefly a laboratory, run by Dr. Richard Croyle.

Stoner's welding/Radiator repair is holding its own and remains unchanged from when I was a kid and used to go there with dad and turn my back to the brilliant light of John Stoner's magical welding rod.

Musser's store is now a beer store, and the real store is a mini mall with such an array of services that my parents would be astonished. Paul Riggs closed his barbershop years ago. We have a Doctor, Dentist, Insurance Agent, and a new office building for the accountants.

The Fisher farm is devoid of buildings, but the ground still "bringeth forth fruit, seed time and planting and harvest will always be with us." We have 2 pizza places, and we have a traffic signal!

Abner Musser called it, "The Biggest Little Town in the USA." Well, maybe. I know I've been blessed to live near it, if not really in it, and I've been blessed to know so many real good, God loving people who like me are proud to call it home.

Buck Company

When driving down Route 272 south from Lancaster, Buck Company Inc. proudly stands as a landmark of the area. Sitting atop a hill in a scenic countryside this now large and modern foundry has emerged from very humble beginnings. The history of this company started in the mid 1940's when William Kohler purchased land in the southern end of Lancaster County known as The Buck. He built a single building on the property for the primary purpose of making brass hinges.

Mr. Kohler sold the property to the Zifferer family in the late 1940's. The Zifferers started the company that would be known as Buck Iron, with L. Robert Zifferer as acting president. Mr. Richard B. Goodall of the Dixon Valve Corporation purchased the small foundry along with machinery in 1951. Mr. Larry Dunn was the president of the company from 1959 until 1964.

During those early years, Buck Iron produced malleable iron castings. In 1953, a non-ferrous shop was started. The business continued to grow through the 1950s and 1960s. Mr. Charles Mooney, who originally resided in the Ohio area, became president in 1964.

In 1969 a decision was made to add ductile and gray iron castings into the product mix. To accomplish this, an entire new foundry was built. This was to be the first step in a major transformation, from a moderately-sized foundry to a highly successful corporation. In 1970, the new foundry was completed. In 1972, the company officially changed its name to Buck Company Inc. The new foundry was separate from the original foundry until the early 1980s, when the buildings were connected by the addition of 22,000 square feet.

In 1988 Mr. Mooney, retired and Mr. Richard L. McMinn became president of the company and is currently president. The company has provided Lancaster County with employment on average of 350 people for over 40 years. Buck Company Inc. now produces malleable, ductile and gray iron as well as aluminum, brass and bronze.

From that single building the foundry has grown to an area of 220,000 square feet. The diversification of the company has been a key in its success throughout periods of tough economic times. Buck Company supplies quality castings to businesses locally and abroad and is highly recognized as one of the industry leaders. Buck Company is a major supplier to Dixon Valve Corporation, its parent company, of hose and coupling parts. Also, Buck Company is a major supplier to the agricultural industry and railroad industry; it continues to supply parts for high voltage and electrical fittings as well as parts for nuclear power plants. Buck Company castings can also be found on horse and buggy transportation. So wherever you may travel chances are you will see a Buck Company Inc. casting and a piece of Southern Lancaster County history.

Black And Blue In The Buck

Heading up 272 North of the Buck, past Buck Iron and Buck tractor pull and across from Rosie's Drive-In resides a large block building. Llads Ventures are the folks that operate this business that evidently specialize in truck tires.

Approximately 40 years ago, this building built and owned by the Paul Riggs and Ike Metzler families was home to a roller skating rink. I recall taking my hoodlums and others, including Townsleys and Stevensons, from our Liberty Square neighborhood there regularly on family week nights to skate. Had this 8-wheel ball-bearing entertainment been located any farther from home we probably would not have attended.

There were undocumented reports of an occasional broken bone suffered by the skaters and the appearance of the local ambulance was noted. My Liberty Square lads and lasses for the most part returned home unscathed. My daughter Jen, however, while lying prone on her back on the hardwood floor following a nasty spill, appearing to be making snow angels in the snow, had her hand run over by the late Richard Stevenson, a fellow Liberty Square comrade and carpool passenger. I had forgotten this 30-some-year-ago incident. She had not!

During my youth in the 1950s we occasionally went to Rocky Springs, which included a well-attended skating rink. It was most embarrassing for this gangly 14-15 year old to observe grade school kids streaking around the giant, crowded floor as I, tense and stiff-legged, held cautiously to the steel bar that surrounded the tiny, "beginners only" rink. It was during this point that both limbs above my waist and below it attempted to disassociate themselves from the rest of my body, with each extended and pointing in the 4 different directions of a compass. I naturally assumed, with every encounter of weightlessness above a hardwood floor, that teenage girls I was trying to impress by being cool, confident and macho, were nearby pointing and laughing. All the while, this bumbling hayseed, fresh off the farm, continued practicing the proper technique to fall awkwardly and never exhibit any pain when landing. As confidence developed, while skating in the big rink, it was best not to closely observe Vern Lefever and those folks skating backwards, dancing to the beat of the music while hoping some of their skating moves and skill might somehow enter my rigid body. Having learned from experience, Vern's face was the last thing remembered as I crashed into the unnoticed wall.

The parking lot of this block building at the Buck along the lanes to and from Lancaster is now home to tractor-trailers. Forty years ago it held captive the bruised occupants and owners of family vans, vehicles from the 60's that by today's standards appeared extended and stretched, farm trucks with a car seat tied with twine beside the driver and an occasional Amish buggy. During every present passing of this place, whether driving or riding and daydreaming, I always utter these 3 long-forgotten words-"All Skate Reverse." In my mind I fully expect all vehicles on 272 to stop, change lanes and head in the opposite direction.

I'm not sure how much confusion this could cause on the highway but it could be worse. Suppose the words I speak quietly while passing the former skating rink are "Ladies Only!" Sorry about that girls, but while writing this I have a recollection of a long-past old farmer who once was quoted as saying, "I have no qualms with allowing females to vote but engineering the propulsion of an automobile best be left to the men."

The skating rink was great nearby amusement for all who were present and delivered confident reassurance as to why the good Lord equipped us all with rear-ends. All sizes and shapes were present, with some better padded then others to absorb the jarring jolt and impact of a demeaning, derriere dismount. Later these discolored cheeks would cause discomfort in sitting, not smiling.

Buck Tractor Pull

The original stockholders who formed the Buck Tractor Pull in 1974 were Woody Funk, Harry Griest, Galen Spickler, Clarence Keener, Elwood Funk and Art Bonholtzer. Art Bonholzter, although now deceased, was a fixture for many years around The Buck, having lived at Truce with his wife Betsy within sight of the tractor pull. Previously, he farmed and resided along Hopkins Mill Road north of Route 372.

Both Ruthie and I remember Art well, as he had a way of leaving a lasting impression on all he met. His blaring, booming voice usually preceded his appearance and the only thing he pushed to the limit more than his tractors and machinery was himself. When work was involved, his personal throttle was always wide open, running in the fastest gear possible, never in neutral and seldom braking. Cocked on his head was his John Deere cap, and the remnants of a cigar were implanted and residing in the corner of his mouth.

Ruthie's parents worked together with Art and Betsy raising tobacco and she recalls as a teenager being the brunt of Art's ire if occasionally slacking off. Supposedly neighbors a mile away could hear a war-hoop delivered by him as he hollered arousing those working with him as a gruff general inspiring his troops. To all who knew him he seemed to be the natural, logical choice of all Buck inhabitants to be part of the original founders of The Buck Tractor Pull.

The first tractor pull was held at The Buck on May 24, 1974 and it has continued regularly on Saturday nights through out the summer months from May through early fall. Regular class pulls are tractors from Pennsylvania and surrounding states all super stock and modified tractors. "Super Stock" refers to farm tractors designed for 120 horsepower, but "Souped-Up" to put out 600 horsepower. "Modified" has tractor wheels, axle and differential, but powered by auto, aircraft or tank engines and jet turbines. At its inception local farmers were featured in different farm class pulls, as farmers would take their tractor directly out of the fields to compete.

Originally this was the first and only stadium built just for tractor pulls. At one time tractor pulling was the fastest growing motorized competition.

Attendance increased nearly 300% over the first year, with crowds of over 4000 spectators.

Since its inception in 1974, the name has been changed to Buck Motorsports Park. Different crowd-pleasing functions and attractions other than tractor pulls have been added at this park over the years, including monster trucks, truck pulls, rodeos, and demolition derby for everything from cars to combines and a large fireworks display at holidays. Buck Motorsports Park is located 10 miles south of Lancaster on Route 272, directly across from Buck Iron Co.

The roar of the engines from the tractor pull on a summer's eve, which rises into the night air, can be heard for several miles in all directions. These fire breathing, smoke belching, tire spinning machines scream across the track, defying gravity with their steering front wheels airborne. This relatively new sport continues to draw large crowds, has ample parking on their large lot and appears to be growing every year. Just as Abner Musser Sr. developed his own Buck logo more than 75 years ago the Tractor Pull also has initiated its own with "See you at The Buck" a reference to all those spectators who regularly attend Buck Motorsports Park.

Locating The Buck Boys

The Buck Boys first appeared on the local scene around 1969. All of similar age and locality this secret fraternal organization moved mostly at night and were seldom seen together in daylight. Their parents were overheard to utter a few disparaging remarks concerning The Buck Boys on occasion. They apparently dressed similar to others of this area and era, not wishing to stand out or be noticed publicly. There were no white sheets, top-hats and manure spreader prognostications as with the groundhogs. Although most were hunters, as far as is known by me, they never carried guns at night. The only thing ever shot by them was the local bull and his excrement. A fun loving group of mischievous lads is how this group was described by their mothers. I'm not exactly sure how they would have described themselves.

I'm told their idea of a wild, uncontrolled disorderly party was to devour several boxes of dunkin donuts and gallons of Fran Metzler's homemade root beer. At this point I've not been able to verify this account related to me by a Buck Boys storyteller.

Most members still remain living in this locality and have not changed their names, at least not "before" this was written. A few names recalled are Sut Mylin, Dave Byers, Rick and Randy Rineer, Denny Findley, John Allen Hambleton, Denny Rineer and Fran Metzler. If you wish to follow up on this local history, many former members are seen and observed daily in this area.

When searching for one of The Buck Boys it is best to approach them with caution. First, before you meet with them face to face with memorized questions and check for positive identification, scan the immediate area surrounding them. If they appear to be traveling with a wife or grown children or grandchildren you best postpone this encounter. Some will swear on a Bible they have no idea of your questions or recollections and will feign memory lapses. They may all at once recall the need to be somewhere else, immediately. Don't further embarrass them by asking "where," as this will only impede your next face-to-face visit that hopefully finds them alone and more at ease.

When this finally happens and you ask to confirm their former Buck Boys membership you may still come away with nothing to show for your interest. A few may have built a mental, metal wall completely around this time in their life and on a dark, starless night deposited it well into the rusty, twisted heap of John Davis's junkyard never to be seen or spoken of again. What you need to focus on when approaching and confronting one of these half-century-old, past mid-life crisis gentlemen is their eyes and mouth. If both remain unfazed, frozen and never change, you're still probably out of luck. But if eyes begin to dance and sparkle as 3 decades earlier and their mouth stretches into a wide grin, followed by unrestrained laughter, then you're home free.

You have encountered a genuine Buck Boy, proud to admit of his past affiliation with this local, long past regiment of land-loving country boys who raised mostly cain but on rare occasions, HELL! What you will now discover is that all are respected, contributing members of this community from regular church attending members to a district judge. Most all would surely agree privately that this transition from soaking a diaper to sipping a cold one to subconsciously submitting to manhood, which usually involved a pretty girl, each contributed to what they are today. Long live The Buck Boys.

Flyin' & Racin' In The Buck

Located in The Buck at this writing there exists a miniature dirt racetrack for radio-controlled cars and also an area for hand-held controls to fly small model planes. These areas are owned by Mussers, as is the hobby shop located in their mini mall where these miniature planes and cars are sold. The activity of these racers and low flyers and the folks involved with this hobby are clearly visible from Musser's parking lot.

I possess a vivid, unsupervised imagination that perhaps may be considered a gift or a curse to visualize into the future. Please read on and remember my predictions that you first encountered in this chapter. Hope you recall this old farmer when my premonitions become reality.

Today the grand metropolis known as The Buck with its many local businesses, points of interest and proposed expansions has recently welcomed an airport and a motor-sport speedway. I believe this airport, known as Dave Byers Inter-Township, currently only serves the Solanco area with daily flights to Quarryville, New Providence, Chestnut Level, Wakefield, Tayloria and Liberty Square. Named for the local man who constructed it a few years ago, I believe this local level plane for planes will in the future be expanded and eventually be utilized by locals both worldly and plain. It will in the future surely serve places such as Lancaster, York, Harrisburg, Philadelphia and perhaps Baltimore, across the vast waters of the mighty Susquehanna. This will be the first inter-county connections for this airport that may eventually be known as Byers International.

At this writing the aircraft using this airport are small because of limited runway length so passengers per plane are very limited. The local air traffic controllers are volunteer residents from The Buck retirement home who, similar to those at larger airports, occasionally doze off while on duty. One hour following these folk's regular meals is not the safest time to be landing in The Buck.

When this airport is eventually expanded, I would hope Dave Byers will once again express an interest in renting the earth-moving and runway smoothing equipment from this non-union old farmer. I don't expect to be compensated, as earlier, for the use of my now antique equipment but would appreciate this "book" to be available to all passengers near the boarding gate or in each plane.

I can envision long concrete runways stretching from the airport terminal north of Clair Linkey's home, past 4 pines and either side of Brian Byers present duck houses with altitude gained near Karl Findley's home north of Dan Sullivan's farm. Hopefully, this constant air traffic of commerce and passengers won't interfere with the daily activities of the thousands of resident quackers located in adjacent pens or those folks living nearby in 3-bedroom ranchers or others located around Tanglewood golf course. FORE! I would assume the control towers for the airport will remain where they are presently located at the residence of Kip Shaubach. Special prescription sunglasses may be required for pilots and crewmembers flying south to alleviate the temporary blinding glare that will surely occur near Gerald Kreider's proposed solar farm.

Musser's parking lot will be extended south to provide increased parking for the cars, tractors, shuttles, pickup trucks and Amish buggies of these future-day frequent flyers. I'm not sure if our local motel, 1 mile south of the airport along 272, can accommodate over nighters. Our airport namesake may likely fill empty campers at Muddy Run Park!

Smoke from the regular, summer-holiday, chicken barbecue in Musser's parking lot could affect landing at Byers International, causing planes to over-shoot the runway with an occasional commuter exiting the plane near the juke box inside Papa Joe's Pizza Parlor. This causes me to consider that perhaps this could be the ultimate way in which a pizza could be delivered in this rural community. I believe a small parachute could be utilized to drop the ordered pizza, sandwich or sub with one's name and credit card number written in large letters on a bed sheet, hung on your wash line. Hope you still recall the purpose of a wash line: It's the going green thing to do in The Buck.

The racetrack at The Buck is usually only open for racing on weekends and holidays. This track will eventually be enlarged in the shape of a mule's ear and will be known as the "Musser Monster Mile." The oblong speedway will run behind Papa Joe's south to the top of the hill behind and very near Ralph Kreider's home. It will continue all the way to Deaver Road with a steep bank turn behind Donald and Frances Kreider's home. This steeped-pitch incline slope will be installed to allow these high-speed vehicles to negotiate this sharp curve and to also block and conceal the panoramic view within the confines of Linda Kreider's in-ground pool. The sight of these bikini-bound, bathing—beauty, brethren-belles would surely cause numerous accidents and possible fatalities if drivers' eyes strayed for a split second and their concentration wavered.

I find it ironic that the Musser Monster Mile will be located in such close proximity to the home of Ralph Kreider, he being one of our most famous southern-end truck, car, tractor and motorcycle drivers. In addition, Ralph, accompanied by brother Robert, will drive the pace car leading the drivers around the track a few laps before the actual race begins, with both smilin' and wavin' to the roaring crowd of spectators. At the Indianapolis 500, the winner always drinks a huge gulp of milk from a glass bottle to celebrate victory. Following this race, Ralph and Robert will reappear with a tanker loaded with fresh, cold milk and everyone in attendance will exit this race wearing a wide smile and a white mustache. At least on his midnight run to the dairy, following the race, Ralph won't be over-loaded.

Ralph, Frank Rohrer and Bob Mellott are considered legendary drivers in these parts at maneuvering shiny-18-wheelers through the twists, turns and mountainous snowdrifts on our local cow-path racetracks of the past. They are equally adept at accommodating narrow, twisting, Amish farm lanes in reverse. These old timers, including Sam Rineer, Dean Mylin, Norm Duvall and Rev. Tom Lefever, are slowly being replaced by names including O'Donnell, Mellott, and Holzhauer.

The roar and whish emanating from the racetrack can easily be detected within Musser's parking lot, with most conversations between patrons muffled by the sound of streak-of-lightning cars. The racetrack contains potholes, rumble strips and large speed bumps simulating Lancaster City and County roads. This causes the speeding vehicles to fly through the air and resemble the former Dukes of Hazard, of TV fame, now referred to locally as simply our "Barnyard Buck Boys."

Our local Tony Stewart's first name is "Gideon." Jeff Gordon, who has stolen a few races, is referred to as "Zook The Crook." Jimmie Johnson's middle name is "Beiler." Richard Petty as we all know is in reality a "King" and Dale Jr., born in The Buck and son of a famous father whose farm was purchased for a looming Wal-Mart is of course a Fisher.

Musser's Market has the contract for all food served at the racetrack concession stands and Buck Beverage supplies all the liquid refreshment. Disabled racecars are removed from the track with lights flashing and horns blowin' by Doulins, Moats or Hill Top Garage. Those deemed demolished are transported to our handy, convenient and appreciated local heterogeneous junkyard owned and operated by our famous and former Liberty Square resident, John W. Davis.

There will be parking near the track for 1000 vehicles and a hitching rail to oblige and harmonize 300 horses that will both welcome and accommodate these handsome yet necessary creatures from around The Buck. Observing their shiny coats, manes, tails and hearing the unmistakable sound of excess oxygen released through vibrating nostrils plus an occasional whinny will certainly diffuse any clippity-clop "neigh" sayers. East Drumore supervisors will receive the revenue from this parking and horse deposit area that will be known as Merill Carter Meadow.

Additional parking will be available across 272 at a proposed Wal-Mart near a sign that reads, "Your Buck Stops Here." Proceeds from this paid parking are supposedly to be used by Drumore and East Drumore Supervisors to install a much-needed traffic light farther south on 272 at the Valero gas station. Members of the Rawlinsville Fire Company will supervise the parking of vehicles, the placement of horses and the road-apple removal.

Traffic that usta zip through The Buck now crawls with most Amish buggies passing these "slow moving vehicles" as they glide past them on the road shoulders. At this writing there is talk of relocating the racetrack finish line near the airport and extending this race-quack onto the concrete landing strip beside, then around the duck houses. I'm not sure what, if any, affect this may play in the expected weight gain of the ducks or in their over active bladders and bowels. S—happens and what happens in the duck houses stays in the duck houses, at least till clean-out day!

For any additional information related to this racetrack relocation check, WWW. Webfeet or the law offices of, Feathers, Bills and Downs. I personally recommend Downs whose great-uncle Billy Downs, 75 years ago, owned 2 small farms along 372 at The Buck. One of these farms was later purchased by Ken and Helen Waltman and now accommodates a housing development on the south side of 372 just outside The Buck proper.

Amish phrase heard as racecars approach the starting line: Boogity, Boogity, Boogity—Wella Mah Springah! English translation: Boogity, Boogity, Boogity—Lets go Racin'

Sparks in The Buck

These are a few of my memories of John and Pauline Stoner and her parents J. Lehman and Martha Burkins of The Buck. Following these thoughts are an appreciated account, written by Jack Stoner, of his parents John and Pauline and grandparents J. Lehman and Martha. They were good people who served this community well.

As a small lad I recall John Stoner and his magic welder and torch, heating and bending steel and then fabricating this into whatever was needed to repair anything on the farm. He always wore a welder's hood to protect his eyes and face. We were told as kids to never look or stare at the source of the flying sparks to avoid damage to our eyes.

I never had Pauline, John's wife, for a teacher, only a choir director. She was from the old school, a good teacher and well acquainted with one-room school discipline. I don't know how teachers of her generation would cope today, forbidden to either crack or hug a student. Ruthie's mother cleaned for Pauline weekly and house cleaned for Martha, her mother twice a year and had a wonderful relationship with both for over 20 years.

As a young farm boy I can still visualize Lehman Burkins navigating his Dodge cattle truck in our lane to haul our cull cows and calves. He also bought and always hauled our wheat. At times I thought Lehman could be the happiest, most jovial, kind man I knew, as he would often arrive at our farm singing. But there were also times when he arrived to haul an old cow looking sour, irritable and grumbling. If the latter Lehman arrived conversation was short and, hopefully, if the cull cow knew what was good for her, she cooperated and cautiously climbed into Lehman's truck. I'm sure years ago, when Lehman was visibly upset, there could have been occasions when sparks and fire were observed on both sides of 272, south. Underneath, though, any who knew him realized he had a heart of gold and would do almost anything for anyone. I recall he held different offices at our church and also supervised the building of the manse in 1960 that stands beside Chestnut Level Church today.

Martha, Lehman's wife, was easygoing, cordial, always smiling, with a jolly demeanor and always the same. To me most times her disposition appeared opposite that of her husband. Ruthie remembers Martha had painful arthritis in her knees. Lehman would park their car in the driveway, in the warm sunshine. She would sit in the car, in the hot sun that temporarily relived the hurt from her painful condition.

Jack, as a preschooler, describes himself as an ornery little boy. He stayed with his grandmother Burkins as his mother taught school at Drumore Elementary. He remembers his grandmother would briefly leave the house daily to get the mail with him inside. He would watch her coming up the walk with the mail and orneriness' would overcome him. He would run to the door and lock it until grandma would say, "Jack, unlock the door." One day when locking the door his hand accidentally went through the glass above the lock. No harm was done when his arm and hand went through the glass but when he frantically pulled it back through the shattered hole a sharp piece slit his arm above his elbow. His mother was called home from school and drove him and his grandma to the emergency room. To this day he carries the ugly scar of an ornery little boy. Jack continues the welding business at The Buck started by his late father, specializing now in radiator repair.

Lehman, Martha, John and Pauline

As recalled, by Jack Stoner

J. Lehman, and Martha Burkins, Lehman known to all as JL, moved to The Buck from the home farm in 1948. After the home farm was condemned via eminent domain proceedings in January 1965 to become part of the Muddy Run project JL, remained very active in business hauling cattle year round, buying wheat, and hauling for Lancaster Milling Company in the summer. Wheat to the "Milling Company" was a summer rite of many farmers. Another rite was waiting in line for hours along 272 at Lyndon in the blistering heat to unload at the "Company's" one bay unloading facility. All before the standard of today, air conditioning in every truck cab. I'm sure this tested Lehman's occasionally short patience. An aficionado of fine Phillies cigars, he perhaps enjoyed a smoke whilst the wait. When burnt down to a stub they would collect in the Dodge truck ash tray, then being the proper length would be stuffed into his pipe, and enjoyed the rest of the way. Why waste 15% of a perfectly good cigar anyway? Enjoy is being objective here, for anyone unlucky enough to be downwind, the aroma would be likened to a junkyard tire fire, or a smoldering burn barrel. The cigar habit evokes memory of a funny Yuletide prank, amusing at least to the rest of us. Last stop on one of the cattle hauling runs was at a neighboring farm. After loading the truck, and exchanging Christmas greeting, this neighbor, whose name will go unmentioned, handed JL a carton—of what else-Phillies cigars. Unbeknownst to the happy recipient, a small explosive charge had been surgically inserted into one of the smokes. As luck would, or would not have it, that cigar was lit around Lancaster, and detonated on the way to New Holland Sales Stables. Filling the truck cab with shredded tobacco and the sulfurous odor of gunpowder and lucky for our Lancaster County Plain Sect and Amish friends in the area that the truck windows were closed, or they would have expanded their vocabulary with words perhaps not likely to meet their approval. JL returned home that night, still visibly agitated, and vowed retribution. How "justice" was served remains unclear, but I'm sure the favor was returned.

All this Martha took in stride with her ready, winning smile. Very active in her Church, local Farmwomen Organization, and Order of King's Daughters, she could set a table, and prepare a meal fit for a king and did on many occasions. Martha and Lehman lived in the southernmost house on the east side of Rt. 272. She, like many women of that era, did not drive, and did not seem to feel that to be a handicap. With many friends and close relatives nearby who did drive, she remained quite mobile. All of the lumber in their house was cut on the farm, including the oak hardwood flooring. A home she took great pride in, and maintained immaculately. Martha and Lehman resided in The Buck for 21 years from 1948 to 1969, both passing within 6 weeks of each other in the year 1969.

John and Pauline Stoner moved to The Buck in 1948. They bought property directly across the road from Lehman and Martha. This would be on the west side of Rt. 272, the last property south in The Buck at the time. This parcel was purchased from Sam Wenger, later to be Wenger Pontiac GMC. John, after a short period of employment with the Musser group in their butcher shop, opened a welding business on the location in 1948. Working extremely long hours 6 days a week, the couple saved, while living in a comfortable upstairs apartment in the Burkins home. In 1955 they constructed their brick ranch house directly beside John's welding shop. They lived there together until John's death in 2004. Pauline lived in the home until 2010, then relocated to an assisted living facility of her choosing, also located at The Buck. Pauline was of course very close to her parents and provided many miles of transportation for her mother, shopping trips to Lancaster, of course, the grocery store, et al. One transport she did not provide was for JL's, monthly sojourn to Smitty's Beer Distributor at Quarryville. See, Dr. Robert C. Helm, who made house calls by the way, had recommended Lehman drink 1 beer a day for his heart.

He maintained this regimen faithfully, doctor's orders! Pauline did not totally approve of the consumption of any fermented beverage, even if for medicinal purpose. As we all know most medications are quite unpalatable, but a cold Pabst Blue Ribbon, for the heart after a hard day's work, can be just what the "doctor ordered." I think JL would agree. As always, Martha took this in stride as well, falling back on the axiom, everything in moderation never hurt a soul.

Pauline, after graduating from Millersville State Teachers College in 1944, began employment in one-room schools in Drumore Township including Chestnut Level, Oregon Hollow and Silver Springs, and then finished her career at Drumore Township Elementary. She was very active in her church, directing the junior choir for many years, teaching Sunday School and serving on the board of Elders. She also served the community in venues such as Meals on Wheels, and much more. Anyone she was aware of that needed help, for whatever reason, she would be there for them. This was her creed until age prevented her from serving others and the community. Even to this day, she helps with what she calls "the older people" at Country View Manor.

John was in his element at the welding shop, adroit at all things mechanical, and with an innate ability to work with people, even the most difficult. The more taxing the problem he was presented, the more he rose to the occasion. He seemed to enjoy working with the most seemingly impossible tasks that his customers would bring in. It was not necessarily about the work, but serving his customers and community. Never to complain about the phone call that came after hours or the knock at the door on a Sunday afternoon, it was all about service to his customers. In that he thrived. John also served his church well, as an Elder, Sunday School Teacher, and Superintendent, and many years on the Cemetery Association. He served on the Drumore Township Zoning hearing board for many years and as an active member in the Tucquan Lions Club. He was very proud of his service to our country. Combat wounded in France during WWII, he like many of those who have stood in harm's way would rarely talk about his experience. Only at one time did he tell Pauline what happened on the night he was wounded, and only one time did he recant the story to his son and daughter-in-law, this shortly before his passing in 2004.

February 1, 1945, his platoon was charged with crossing behind enemy lines to capture prisoners in hope of gathering intelligence. As with many of these forays, things did not go as planned. Encountering German infantry in a small hamlet, a violent firefight ensued degenerating into hand-to-hand combat. John was severely injured. His squad leader asked John if he could make it back to friendly territory on his own as there was no one available to help him. After an unknown distance due to loss of blood, he became aware he could not go on, and decided to rest where he hoped his unit would find him on their return in the morning. By the grace of God they did find him, unconscious, but still alive. He awoke in an Army Hospital where a doctor told him, if not for the severe cold, he would have bled to death. There is no glory in a foxhole, only honor, and those of us who have not been there cannot possibly imagine the horror of war. We are forever indebted to those who have put themselves in harm's way.

Lehman, Martha, John, and Pauline led a life of service to others and community, and pass on a legacy very difficult to live up to. We need to look back and appreciate where we came from sometimes to enable us to look ahead and determine where we should go. Jack Stoner

Concerning Jack's vivid description of exploding Phillies cigars, I'm told that 2 pranksters of The Buck during that era were Billy Downs and Dave Byers.

Some have said that the taking of the Burkins farm by Philadelphia Electric for the Muddy Run project broke Lehman's heart and his son Bob's spirit.

Folks Remembered

The following are a list of folks recalled by Ruthie residing in The Buck more than a half century past. We apologize for those forgotten, as we are also both from a time more than a half-century ago. Sadly, the vast majority of these mentioned are deceased but we believe they deserve and would be both pleased and grateful to have their names once again associated with The Buck.

Park & Iva Moore
Abner & Esther Musser
LeRoy & Naomi Wenger
Lehman & Martha Burkins
Harry & Ida Good
Billy Pleger
Leon & Martha Kreider
Francis & Dolly Wenger
Naurie & Pearl Boyd
Bobby Reinhart
Roy & Dot O'Donnell
Ralph & Edith Reinhart
Rex & Esta Cully
Claude Herr & Family
Tom & Mazie Newswenger
Herb Mylin & Family
Keel & Clare Hambleton
Tom Giberson & Family
Grace & Ernie Shaub
Don & Ruth Moore
John & Nora Lefever
John & Pauline Stoner
John & Louella Byers
Paul & Hazel Riggs
George Rhoades
Raymond & Jessie Testerman & Family

Wayne & Mabel Byers
Sam & Pearl Wenger
George & Maggie Knight-Walt Eberly
Elvin(Shorty)&Elizabeth Herr
Paul & Lena Dombach
Wilbur & Grace Pollock
Everett & Flossie Kreider
Harry McCombs
Harry & Lib Keene
Billy Downs
Frank Lyons
Irene & Gussie Garner
Paul Shotzberger
Sam Sinopolli
Charles & Ruth Myers
Harry Woerner
Joe Holabein
Herb & Della Creter
Kay & Robah Hess
John & Dot Jamison
Dick & Marian Lefever
Charles & Mim Kachel
Ken & Helen Waltman
Dick & Lois Myers
Buck Hotel, Banzhoff, Weaver,
Riggs & Waltman

A few facts that recently surfaced from those atop The Buck hill north from that era are as follows: Paul Shotzberger had a restaurant there that contained a lunch counter and stools. Park Shaub conducted sales Wednesday evenings near Rex and Esta Cully's. Sam Sinopolli started the junkyard and Tom Giberson worked for him. John Kohler started the foundry. Rex Cully started the sawmill with employees, Tom Giberson, Ken Wentzel, and Ray VanCleve. Esta Cully ran the Star mail route then later Doris & Dick Lefever. One of the most famous softball pitchers and bowlers from Lancaster County during this last half-century was Charlie Rhoads, also from The Buck

PART TWO

EVERYWHERE "AROUND" LIBERTY SQUARE

Farmhouse with a view

A nice assortment of fine-feathered friends frolic at the feeders outside my kitchen window this frosty February morning. The finches, always more interested in confrontation with one another and evidently enjoying nothing more than a good argument before breakfast, must be Irish. The chickadees, titmouse, cardinals and sparrows pay no attention to the finches' heated debate as they enjoy the breakfast buffet. The clothesline behind the buffet is lined with latecomers who evidently didn't have reservations. Waiting patiently, evidently Mr. and Mrs. cardinal, party of two, dressed in their finest plumage, were summoned to the awaiting food. A few drab sparrows, observing the cardinals' arrival, glance their way, thinking they are a tad over-dressed for a week-day breakfast.

Through the slowly thinning evergreens behind the clothesline, I can see all the way to the woods at the top of the hill this clear morn. Our two resident red tail hawks, high on a limb in the still barren trees of winter, seem to glow as two angels on a Christmas tree as they each face the warm morning sun and me. Even from a distance of several hundred yards, their white breasts are gleaming as they, like all living creatures I observe today, appreciate and welcome their sun.

As I rise from the breakfast table, a smaller hawk about the size of a crow glides unnoticed in behind the outhouse near this bird buffet. We always referred to this bird as a chicken hawk, for obvious reasons, when we raised fowl many years ago in outside, open pens. The startled screams in daylight from a half-grown Rhode Island Red could mean the swift, silent attack for a hawk McChicken to go.

The chicken hawk, still hidden behind the outhouse and from all the tweety-birds, finally penetrates its beak and eyes through some weeds and a dead peony bush. Perfectly camouflaged, had I not observed its obscure landing from the north I would never have noticed it in the dead foliage. I'm reminded what experienced hunters have told me: more creatures observe you than you will ever notice when hunting. Now begins the waiting game by the predator, as it remains motionless, realizing it is unseen, except for me. Patience is the greatest attribute and virtue of this two-pound killing machine as it surely must be in all predators.

Suddenly, a pair of unassuming doves drop from the sky like two miniature toy helicopters landing halfway between the buffet and the hawk. In a flash, the hungry hawk appears to be shot from its hideout, grabbing one of the startled doves with clenched claws before it lands. This effortless motion evidently caused it to eye its prey for a split second too long—and—kerplunk—it crashes into the steel pole holding the bird feeder. The unforgiving metal pole caught the hawk near the base of a wing, causing it to spin wildly 180 degrees. But with wings spluttering it never came in contact with land. In the ensuing confusion of crash, exploding feathers and panicky birds, the hawk relinquished its grip and the terrified dove escaped.

I am astounded, spilling half of a second cup of coffee on my Penn State cushion at this instant confrontation right outside my window. The crash was muffled and absorbed by thick layered, ruffled feathers on this miniature, silent, land hugging fighter jet of nature obviously equipped with undetected yet useless radar. While gaining altitude the hawk regained its composure, then streaked outta sight, apparently unhurt and only suffering possible embarrassment. The bird feeder attached to the pole, however, swung wildly, causing windrows of seed to be scattered in all directions at pole clanging intervals. For some unknown reason while observing this mini-second beak-to-beak physical combat, nearly tragic for both participants, a roadrunner cartoon scene flashed across my mind. It will be hours before the smorgasbord breakfast buffet reopens. When the patrons finally return they will be scarce, fidgety and later experience heartburn as they gulp their meal while expressing nervous head and neck contortions.

The weather remains cold this last week in February, just as our local prognosticator, Octorara Orphie, predicted. Those who frequent the bird feeders remain active and are slowly reviving their silent winter conversations with sounds and songs coaxing spring. The song of the chickadee immediately transposes my drab landscape into a luscious green, flowery fragrant golf course (perhaps the Masters at Augusta). Occasionally I watch this golf coverage with both sight and sound clearly visible and audible and delight in hearing the sound of the tiny black-capped chickadee over and over. I'm probably the only one of you intently watching the methodical moves of Tiger Woods and other participants that enjoy the chickadee sharing its repetitive song live from several hundred miles away. Perhaps like those who watch and play golf I also look forward to and appreciate a birdie now and then.

Before you jump to any conclusions, I've never played golf, although the exercise would probably be beneficial to my far from fluid body. My hang-up is that I've never been able to hit a ball solidly that arrives or lies below my knees. I'm not a good low-ball hitter and further more if I do make contact on the diamond at least someone else has to chase my errant drive, not me. In this present environment, when others from the government to the trash man influence my daily decisions, I'm still independent enough not to be influenced or led around by a tiny mindless, white ball that would seldom, if ever, travel in the direction I intended. Hopefully the Tom Tom that determines the course I will follow and navigate will remain Tom! "FORE!"

Amish Winter Olympics

With cold weather arriving in early December this year, the local farm ponds have prematurely frozen over, permitting resident ice-skating to commence. Along with a few others, plus local farm dogs, we enjoy being spectators of our neighborhood Amish children, along with a few dads, that participate in this blast from the past frolic. I grew up listening to parents and grandparents speaking of this activity with reflection and long—ago smiles. They also spoke of winters 100 years ago when skating continued continuously for 3 full months. Weather patterns have evidently changed somewhat as I recall local ponds unfrozen for skating for the entire winter with the exception of a week or 2 in January.

We didn't have a farm pond but had access to a couple nearby, one being that of Dick Nicodemus that was occasionally skated on. Consequently, I was always unsure of my ability to cruise around, on 2 single, shoe-length-thin steel blades. Lack of participation in this activity relates directly to lack of confidence; therefore, the only aspect of ice-skating ever practiced sincerely by me was the art of falling down gracefully while being able to hide pain or embarrassment.

I much prefer roller to ice-skating and my old truck to a sleigh, although falling while roller skating on a hardwood floor can, upon observation by a close family member, transform your rear-end into a majestic, colorful, Doris Hough painting of a Liberty Square sunrise amidst dark threatening clouds.

No offense intended girls, but lately I have observed a few ladies, who should they fall skating, appear to be well padded with all the cushions from a 3 piece sofa inserted inside the back of their slacks. If these "curves" dropouts, whose favorite word is smorgasbord, should fall and suffer discomfort I imagine their backside could also appear similar to mine. However, this painting would most assuredly become a breathtakingly beautiful, Bill Ressler, river hill sunset "mural" framed by my Amish neighbor lads using weathered fence boards.

Sorry for the distraction—back to the skating before the weather changes and the ice melts.

As we approach our local ice-rink, a farm pond located on the John Adams farm beside our acres, it appears out of the blackness of a moonless December night, totally foreign to our rural environment as the home of the Hershey Bears. A small gasoline engine drives a generator that powers the lights that crisscross above the skating area. This illuminates the ice and surrounding area for spectators and probably the startled blue gills, bass, minnows, water snakes and the resident snappin-turtle glancing up at the black-figured predators circling their ice-encased habitat.

The ladder still rests on the tree limb where the final string of lights was attached. When invisible breezes appear, the tree limbs sway gently, the lights refocus cautiously and the shadows on the ice and area surrounding it appear to dance. With arms flapping wildly from a distance, the Amish children appear as prehistoric crows on this bright as day night, although their young voices are more soprano sounding than the boisterous, baritone birds they resemble.

Hockey is evidently the sport of choice tonight as a low fence encircles the rink, with goals of netting at either end. All players carry hockey sticks, some store bought, some home made with a knot attached and growing on the end that absorbs the punishment. Evidently the puck is genuine and not homemade. The boys play rough but seemingly without altercations or fist-a-cuffs.

We observed a wild shot that soared astray and into the small creek that flows behind the open arena. This relegates a few older players to slog upstream and down in freezing but unfrozen spring-fed water in search of the errant escapee. One would think trudging, with skates attached; through this ice cube water would later cause foot and skate to be amputated as one.

Young Amish girls skate continually around the perimeter of the rink but don't engage in the affairs of net, stick and puck that is still not located and has now required lanterns and flashlights to aid in its recovery. The girls cannot hide their complete satisfaction and enjoyment as they skate back and forth across the hockey rink, with the game still on hold as those dedicated to the search holler words of their language that I don't understand back and forth to one another. The stream examination has evidently expanded as flashes of light and voices are seen and heard halfway to the river. As the young ladies continue to glide effortlessly across the pond, their cold eyes sparkle above the uncharacteristic color of red observed on rosy cheeks but never seen in their attire.

Hooray, plus a conglomeration of Amish exclamations ungrasped by me, rises from the adjacent stream as the puck is recovered. The hockey game soon resumes in earnest as the girls scatter to safety around the edge of the rink. A hatless, fair-haired 12—year-old along with the puck go flying into the net, driving it completely off the ice. Sitting on their hunkers behind the purring generator, 3 little boys suddenly appear, apparently startled by the flying goal that lands beside them. Totally unnoticed by me until this moment, they were evidently graciously soaking in the heat expelled by the warm motor before they attempted to provide assistance to the older boys trying to relocate the goal with net backing to its necessary position. I then realize these little guys are no more than 3 or 4 years old and dressed in appropriate Amish garb with black hats firmly perched atop hair-thatched heads. Their tiny steps in the frost around the ice appeared as one continuous, narrow, tender trail. They soon return to their nest beside the welcome, cozy generator.

The Amish kids constructed the entire fence around the rink, the lights and the goals. They were quite proud of their skating ability and their makeshift facilities. I didn't recognize all the hockey players, but do recall a few of their names. The player whose errant slap shot had gone into a Susquehanna tributary was Gideon Gretzki. Sylvan Sidney Crosby is recalled, as is goal tender Benuel Boricher and also Gideon Giroux. Bobby Beiler Hull, sporting a beard that indicates he is now married, made an appearance. Gordie Glick Howe, also evidently married, scored 3 goals this particular game, referred to as a Black Hat Trick. Nicklas Lapp Lidstrom was awarded and made a penalty shot for earlier icing a shoofly pie. The Stoltzfus brothers served as referees.

Later, skates were removed and lights were outed. Those with transportation made their way to wagons, buggies and 2-wheel runabouts hitched to patiently awaiting 4 legged corn and hay crunchers. The remaining lads and lassies, skates tied together and draped over willing shoulders, walked home. All ice age impressionist and transportation providers look forward to home and stall. Each will sleep soundly and dream vividly tonight despite an occasional midnight outburst of GOAL! As my head depresses my pillow and closed eyes encase another day, I visualize that which I have observed tonight and will dream of my ancestors skating across a local, moonlit, frozen pond. An imagined, animated Currier and Ives print coaxes me to sleep. Rest well my friends.

A couple weeks following the writing of the Amish Winter Olympics, I spoke with a few English acquaintances that hire some local Amish boys. With ponds still frozen, these local Amish lads have formed teams from different near-by areas and have gotten serious with their hockey playing. Evidence of this is indicated by the appearance of these participants sporting black eyes, gashes on heads, bruises seen and unseen and a noticeable limp. I don't believe all-out fighting is involved but evidently a series of checks and balances continually enter this ice-covered arena. Ferocious, nonnegotiable, bouncing checks and the temporary loss of the even distribution of one's weight causes an imbalance of an upright position and is responsible for these battle scars.

April showers may bring May flowers but it seems a January freeze brings bruises, bumps and shattered knees, at least in our surrounding Amish community. A February thaw will most likely bring closure to this rough yet enjoyable winter sport and hopefully most abused bodies will be completely healed at the arrival of spring chores!

Liberty Square Lions Club

The following are excerpts from a brief speech I delivered at a meeting of the Quarryville Lions Club. Along with my cousin, sports writer, Ken Denlinger, who spoke of his sports experiences worldwide but especially of Penn State football with insights into the character of Joe Paterno. I divulged memories of writing my first book and remembrances of my life down on the farm.

This evening occurred approximately 6 weeks before the last presidential election, which explains my reference to the candidates. While experiencing an unrestrained impulse, I also contrived a Lion's Club story of my own. I include this feeble attempt at old farmer humor because a few days later I received several calls from Lion's Club members for copies of this uneasy oration.

Ken and I were originally gonna do our Laurel and Hardy routine but we came here tonight and forgot to wear our suits, ties and top hats. Right about now I was gonna flick my necktie at him and declare, "Well, here's another fine mess you've gotten us into."

I hope you don't mind my reading most of this. I've reached the point in my life where my "senior moments" are sometimes measured in hours.

Because of all the present multitude of campaign ads, I am currently suffering from a "senior stupor" that my psychologist has determined can't be treated or cured until after the presidential election. I offer a couple of observations from the current presidential campaign that has helped me greatly with my political therapy. My observations and opinions are those of an old, uneducated corn-cob-college academic and don't necessarily reflect those of family members present here tonight.

If you are for Senator Obama and Senator Biden then it would seem to this old farmer the key word for you and their campaign is "change." That's right, it's all about change as I hold up a quart jar filled with pennies, nickels, and dimes. With the Democrats it's always about change. There has been much written of late of Sen. Obama's association with William Ayers, a former radical war protestor linked to Vietnam-era bombings. Ayers was a member of the Weatherman Underground Organization. I don't know much about the Weathermen but I don't think I want my president hanging around with the likes of Joe Calhoun and Al Roker.

If you're supporting Sen. McCain and Gov. Palin, I offer the following. Some folks up Lancaster way refer to where I live as the edge of civilization and that I have no idea or comprehension of all the problems occurring everyday outside my neighborhood and around the world. Well, doggone it you guys, that's just not true. From where I live, for instance, on a clear day I can see York County. If the Atomic plant, directly across the river from me at Peach Bottom, blows up some night, who do you think will be the first to know, some politician in Washington or me?

I'll tell you something else, these high paid Wall Street executives and my Amish neighbors each have something in common, they're both now looking for a free ride. You know the only difference between a Wall Street Executive and an Amish man—"deodorant." Darn right! Now that I've succeeded in insulting most everyone, including the Amish, I best move on. I have a feeling it may be sometime before we're invited back to Black Rock and the Lions Club. I probably have also eaten my last free Amish whoppie pie!

Ken, trained in Journalism and writing has for over 40-years built a career writing of sports events worldwide and also authored several books. I, on the other hand have spent my last nearly 50-years down on the farm, on top of a John Deere or under a holstein. But regardless of what you're thinking our careers have had some similarities because you see while he wrote about exciting sports events that were "udderly" long remembered I handled the "udder" part. We both took our particular jobs seriously and literally milked them for all they're worth. If you have the urge, this is the appropriate time allotted to "BOO." Our lifetime of work, however, may have each appeared together on your breakfast table every morning. His work you poured through in the sports section of your morning newspaper and mine you simply poured on your cereal.

I've been asked to say a few words about my book titled "Liberty Square Observed and Noted." As a little background for those of you who don't know our tiny village of Liberty Square it is very small. Comparing Liberty Square to Quarryville is like comparing The Buck to Philadelphia.

Someone once told me that reading my book was like visiting with me in an old country store many years ago, with me telling you a few stories from the past. With that in mind I would like to tell you another old story, one that you folks in particular, may be interested in.

This story is told around home that many years ago a few old fellas decided they also wanted to form a Lions Club in Liberty Square. Not knowing all the rules, regulations, purpose and by-laws of the Lion's organization they relied a lot on here-say and went forth blindly and formed The Liberty Square Lions Club.

This proved to be both disastrous and disheartening for all the local members when they arose before daylight one cold February morning and headed for the river hills. You see they were hoping to observe a lion at daybreak to check and see if it saw its shadow. No luck. Later in the day large appetites and compelling thirsts were quelled and quenched by a hearty breakfast and a barrel of hard cider.

With stomachs full and fermented cider bolstering their courage, they again set off in search of a lion. One of the members had heard that the tail-twister was a most important office in the Lions Club. They decided if they captured a lion, whoever could tie a knot in the large cat's tail would become tail-twister for life. The story goes, after a futile search and no sightings of a lion they found an exceptionally large Tom Cat, sitting in a fencerow, sunning himself on a farm years later owned by Ben Herr.

They cornered it and a rugged old Irish farmer spit tobacco juice in the cat's eyes, temporarily blinding it. Perhaps the old farmer wanted the honor of tail-twister extraordinaire or maybe it was the hard cider that fueled him, but he dove into the briars and honeysuckle on top of the miniature lion and through a maze of blood, spit, fur and tobacco juice tied a perfect square knot in the tail of the startled cat. As eyesight retuned to the puddy-cat, it escaped and was last seen streaking past Rawlinsville Hotel by a couple of patrons who claimed the cat, still moving at top speed, kept glancing back. The old farmer was taken to a local doctor in Holtwood and treated for scratches, bites, loss of blood and intoxication. A short time later the Liberty Square Lions Club disbanded forever!

Following a talk on my previous book I concluded this evening with the following:

On behalf of Ken and myself I would like to thank all of you for sharing this evening with us. Thanks not only for your attention but also for your smiles and laughter.

When we were young we thought little of how we would handle heartaches and disappointments "IF" they came into our lives. Today we no longer wonder "IF" they'll come but "WHEN."

I am one who believes that a sincere smile and hearty laugh will not eliminate life's problems from entering our lives. But, if they are mixed with our heartaches and frustrations they will in this life eventually drive them from our soul and are an essential ingredient for all of us, from the cradle to the grave.

If you have any questions for either of us we will be happy to try and answer them, but if you wish to gain some insight into the exact time of Joe Paterno's retirement please refer those questions to Ken. If you have a question pertaining to the exotic life of an old farmer, down on the farm, you best address them to the "UDDER-GUY."

Sounds From Behind The Barn

With our home farm located in close proximity to Muddy Run Park, we've been able to hear some of the activities that occurred there over the last 40 years. When a calm breeze is blowing from the northwest, these sounds that originate nearly a mile away appear to be occurring directly behind our large 120-year-old barn. One of the first to be heard was the creation concert, held in June of 1979 when several thousand folks descended on the open green grass, former fields and woodland adjacent to Muddy Run Lake. This local faith-oriented Woodstock, evidently shrouded in prayer instead of drugs, attracted folks far and wide to this open-air religious festival. More about Jesus than Joan Baez, Janis Joplin, Jefferson Airplane, The Grateful Dead and others, this gathering was later discontinued when the area was designated as too small to handle the enormous crowd. It continues today in west central Pa. and draws more then 100,000 people.

I recall hearing excerpts from praise songs and words from those who spoke through speakers with not every spoken word audible that was blowin' in the wind. What is remembered most by this old farmer from that festival was the applause, cheering and roar from the crowd that had never before occurred in this once very rural place. It sounded similar to the parking lot at a Phillies game when a home run was hit or the area around Beaver Stadium in State College when a touchdown was scored. You had to live in this remote, rural area for half a lifetime to realize how out of place this crowd roar sounded to us natives both 2 and 4 legged. Those of us who witnessed the building of the Muddy Run Project and survived the unforgiving destruction of earthmovers, fires and the complete annihilation of nature and man once again shook our heads.

The tractor pulls also are heard regularly when held at Muddy Run. When conditions are just right, these forgotten farmer furrow followers of yesteryear driven by our local Tony Stewarts and Dale Juniors, dressed in overalls, work shoes and wearing farm advertising caps appear to be somewhere in our back fields pulling a plow instead of a sled. The public address system that blares out, "167 feet, that's good enough for second place," reminds me that many old and young farmers have now developed a sport out of tedious tractor-tilling tasks. Although I've been driving tractors for nearly 60 years, I have never participated in coaxing a tractor pulling a weighted sled, down a track.

Our minister, Rev. Dr. Michael Wilson, and youth director Joe Garrison approached me a couple of years ago indicating they wanted to enter the tractor pulling contest at Solanco Fair with me supplying the tractor. I told them it is not something to be taken lightly and cautioned these non-farmers with no experience to the unforeseen danger that can occur. When they still wished to pursue this man and machine drag to the demise of engine or traction of spinning tractor tires, I finally forcefully told them, "You guys better stick to the cow milking contest." Naturally, they were both "udderly" disappointed; I was relieved, and that's no bull!

In the opinion of this old farmer, one of the best things to happen from the tractor pulls is the resurrection of hundreds of old tractors from barns, fencerows and iron and steel graveyards. Some appear to have been completely forgotten and are visible on the pulling track in that same rusty, faded, battered skin in which they were found as they last criss-crossed our farms years ago. Others appear with shiny, fresh-smelling new paint, new decals and lettering, looking identical to their first day on the farm. As I've grown older I've forgotten many things, but I've never forgotten the smell of fresh red paint on our brand new Farmall M tractor. It gives me a great deal of satisfaction to observe these tractor pullers of all ages, sizes and both sexes and the pride they display for these old machines that replaced horses and mules when I was young.

The sight and sound of this old iron is rehearsed and rewound inside my head and always coaxes a smile. A few others have developed modern engines for tractors but they may seem more at home cruising at 30,000 feet above the Atlantic Ocean than in the belly of a tractor, although they also have quite a large following. But for this old farmer the old iron, whether freshly painted or rust upon rust, is my preference.

I recently heard a sound behind the barn that was different and unfamiliar to any ever heard before. The rhythmic sound of drums caused me to glance in the direction of other sounds heard over the years. As I slowly walked behind the barn, the unmistakable sound of Indians chanting and singing was heard to the beat of drums that resembled the heartbeat of Mother Earth. I had heard this sound in every cowboy and Indian movie on TV, which was now clearly audible, tempered by the soft breeze blowing across the lake caressing my face. It was only then that I recalled reading of these Indian descendants appearing at a celebration at Muddy Run Park.

As one who fantasizes when recalling our local history, I couldn't help but smile as I thought: this is not the first time these rolling hills along the mighty

Susquehanna have heard these sounds that surely occurred hundreds of years before the white man ever walked these woods. Perhaps they seemed more authentic to me, originating and arriving from a distant hillside, and for a brief moment I lived among the Redman who first settled this once remote area. As I continued to daydream of attacking Indians, with drums and shouting, screaming savages in the background, I decided not to take any chances. I relocated much of my available machinery and realigned it forming a circle, as my ancestors surely would have done. Although my assortment of old guns is limited, varied, rusty and not fired in decades, I placed them pointed outwards among corn pickers, balers, tractors and manure spreaders. Hope the Indian braves never realize these weapons are unmanned and unloaded. If they are performing a war dance and planning a local attack, they will surely be disappointed when they realize my head is hairless and has evidently already been scalped. If this war party of Susquehannocks approaches my farm, I'm hoping they become disoriented and disillusioned as they observe me totally immersed in my own Presbyterian war dance. Dancing in a circle around my Weber gas grill and wildly singing these 4 rhythmic words—Hi How are Ya, Hi How are Ya over and over will hopefully cause them to pause. Having no peace pipe I intend to hand out Phillies Tiparillos and tickets to our Chicken and Waffle supper at Chestnut Level Church, which should produce complete bewilderment. My imagination sometimes runs wild in downtown Liberty Square as I temporarily escape from reality. Hope you listen to and appreciate the everyday sounds that occur in your world.

Motivating Morning Meditation

Early one spring morning while spreading the excrement of my confined 4-legged, T-bone, rump roast and quarter pounders I observed an Eagle resting majestically atop a large oak tree at the edge of my woodland. Although it is not uncommon to view this stately creature in our area, it is not any everyday occurrence.

Spreading the steamy manure on this dewy field adjacent to the woods, I pay little attention to my smelly task, staring intently at this white-capped wonder. Through dusty glasses and glaucoma-impaired eyes I focus intently on this symbol of our freedom. Through the eyes of an Eagle, it seems to focus intently on me.

Gracefully the bird leaped from the oak branch, bending it slightly at its departure and, with unfurled wings appearing to be in slow motion, soars directly toward me. Banking slightly before me, it looks both dignified and imposing as it gains altitude with a couple of effortless flaps of its impressive wings.

Silently the eagle hovers above my slow moving John Deere caravan and me, similar to a news helicopter covering an important story. During these brief moments I'm both startled and confused by this creature's unusual, unnatural interest in my machine and me. Then as the spreader discharges a partial page of newspaper that is located in my load of manure, in an instant, it all makes sense to me. After reading our local newspapers they are disposed of in the feces of our cattle to serve as bedding. They are trampled by the steers into the animal waste and completely disappear in a matter of hours, soaking up any urine and then completely disintegrating in the manure. Occasionally a small piece of paper is not trampled and ends up on a manure-covered field.

There are also some local poultry farmers who periodically have fowl that may die and a few end up in their fields. I have seen vultures and an occasional Eagle search from the sky and find one of these white, deceased chickens, drop to the earth and devour all but feathers and bones.

Thinking the sliver of newspaper is somehow related to Colonel Sanders is the reason for this Eagle's interest is my immediate thought. It drops to the ground beside the Lancaster New Era column of Jack Brubaker and looks disappointed and unimpressed, then rises 5 or 6 feet above the earth. Flying effortlessly a mere 10 yards beside me at the same altitude as my hat and same speed as my tractor, we move across the field side by side with each of us riding on air, its flowing under each wing and mine compressed inside 4-Firestones.

During those few brief moments as we shared a common habitat I look directly into the eyes of this beautiful creature and it looks directly into mine. Gliding into the first streams of glorious morning sunshine, with white gleaming from beak to breast and snow-white tail feathers spread in a plume, it truly is a breathtaking sight to behold. Then with a couple of effortless strokes of its powerful wings it rises above the trees, turns and flies above me one last time surveying the landscape below. My mystical morning companion then soars gracefully above the treetops, disappearing into the damp, dense, morning mist. I silently give thanks for having shared this brief time with something so revered and knew I would never forget it. I later wondered if I had encountered the very best of nature and if I had looked directly into the eyes of God.

Halloween in Liberty Square

I perhaps don't fully understand each and every one of our Amish neighbor's holidays and they may not comprehend all of ours. I think I might have some difficulty explaining Halloween to them. Folks young and old dressed in the scary attire of a ghost, demon or George Bush, Bernie Madoff and Barack Obama, going door to door expecting folks to deposit candy into a plastic pumpkin just because they showed up really is hard to figure out. Locally grown pumpkins, scooped and stripped of their innards, then carved into various facial expressions with a candle burning inside, makes even less sense. If allowed to remain on the front porch for a couple of weeks, this form of wrinkled human facial anatomy depicting 80 years of life is fast forwarded for all to view, which is the scary part for me.

I remember as a young Liberty Square lad when an occasional local farmer would awake some autumn morning and sometime during the day realize a tractor or some piece of farm equipment was gone from the farmstead. Irate with anger, the farmer never factoring in Halloween, police were called. They were always telephoned a few days later by the embarrassed farmer informing them the missing equipment was not stolen but relocated by pranksters to a remote area of the farm or in his woods.

Years ago before the mechanical corn picker appeared locally, corn stalks were cut by hand and put in shocks to dry with the ear of corn later removed. These dry corn shocks were evidently tempting to local Halloween firebugs, who set them ablaze in the middle of the night. This may have occurred in the middle of a field or in the middle of the road that always drew more attention but involved more work in moving the shock by those creating mischief. It seemed Halloween night was the allotted time for local youth to deliver payback to any they thought had irritated them. One story is told of a local mean-spirited farmer who found his large hay wagon atop his barn roof one morning. How it got there in the middle of the night, resting on the slate-covered peak, is to this day considered one of the 7 wonders of Liberty Square. None of those involved ever stepped forward to take the credit. Some speculate the wagon was dismantled on the ground, raised to the roof and then reassembled. Others believe it was somehow raised mechanically, then pushed and pulled to its resting place on the peak.

Around Liberty Square, soaping windows of houses or vehicles or tossing a roll of toilet paper over a tree was something city kids did at Halloween. Country kids put a lot more effort and thought into their pranks that were always accomplished under the cover of darkness and sometimes involved a certain degree of danger for them.

Wild and domesticated animals were sometimes involved in these seasonal pranks. There were undocumented stories of coons and or groundhogs, alive and dead, appearing inside closed mailboxes. This causes me to wonder if these pranksters disliked the homeowner or the mailman? Also a Rhode Island Red hen was evidently startled and left cackling, as was the mailman when he raised the old-time mailbox lid. Showing no animosity toward anyone, she left behind a large brown egg.

The relocation of farm animals was for the most part a simple practical-joker task. Cows that in those days were confined in a stall could be led and tied to a front yard tree clearly visible to the owner on Halloween morn. I have heard of a couple sheep or hogs waking up disoriented in the milk house, and a rooster crowing his wake up call inside the old farmer's automobile. A couple eggs from a forgotten nest by the one that laid them is remembered and a source for revisiting by another lad. He cautiously selects a couple that are surely rotten. Our mischievous lad then places them on or beside the motor of our farm owner's car, reminding the driver of Halloween on his next roadway jaunt. The relocation of farm machinery placed to block the farmer's lane was also popular and didn't involve the police. The farmer moved this machinery immediately, I'm told, some with smiles and some swearing.

Traveling between farms at twilight a few evenings before Halloween, I noticed some strange figures moving across the horizon. There were black bodies with amputated legs followed by legs moving in different directions and in odd contortions evidently trying to match up with their proper corpse. Headless trunks of bodies were moving in unorthodox, jerking motions all seemingly now headed in the same direction and disappearing behind an old stone dwelling. On the horizon the silhouette of a galloping, riderless horse appeared briefly as the skyline darkened. The legend of Sleepy Hollow came to life and, briefly, I become Ichabod Crane viewing the headless horseman now absent of his entire body.

Wanting to observe this Halloween phenomenon more closely, I stopped my already slow moving, drifting truck, turned off the engine and sat, surrounded by darkness and silence beside my woodland. This absence of sound accompanied only by the trickling water from a nearby spring was broken by the hoot of an owl. It was evidently perched on a low hanging limb directly above my vehicle and me, with every eerie sound it made questioning my location and motive. Although startled, I continued to hold my position as this creature of the night maintained its. Finally, I rewarded its patience and perseverance and quietly drove away, allowing my pointy-eared acquaintance to remain in its familiar, silent, dark world. But this old farmer would remember what I had seen and heard at twilight that seemed appropriate so near to Halloween.

What I had observed at dusk was the Amish farm of Jonathan and Fannie King. The running, riderless horse most likely was heading across the hilltop pasture to its welcoming stall and nutritious feed. The black headless, partial bodies were clothes of the male members of the King family being coaxed and pulled toward her on a rotating wash line by the Amish wife and mother hidden behind her house. BOO!

Amish Summer Olympics

The activity of which I write today occurs at the farm pond of neighbor John Adams. Located between our 2 farms, we travel the road past this place several times a day on or in tractors, trucks, a lawn tractor or car. Only a few feet from the road, the pond is always observed as is the wooded landscape surrounding it. Mentioned in "Liberty Square Observed and Noted," my previous book, this watering hole is recommended by the local wildlife as an uninterrupted stopping-off place for relaxation and a cold one.

Deer, foxes, raccoons, wild geese, gulls and ducks, rabbits, pheasants, squirrels, groundhogs, an occasional wild turkey or blue heron and a local stray horse, mule or cow have all been observed on or crossing the road for liquid refreshment by this passing, resident zoo keeper. Consequently, my speed through this Liberty Square Serengeti is greatly reduced from my normal 15 miles per hour. My senses are each initiated to function at full capacity while one foot gently coaxes the throttle or accelerator as the other cautiously anticipates the brake.

But this day I wish to relate another activity that occurs mid-summer at this nontransparent, cloudy, local Lake Louise. This involves my local Amish lads, who may number 3-dozen, and takes place many hot, humid evenings till and sometimes well into the encroachment of darkness that may be as black as the daily clothing worn by the boys. They arrive along the shore of this man made pool that provides for fish, mammal, amphibian and boys totally clothed with swimwear evidently underneath. If there is the occurrence of a total change of attire it must take place behind a tree or in an enclosed buggy as bare butts are never flashed. When I drive past, with all in the water, the only items flashed in my direction are smiles with voices echoing, "Jump In Tom!"

The diving board, installed earlier in the season is located off the west bank of this pond that supports both summer and winter Olympics. I'm not sure of the ancestry of this particular diving board but it seems to propel the participants to heights enabling the rotation and somersault of a water-soaked, flying carcass. The board itself is fastened securely at one end and rests upon 2 airtight metal drums that float on the surface of the water. The end that initiates the thrust protrudes several feet past the barrels and above the receptive water.

Because this Olympic pool is constructed entirely of dirt, within 30 seconds of swimming and diving activity, the water is so cloudy and muddy that anyone in the water completely disappears if they're 2 inches below the surface. This dirty water neither discourages the activity nor suppresses the enjoyment. There may be over 2 dozen boys swimming or diving and splashing in the swimming hole, but as I approach and drive by they all sometimes completely disappear at once with the only sign of life observed by me being a few bubbles rising to the surface from various depths of the pond. In my rearview mirror, I notice wet, clinging hair attached to waterlogged, submerged heads, all surfacing throughout this pond and then ensuing laughter. At the ocean, most folks usually take a shower to remove the sand and grit following some time on the beach. One could surmise these guys would later take a shower to remove the soil and dirt adrift in the thrashing waters of the pond.

The resident swimmers, when out of the water, display golden brown faces and similar tones from elbows through the 10 residents of winter time gloves but are otherwise as white as a January snowman in appearance. An unfamiliar observer might conclude these lads have not only sprung from parents of 2 different sexes but also separate races. Possessing these 2 uncoordinated shades of color myself when modeling a swimsuit, I simply refer to my local lads as 2 toned.

On an occasional weekend drive-by, I have noticed a small, white, square floating in this watering/swimmin' hole. Upon closer inspection it appears to be a cake of Ivory soap. I suppose this could account for the soapsuds observed hugging the edge of the pond, particularly on a Sunday morn. It has been reported to me that 70 years ago a couple local farm boys were known to regularly enjoy a Saturday night bath in this earthen tub, their clothes draped over a nearby tree limb. This activity supposedly ceased when someone secretly removed all their awaiting dry clothes, never to be seen again. I'm told the boys didn't leave the appreciated confines of the muddy water; constantly stirring it up until total darkness was upon them. Later when walking home, completely naked, they were thankful that clouds had concealed a full moon.

Could it be our local Amish lads have also taken and revived this 70-year-old local practice? I'm not sure of the effect on the resident bath tub bass and blue gills but have been advised a few have recently been caught and reeled to shore blowing colorful bubbles. A local outbreak of suspected rabies was recently put to rest when a foaming-at—the-mouth raccoon was trapped near the pond with the undeniable odor and appearance of Ivory soapsuds on its masked face.

The swimming and diving to prepare our local fellas for the upcoming Olympic Games continues nightly through July and August. This regular flailing in the Olympic pool causes the organic natural white caps to remain brown for at least 24 hours following all this activity until it again resumes. There is never the appearance of anyone assumed to judge the constant swimming and diving activities. In my imagination, this is simply a practice pool, with the best water entrepreneurs eventually moving on to the finals at larger ponds with greater crowds of spectators. Located near flourishing Amish communities at Kirkwood, Ronks, Georgetown and Bird in Hand, these Amish summer Olympics will conclude amidst frolics, food and fun.

At the conclusion of the events, the judges, older men with white beards, will award the coveted bronze, silver, and gold horseshoes. This will occur as individual scores posted are in Roman numerals on the backs of last year's calendar months. Supported by baler twine, the appropriate horseshoe is placed according to the best of each class, around the neck of the winners. As all walk solemnly from the meadow, the fire under the remaining cooked food is extinguished as all return home.

There is talk among the days participants that an Olympic sized concrete pool could easily be adapted inside a local abandoned, manure pit requiring little effort or expense. From a distance, the various personal rings of cell phones are heard amidst the young clippity clop spectators departing the games. Most calls are from those of their buddies unable to attend, seeking the results of the Amish Summer Olympics.

Appreciating Susan Boyle

Another humid, 90-degree-plus day expires reluctantly this first full week of July, 2010. This unusual desert heat remains, even though the red fire ball that has conveyed and surrendered it is now absent. Quietly, confidently and without the assistance of man it has plotted its customary course West and, although completely out of sight, nevertheless relinquishes the final rays of light of another non-refundable day. The motionless green leaves that chaperone my self-propelled to-and-fro porch rocker and myself, hang humbly and long for an exhale from Mother Earth. Not a breath of air is how we old farmers would describe this humid summer eve. An occasional cool, soft breeze to gently caress my sunburned hide would be as appreciated and welcomed as a smile and compliment from a stranger.

Each of the songbirds that surround me performs one final solo for me alone before retiring for the night. The robins, cardinals, wrens, finches, blue jays, doves and even the crows are evidently all situated for the next 8 hours of relaxation and slumber. Not to be forgotten, the frail, spinny-legged killdeer cries frantically from its well—camouflaged on-ground nest. How often I've observed this protective bird display its well-choreographed, broken-wing dance to lure predators away from its young. Everything from hungry rodents to an approaching large, 4-legged green and yellow prehistoric praying mantis, referred to now days as a John Deere, is enticed away from its nest.

I know many animals supposedly dream, but I wonder if birds dream about the one that got away, worm that is. Perhaps they have nightmares of being pursued by a hungry hawk that frightens them awake. In reality, perhaps these songsters are not performing for me at all but are simply communicating one last time to one another before darkness and I am simply an uninvited observer seated in their audience. My pompous, self-centered attitude that man is always the center of everything is shattered by the realization that we humans only play a small role in the vast scheme of things.

The star of the show, the mocking bird, sits high atop the lone pine tree branch nearest the stars seemingly surveying its kingdom. It appears to be only practicing when it occasionally chimes in as the other members of this feathered local choir each performs one final twilight solo. Following a brief intermission of silence, with darkness increasing, the one that mimics and mocks its other acquaintances begins its non-stop concert that includes a complete repertoire of repetitive voices of all its fellow colleagues. This solo concert continues into the descending darkness as throngs of fellow fans known as fireflies or as we refer to them, lighting bugs, join me. They dazzle this open air-theater with their soft glowing, flickering light similar to the light we hold in our hands, swaying back and forth in the darkness at a concert of one of our popular singers.

Shrouded in gray, drab plumage with a splash of white in an unfurled tail, this plain-looking creature displays a voice that is unrivaled by any of its acquaintances. At times these colorful vocalists appear to be jealous in that this ordinary-looking creature can sing "THEIR" song even better than they. I'm reminded of a frowzy, ordinary looking Susan Boyle, who recently appeared on TV possessing a stunning, angelic voice that moved folks to tears. A human mocking bird is what I remember thinking when seeing and hearing this middle-aged lady from England. The mocking bird, evidently gratified by the gathering throng of lightning bugs, unseen others and me sings on and on and then even flies to another nearby dead, barren, locust limb for an appreciated encore. Now in complete darkness, only its silhouette is visible as today's final curtain of earth's shadow descends on the last dim glow of the western sky.

Sometime later that evening, during a late-inning Phillies meltdown and loss, our mocking bird friend that has been known to patriotically provide outbursts of its own version of the National Anthem before a ball game, has become silent. Following the 11 o'clock news and before bed, bathroom banter, one final flush and the outing of the light, our favorite late and early bird begins once again to sing in the dim, shadowy moonlight. Accompanied only by a distant, mournful train whistle, this bird of a thousand voices and tunes is the very last sound I hear while whispering a silent prayer and welcoming unconscious slumber. I sleep very well.

Next morning, before the first ray of light peeks over the hill to the East, my traveling alarm clock, reassuring my notion that time actually does fly, begins anew with a wake up call of inspirational praise songs. When first light literally appears, its surrounding companions residing in nature's local birdcage, reluctantly at first, join in. Soon all sound every bit as enthused as their self-motivated choir director in joyously welcoming a new, appreciated day. Take time to listen to nature's surround sound system and welcome each glorious new day as those full-feathered, humble creatures singing outside your window. I sometimes wonder, do these serenading space streakers reside in my world or I in theirs?

Thanksgiving

As a lifelong farmer, I can honestly say that all holidays are anticipated, enjoyed and long remembered with the gathering of family, friends and food. While one holiday involves shopping and the giving of gifts and the frills of decorated trees and colored lights, that is for a later date. There are other holidays that involve hand painted eggs to hide, flags to wave, costumes and masks to wear, Super Bowls or toasts to be made while ushering in a new year. At Thanksgiving, it all boils down to just us and a naked bird.

Those of us who are older and have been seated for years with our same, familiar, present family members are also as naked as the center-piece on the table, having been stripped of our frills, our youth, our pride and now most of our dreams by circumstance, life and age. Hopefully, by this time we accept one another for what we are and not for what we could or should be or for what we may or may not become.

Thanksgiving is the time of year when all crops have usually been harvested. Being an old farmer, I recall sitting at many a Thanksgiving table selfishly being thankful for that fact second only to the health of our family. I have found that if you don't truly appreciate the simple, basic things in life you will never fully appreciate anything else. Sooner or hopefully later someone from within the family circle will be missed and only be present in our memory. Those who have set the table, cooked the Thanksgiving meal and served us as children have continued a tradition for another generation, passed down by their ancestors. This tradition is unceremoniously then passed to the next generation to hopefully continue.

I am one who believes in miracles and that each of our lives is nothing less than one. I also believe each of us knowingly or unknowingly contributes something to our world even in the short span of time we spend here. How others and our God remember us is the ultimate and final test of our worth.

My wife is from the old school, with tradition mandating that she buy her fresh, unfrozen turkey from the world's oldest turkey farm. Located in Lancaster County, Esbenshade Turkey Farm was established in 1858 and every year, the day before Thanksgiving, she makes her annual jeep-transported turkey trot for our holiday bird. She wants no parts or giblets of a frozen gobbler or hen fitted with a heart monitoring defibulator indicating when cooking is complete.

Usually in a hurry, with other food stops in the general area of our preordered, awaiting bird it is most helpful and less stressful for her if the local Amish buggies are limited on the Audubon that leads to this farm in Paradise. Our turkey has succeeded in serving its purpose in life by becoming the main attraction on another food-laden Thanksgiving table. I find it most ironic that this particular bird, hatched and living out its life in Paradise, eventually dies and unknowingly departs from this place. We humans also dwell within our own circle of turkeys and are hopefully successful in serving our purpose in life and with death eventually wish to reside in Paradise.

I suppose the tradition of eating turkey goes back to the 53 surviving pilgrims and their 90 Indian guests, including their leader, Massasoit, at the first Thanksgiving. I seem to remember reading the turkey, although appreciated in 1621, was scarce that day but there was an abundance of turnips. I would bet those pilgrim ladies told their family members to limit their portions of turkey so their Indian guests could have plenty. I imagine a religious English lady saying, "Mr. Massasoit, would you care for another drumstick?" while passing the turnips to a somber Myles Standish. I recall a similar incident 60 years ago when Mom cautioned me, before Thanksgiving dinner, to limit my portions of oyster stuffing and fill up on mashed potatoes. This must be a European female tradition to always attempt to treat all guests as special.

With deer along with wild turkey also inhabiting the area around Plymouth, I'm sure venison was also an available food at that first Thanksgiving. Evidently later, these strutting gobblers and cautious hens were more easily domesticated and then raised in greater abundance than Bambi. Also it would have taken a woman with a disproportionate lengthy arm to stuff a deer. It took over 3 centuries later and Gene Autry to rewire Rudolph's nose, elevating the elusive deer to new heights above housetops and chimneys during another holiday.

The first Thanksgiving that occurred in this land that included both the white man and the red man would surely never have happened without the involvement of the Indians. Our forebearers would most assuredly have perished in that first bitter New England winter without the assistance of those who lived and hunted in this land hundreds of years before the white man arrived. Later, many of those referred to as savages suffered terrible losses throughout all their territory from infectious diseases incurred from contact with we Europeans of which they had no immunity. Thanksgiving for the pilgrims was the beginning of our rich American heritage. For the Indians, it was the beginning of their demise at our hands into total oblivion. I believe it was Will Rogers who many years later stated the history of America would be written in 3 phases, the passing of the Indians, the passing of the Buffalo and the passing of the Buck. We are well into Rogers final phase my friends. To quote the late Abner Musser Sr., "Don't pass the Buck." Hope I never live to see a proposed Wall-Mart to be built at the very fringe of the Buck. I'm afraid their logo may well be, "The Buck Stops Here." We live in the greatest nation this world has ever conceived, but we have and continue to make many mistakes and are far from perfect as a free country. Humility may be what eventually saves us from arrogance that could destroy us.

50 years ago and earlier in this area, small game hunting was a familiar part of our Thanksgiving Day tradition, especially in the morning. Following our table-laden turkey dinner, with the overstuffed bird picked clean and devoured by the mighty hunters who now themselves are over stuffed, the hunting is continued within the confines of the living room. If the wives and ladies who cooked the meal were unable to eat with Daniel Boone and Davey Crockett because of limited seating, this was their time to enjoy all food that was remaining.

Most of the living room conversation delivered by those on sofas, over-stuffed chairs and lazy boys concerns the game that got away before dinner. Belts are loosened amid sighs and groans of discomfort. Less than an hour into discussing tails and tales, half the hunting party is asleep while the rest speak with drooping eyes and slurred speech, drunk from overeating mashed potatoes, filling and gravy and occasionally belching turkey breath.

Following a couple hours of relaxation, a few of the more energetic and enthusiastic hunters return to fields and fencerows in search of feathers and fur. All this uncommon walking eventually tires our weary hunters, while their wives also appear exhausted from all the cooking, dishwashing and constant conversation. Perhaps this was good in that it remained, for the most part, similar to the first Thanksgiving, minus the Indians, nearly 4 centuries earlier. We haven't commercialized it to the point where the true meaning of this American holiday is forgotten. With all that happens around a family Thanksgiving table, as all participants contribute to ongoing conversations, what remains at the end of the day are everlasting memories and temporary heartburn. More turnips, Myles?

Public Farm Sales

Public farm sales, 50 or 60 years ago, may have occurred at various times but in this area they were held mostly in late winter through spring. January through April was the allotted time to have a local auctioneer engaged for a dispersal of livestock, machinery, household items and perhaps even the farm itself. Factors that influenced this auction season were—spring work had not yet commenced, if farmers raised tobacco or other cash crops they actually had a little money in their overalls and may have been interested in a tractor, implement, or years earlier a needed work horse or mule. Perhaps a dairy cow or 2 were required as replacements in their herd and Mrs. Farmer could always use a household item that usually was sold at a sale for much less then new price. It was also considered a social time for friends and neighbors. If the items to be auctioned were strictly livestock and or machinery, those attending were mostly men and boys.

When I was a boy 60 years ago it would have been possible to attend at least a dozen sales every spring less than an hour from home. Most local farmers attended a few, depending on work at home while others, namely Bill Douts, a local Chestnut Level farmer, unless an emergency arose, missed none. This "rite of spring," occurred when there was an abundance of English farmers locally with the Amish only appearing in this area in large numbers after 1980.

All in attendance appeared to be enjoying themselves, including the auctioneer, as laughter was a constant throughout the cry of "SOLD," by the man conducting the sale. Those in attendance were there to get caught up on the local news and gossip, buy and devour delicious home-made food provided by ladies from a local church, fire company or charitable organization and perhaps bid on an interested item.

Bidders each wore a variety of work clothes usually hidden by a suit of coveralls. Boots or rubbers covered all footwear taking the brunt of Lancaster County spring mud or snow that always seemed to accompany most spring farm sales. Although the weather could be quite nasty and below freezing, anyone who engaged ear flaps or ear lugs as we referred to those additions to winter caps caused old timers to snicker. There was such a variety of animal smells represented on the auction-goers that there never appeared to be any distinguishable, noticeable or familiar odor present.

The auctioneers, constantly engaged in the exchange of oxygen, appeared to never get cold on the most frigid day as they remained in continuous physical motion while practicing and producing tongue aerobics. Most auctioneers always wore the same hat at every sale that served as their trademark distinguishing them from one another. If a property was to be sold at auction, an attorney representing the seller was present to read aloud the conditions of the sale including boundaries, money paid down at the sale and a settlement date. This attorney always stood out in his 3-piece suit and $500.00 overcoat.

Kersey Bradley on the left, with hat and gavel in hand conducts a horse auction at New Holland Sales Stables. Paul Synder is to his right.

Kersey Bradley, who supposedly was apprenticed by Quarryville auctioneer Simon Groff, was the caller of sales I most remember and the most popular locally from the 1940s through the 1970s. He was my grandmother Shoemaker's brother and his brash personality seemed to suit and befit his occupation perfectly, which probably attributed to his success. Others I recall from that era were Lee Work and his son Bob, Park Shaub then later his very successful son Howard, Stanley Dieter, Everett Kreider and Carl Diller, Lloyd Kreider, Norman Hart, Abe Diffenbach, Elmer Murry and a personal favorite, the late Roy Probst and his son Eric. Along with his family, including wife, sister and mother, Eric continues this auction enterprise started by his late father, who died tragically in an auto accident. The Probst clan have a way of including enjoyment and fun into every one of their auctions.

Every auctioneer developed his or her own style, sound and chant distinguishing each from the other much like a popular singer. Today each individual bidder is assigned a number after their driver's license is checked for identification. In years past your name was your identity and there were few folks the old auctioneers didn't know by name. I recall Sara Lee, Kersey's daughter, telling me that the very first sale her dad conducted following the switch to numbers was near Oxford and a man unknown to Kersey bought a couple thousand dollars worth of antiques, then left with his merchandise without paying his bill. Kersey claimed that not knowing him, a stranger would not call out a fake name after purchasing an item for fear someone in the crowd would recognize him. This bidder evidently used fake identification when acquiring a number. The number as an ID is still used at public sales to this day.

If no bids were received on a trivial item it went to the predetermined nickel-man, who got the item for a nickel. Today with inflation, this predestined person still exists but is referred to as the quarter-man. If household goods were to be sold all upholstered furniture in those days was fumigated and tagged before the sale day. Originally this was accomplished in an enclosed room by lighting a formaldehyde candle floating in water in case it tipped over. It occasionally went out and had to be relit by someone reentering the encased room filled with this colorless gas that served as a disinfectant. I'm told this person many times later suffered a severe headache. Later a pump sprayer was used to lightly spray the stuffed furniture and bedding. I'm not sure how this process is handled today in the 21st century.

Many factors may contribute to the decision to hold an auction or public sale. Death of a spouse, a dream and old age infirmities have each played a part for this reasoning. Unable to care for a once busy, active farm, a large now quiet house once over-flowing with children and financial or personal difficulties may also bring about these changes.

I recall a conversation with Kersey during a reflective moment apart from a public sale or the frantic sales ring where he served as the ringmaster and the one in charge. His closely guarded brash, self-assertive demeanor was briefly absent as he spoke of the responsibility of conducting a sale for folks whose entire life and livelihood, during a few short hours was transformed and turned into monetary value following a life long struggle. During Bradley's early auctioneering days he stated many hard working older folks were disappointed with the money received following their life's work. They realized this would not be sufficient to sustain them till their life was over. Yes, laughter and a good time were enjoyed by most folks at these public sales but behind the scenes, before, during and following the sale tears were always shed. This continues today. Perhaps this poem written by S. W. Moss a century ago may convey to you these appropriate feelings of those whose personal property, memories and life is exchanged for currency. This necessary trade-off, no matter the prices received, causes the seller to ponder that they have lost so much more than they have gained on sale day.

The Auctioneer's Gift

The auctioneer leaped on a chair, and bold and loud and clear,
He poured his cataract of words, just like an auctioneer.
An auction sale of furniture, where some hard mortgagee
Was bound to get his money back, and pay his lawyer's fee.
A humorist of wide renown, this doughty auctioneer,
He joking raised the loud guffaw, and brought the answering jeer.
He scattered round his jests, like rain, on the unjust and just;
Sam Sleeman said he "laffed so much he thought that he would bust."
He knocked down bureaus, beds, and stoves,
and clocks and chandeliers,
And a grand piano, which he swore would "last a thousand years;"
He rattled out the crockery, and sold the silverware;
At last they passed him up to sell a little baby's chair.
"How much? How much? Come, make a bid; is all your money spent?"
And then a cheap, facetious wag came up and bid "One cent."
Just then a sad-faced woman, who stood in silence there,
Broke down and cried, "My baby's chair! My poor, dead baby's chair!"
"Here, madam, take your baby's chair," said the softened auctioneer,
"I know its value all to well, my baby died last year;
And if the owner of the chair, our friend, the mortgagee,
Objects to this proceeding, let him send the bill to me!"
Gone was the tone of raillery; the humorist auctioneer
Turned shamefaced from his audience, to brush away a tear;
The laughing crowd was awed and still, no tearless eye was there
When the weeping woman reached and took her little baby's chair.

Usually a farm sale began with small items piled on a, flatbed wagon or wagons. The amount of these items to be sold was directly related to the amount of years the seller spent on this farm. If the farmer had been farming this farm for less than 10 years, one wagon could hold most all of the tools and small items. Depending on the size of the crowd, the farmers would surround the wagons of goodies 4 or 5 deep, pushing ahead to get a closer look similar to teenagers surrounding the stage at a rock concert. The auctioneer and one helper untangled and identified each item from another as they stood cautiously, at first, on these items on the wagon. It would be sometime before these 2 had feet fitting wolverines that actually come in contact with the wagon bed beneath them.

I have been to sales when the seller had been at the same location for a lifetime and the red-faced auctioneer was still hollerin' while perched on the wagons at noon from a sale that began at 8:30 in the morning. An old tool, an oil can, a grease gun, a 3-year old opened bag of seed corn, a rusty milk can and a 5 gallon bucket half full of unknown items, somehow miraculously finds a new owner if "the price is right." If household goods are to be sold these items are usually sold next followed by the machinery. The large furniture usually is set outside in the yard if the weather cooperates. The small items—dishes, kitchenware and cloth items are-handed out to the auctioneer through an open door or window, as the crowd gathers before him.

The machinery was usually cleaned and washed beforehand with much of this old iron formerly encased in dirt, dust and manure and now unrecognizable by the seller's neighbors. It is placed in lines in a field or pasture away from the buildings. The first row contains the smallest and cheapest items gradually increasing in size and price. This gradually builds culminating with the tractors and the more expensive machinery and the sale's conclusion.

The owner of the machinery usually paddles along behind the auctioneer like the hen-pecked husband of a domineering wife to answer any questions raised by a bidder on an appropriate implement. Questions concerning a tractor or years earlier, a horse or mule were those most voiced. Pop stated at Wilbur Pollock's sale on the farm owned today by Tom and Marty Henry, the auctioneer asked Wilbur to describe a dandy pair of his work horses to be sold. Wilbur stated, "They'll move anything they're hooked to and if it's really tight, they'll loosen it." The physical appearances of a tractor, tires, rust and wear can easily be observed by a potential bidder. The question most asked by someone interested in a tractor is, "does it use any oil?" A farmer may be accused of many things but most won't lie publicly to a fellow farmer. Most neighboring farmers know one another and their habits very well. I once was at a sale when this oil burning question was proposed to the owner of a tractor in front of 100 encircled farmers. "Not a drop," was his instant reply. His old neighbor standing beside me grumbled, "How would he know, he never checked it."

Sometimes the loud conversation and laughter at a farm sale becomes distracting, inundating and disturbing to the auctioneer, who must remain alert and aware of the ongoing proceedings surrounding him. I've witnessed a few cane carrying; chanting conductors of sales at an unexpected moment swing their cane against a board, bin wagon or any exposed sheet metal on machinery to quiet the boisterous crowd. The ensuing, startling sound reverberates through the shocked onlookers similar to that of a fired 12-gauge shotgun which brings immediate silence. During this brief hush someone from the rear usually hollers, "Give um hell Kersey." The clerk, who keeps tabs of buyers and prices paid for items, always remains beside the auctioneer. He or she must also endure all types of weather when selling outdoors, the confusion of the crowd and the occasional flying spit of the over-zealous auctioneer as he works himself and the crowd into a frenzy.

Practical jokes by farmers were always a given at farm sales years ago. At John Denlinger's sale, auctioneer Kersey, who had held a property sale earlier that morning, was late arriving at this particular 12-noon auction. A few farmers and neighbors chided him for his tardiness. During the sale of the dairy cattle, Bradley complained that the locals, moving the cows one at a time, in then out of the sales ring, were not keeping up providing the next cow to enter as the one just sold was existing. The workers inside, disgusted and evidently unappreciated, then released an ornery bull in protest. One of the livid cow-moving farmers inside was heard to holler, "That'll keep him quiet for a while." It did, as bidders and onlookers seated on straw bales surrounding this sales ring with only their presence providing for the enclosure and escape of the cows. At the appearance of the Guernsey bull spectators scattered amidst a blizzard of straw and chaff and for a few seconds, the startled Kersey, appeared to be frozen as a matador in the center of the bull ring with the confused, disoriented bull. Although this lasted but a few short seconds at the time it seemed much longer as these 2-creatures stood approximately 10 yards apart staring at one another, the 4-legged one evidently daring the 2-legged one to try to get away. Kersey, knowing he couldn't out run the Guernsey, remained paralyzed. Unexpectably, the bull then wheeled around and ran back into the barn as Kersey, whose face appeared ashen, cockily walked after him swingin' his cane, offering a few unflattering words at the bull as he disappeared into his darkened stall. Needless to say the bickering between the auctioneer and sale helpers ceased and no one in the auction crowd even offered a bid on the disruptive bull.

At another years ago sale I attended, Paulie Weaver, a small, loud voiced, crude, red-faced Dutchman, was occasionally made fun of by a few. Paulie bought a whole lemon meringue pie at this particular auction and began eating it without utensils. While holding this delicious, homemade dessert up to his face, devouring it as one would a sandwich, temptation completely overcame Stanley Kreider, standing nearby, who knew Paulie well. He abruptly pushed the entire pie into Paulie's startled face. Although this pie-promoting mug was surely as red as the Farmall tractor being sold at the time it was not visible to the laughing on lookers or Stanley. It was hidden behind the yellow lemon and white meringue squashed and plastered to his countenance. Paulie evidently wasn't one to get mad as he also smiled while he appeared to be shavin' his face with his index finger, placing the clinging facial pie ingredients into his mouth.

Stanley Kreider, and his brothers, Bill Douts and a few others more than once during their lifetime seemed to participate in this amusing devilment that was not always amusing to a few receiving it. Jay Maule was another southern-end character who was the butt of much teasing, trickery and practical jokes. Those scheming then carrying out these pranks soon learned the ones that wouldn't take this public humiliation. Occasionally one of these pranksters would be observed with a black eye that usually meant they messed with the wrong guy. This discolored eye socket also generated smiles and in some cases, satisfaction to those viewing it.

My late father and his deceased cousin and neighbor, Bill Bolton, usta talk of a neighbor, well known to be frugal. When this man had sale, he unscrewed the 2-light bulbs in his small barn, handing these fly-specked, and persuaders of light to the disgusted auctioneer to sell. I find it amusing that this frugality continues and remains significant in the lives of this man's descendants today.

Kersey Bradley possessed not only a strong, long-lasting constitution but an even more potent, durable, compelling voice. Hollering and chanting continually for 49 years, he conducted his first sale in the early 1940s and his last sale, for Edna Beck, in 1992. He not only seemed to have most of the local auctions but also regularly sold horses every Monday, dairy cows and heifers every Wednesday and steers and beef every Thursday in New Holland. He also for years sold steers at Vintage on Tuesdays.

Clerks he employed at his public sales over the years were Warren Kirk, Dave Eshbach, Stoney Eshbach, Everett Eshbach and Kersey's daughter Saralee. At his local sales he never had an assistant auctioneer, as most do today. He supposedly ate very little during or before calling a sale-only soft food, warm milk or a raw egg. He stated his most difficult sale was held for John Waggoner, a Quarryville merchant. This was his first sale following the unexpected death of Kersey's wife, Peg, in 1962.

Kersey besides an auctioneer considered himself a farmer, farming the farm where he was born and raised. He also was a long-time bank director at Quarryville National Bank, a member of the local school board and an active member of Chestnut Level Church. Considered a conservative school board member, he was popular with his constituents (the tax payers) of his generation but not always with teachers and administrators, especially during salary negotiations. I recently thought of him during our local salary contract bargaining with teachers, staff and administrators. When the present contract was approved and the teachers union representative was quoted in the news as being elated with the results, I wondered, "What would Kersey say?" Kersey Bradley died in 1998 at 95 years of age.

The late Bob Work related this story to me before his unexpected death a few years ago. He said it was a favorite story his mother often told. Auctioneer Lee Work and his wife had 3 sons, Don, Dick and Bob. When very young these 3 lads would play together and with other local boys. Imitating their father, as most boys were fond of doing, no matter dad's occupation, these 3 Quarryville boys and their friends would conduct a farm sale.

After each was assigned their part-to-play, auctioneer, clerk and buyers, the sale was begun in earnest. All of this was overheard by their mother outside their bedroom door that both entertained and amused her. Bob Work stated that before beginning the sale the plastic farm animals were all placed in pens made of Lincoln Logs, blocks and various forms of fencing. The auctioneer assumed his position standing near the miniature machinery at the far end of the room with the clerk, pad and pencil or crayon in hand. The buyers were all seated on their hunkers on the floor in a semi-circle.

The sale began in total sincerity with each participant showing serious interest as each winning bidder was given the item he purchased. Talk among the bidders was similar to what the Work boys had heard attending their father's actual auctions. One was heard to say disgustedly to the other, "You paid to much for that old tractor" or "you know that wagon you just bought only has 3 wheels."

Later the livestock was sold, at first individually, with dairy cows bringing between 50 and 100 dollars and all items paid for using monopoly money. Next was the sheep with no one bidding on them. The auctioneer decided to sell the entire pen of these wooly creatures to complete the sale and head to mom's kitchen treats for all attendees of the auction. The frustrated auctioneer tried and tried, hollerin' until he was hoarse but none would bid. Finally in desperation he said to his brother Dick, who had bought several of the cows, "Will you give me a dollar for the whole pen of sheep?" Dick's thoughtful reply to the auctioneer, "I'd like to help you out but I just don't have a damn place to keep'em." I'm sure this was not the first time these boys had heard this phrase uttered at a sale, but Mrs. Work completely lost it and burst out laughing behind the partially closed door. This ended the sale as the boys, still playing their parts, began arguing as to who was responsible for feeding and watering the unsold sheep till the next sale.

For the last 3 decades of the 20th century, one of the most prevalent and popular local auctioneers was Howard Shaub. I shall allow him to conclude this chapter on public sales in his own words of "auction chant."

Ladies and Gentlemen—here's your spittoon, theres an old one and a fine one, right there, I got 25 and a bid 30-35 now 40-45 and 50, ride your bike-I got 55 and 60, 65 and 70 a voit-now 75 and 80-now 85 ride your bike and 90, I'm bid 95 a voit now 100-100? Sold RRRight there, 95.

PART THREE

EVERYWHERE "BUT" LIBERTY SQUARE

The Old Farmer Duz Stone Harbor

Although the reservation for my next life has been confirmed and my ticket has already been stamped, I still find great joy each and every day experiencing the present one. Ruthie and I recently spent a couple of days in Stone Harbor, New Jersey, at the home of my brother and sister-in-law. From this house, the mighty Atlantic Ocean can be both seen and heard. You tend to truly appreciate your senses when viewing the sea seated at the dining room table or from the decks located at either end of the home. Whether drifting off to sleep or awakening totally rested and relaxed the following morning, the constant roar of the ocean is every bit as present and as comfortable in this king size bed as me.

Although my brother is certainly not his brother's keeper, he did provide for those few days of total relaxation and peace of body, mind and soul seldom experienced by this old farmer. I not only began again to write some of what I observed but when not writing I was reading "John Adams" by David McCullough and one of James Harriot's books. I was totally engrossed in all I read, wrote and observed and never for one instant felt any remorse or guilt that usually accompanied these fits of folly at home. The following are but a few observed and noted thoughts and memories of those couple of days by the sea.

The crows all facing us, sitting on an electric wire, that wished us well and waved good-bye at home looked very similar to the ones, also in a line on a matching wire, that welcomed us as we unpacked our suitcase. I'm not sure if these gulls, all fitted in black tuxedos, have a permanent home in Stone Harbor or, like us, are just mooching at the residence of another old crow next of kin affiliated with the banking business.

The weather could not have been more perfect, with the sun never interrupted by a cloud and the ocean breeze a constant both day and night. Flags placed periodically on the beach homes along the ocean stood constantly unfurled, flapping proudly in the salty ocean air. It had been a few years since this farmer's feet in flip-flops had carved tracks and imprints upon the warm welcoming sand leading to the awe-inspiring, never ending breaking waves. Although I was greeted by the sea as the returning prodigal son, I saw no sign of the fatted calf. I did however notice a few dolphins occasionally surfacing above the water on a trek north not far from the shoreline. I had forgotten this inspired feeling of standing on the beach observing this ancient ocean, and all the thoughts conjured up inside my mind that were now awakened as an incoming tide of fond memories.

My first visit to the ocean occurred around 1950. We farmed together with the Denlingers of Chestnut Level. John and Lib Denlinger, my father's sister, and their children, Ken, near my age, and Margy, my sister Lane's age, and my brother, Scott, were together constantly during this time from my birth in 1943 through 1960, when Ken left for Penn State. The Smiths and Denlingers farmed their respective farms separately but the summer jobs of harvesting grain and baling hay and straw were all accomplished together.

Sometime during this hectic work schedule, a break occurred and all of us traveled together to what we referred to as the seashore. Having journeyed very little outside our rural community and only periodically to Lancaster, this vacation was greatly anticipated by all, especially us kids. So much so that an exorcist named "car sick," or motion sickness as it is referred to today, was always an invisible passenger of every seashore excursion. We kids were the only participants, as I recall, but when one vehicle stopped, immediately in tandem, the other also pulled off the highway as doors flew open, close-at-hand-basins and buckets rattled and old towels appeared from underneath seats. This first up-chucking of supper, breakfast and nerves usually came to the surface in the vicinity of Nottingham Presbyterian Church. Being Presbyterians, this allowed all participants to remain true to their religious affiliation in both sickness and in health. I'm sure more than once I was a willing, cooperative shareholder in this yearly exorcism ritual that transpired from bowed heads on this church property.

Atlantic City was always our chosen port of call and in that era was the most popular spot on the Jersey shore. We always stayed several miles from the ocean at a place called Pleasantville in New Jersey. I really don't know why this place was chosen so far from the sea but I'm sure money was the most important factor in that decision. I'm sure our two-night layover in Pleasantville cost less than the gas today for a round trip to the ocean. Pop said, "I remember these accommodations being crowded, but we made it work and all got along."

Our parents never spent any money foolishly and I had the feeling John Denlinger may have been the most frugal of the four. Even today my folks shake their heads at how children and grandchildren, "throw money around" as they refer to it. Mom's comment, "they might need that money some day, then what." At ninety two (my father and Lib and John all now deceased) and my mother remained frugal to the core, which I believe is directly related to all of them living through the "depression" and the effects it caused their parents and families. Although it occurred nearly eighty years ago, the "depression" left a lasting impression on my parents and probably was the underlying reason why we stayed miles from the ocean in Pleasantville. Our parents would never have gotten caught in the financial bind so many folks find themselves in today. For although our parents made very little money throughout their lifetime they survived very well, thank-you, because they always spent much less than they earned.

Two small cabins situated in a wooded area would be our home away from home for two or no more than three days. My mother and Lib Denlinger would first inspect the two primitive wooden structures before any money changed hands or unpacking commenced. If they met their approval, we each moved into our appropriate 1950s condos. By this time Ken and I were already throwing a baseball back and forth. Baseball gloves and a ball were always packed long before swimming trunks for any vacation we ever took together. Most all food to be eaten was prepared at home by our moms and transported in coolers similar to a three-day picnic. As I recall this today it doesn't seem much like a vacation for our mothers.

What made this cheap, primitive place so impressive to us kids was something we had seen photos of but never experienced. It was called a swimming pool. Until this point in time our swimming consisted of picnics two or three Sundays a year along Fishing Creek located in what we called Burns's Hollow, now referred to as Scalpy Hollow. This crystal-clear stream had a few places we dammed up, making the water in these small areas nearly three feet deep. The fancy concrete swimming pool we now enjoyed was way over our heads at the deepest point and also provided a diving board that no one of our group dared to use. We thought our parents must surely be well off and imagined them to each be worth at least a thousand dollars to afford a vacation place such as this.

In the morning, after a farmer's breakfast and some ball playing, we dressed in our swimming attire and headed to the ocean approximately a half hour away. The fact that we were all together is what made this so memorable. Later in the afternoon we headed back to Pleasantville and ate hamburgers, hot dogs and our picnic snacks.

One evening during our stay, we would return to the nightlife of Atlantic City and the Boardwalk and Steel Pier. I really don't know if any of this area is still there with the infiltration of new hotels, casinos and Donald Trump. The Steel Pier featured a diving horse, ridden by a girl, which leaped from a platform several feet in the air into a tank below filled with water. There were also divers performing a water show, a movie theater, places to buy all assortments of food, games of chance and an auditorium where live acts appeared. I'm not sure of the year, sometime in the 1950s, two acts that were presented live the night we were there were Georgia Gibbs, whom I had heard on the radio singing her popular song at that time, "Kiss of Fire." Also a new group I had never heard of called Bill Haley and the Comets performing their song that later became a rock and roll classic, "Rock Around The Clock." Considering this all happened sixty years ago, I don't remember a whole lot more but have come to realize and appreciate that it was parents and one another that made it all so special.

    I'm ushered back from those fond memories as a tiny, cold wave slaps my less—than-fatted calves. The familiar lifeguards that patrol the ocean beaches today seem to grow younger with my periodic visits. The ones I observe today resemble boys from middle school. They still blow their whistles, as I first remember, with the emphasis on the beginning and the end of one long attention-getting abrasive sound. I've always wondered if they, at sometime in their training, attend a whistle-blowing seminar? Being a Smith, I have never ever been whistled at by a lifeguard for journeying too far into deep water. The story is told that we were forbidden by parents to take a shower until at least twenty minutes after eating a meal for fear of drowning. Because of the close-at-hand spectators, being whistled by a lifeguard for an infraction would be worse than being stopped by a cop for speeding. The embarrassment would surely be unbearable when the fact that I could barely swim surfaced along with my life vest and me.

    There are those who still read at the beach, but not to the extent that I remember. I didn't observe anyone reading David McCullough except me. I didn't even notice any one reading "Liberty Square Observed and Noted," although I have in my possession a photo of a friend, Mitch Huber, reading my book on a white sandy beach in Jamaica. This photo is one of my treasures.

    Hunkered down in a beach chair, my lily-white legs that haven't absorbed or visited direct sunlight in decades remain hibernated and hidden beneath a beach towel. There are folks on the beach that are light skinned and there are folks that are dark skinned. But just like the coloring of the cars of the 1950s, on the beach at Stone Harbor I'm considered two toned.

    At mid-day the water remains cold, with many on the sand and few in the surf as a small plane pulling a Heineken Beer sign passes in front of all. Silent sea gull shadows move across the sand and me. To me this generation of sea gulls seems larger and even more bold than its ancestors. Apparently, most of the sun worshippers who profess to going on vacation and getting away from it all have had their cell phones surgically implanted into their palms and can't leave home without them. Evidently, the reception is excellent at the beach and no incoming or out going calls are missed or altered. Can you hear me now? What ever happened to portable radios that were once a status symbol sixty years ago? Would I be dating myself if I said I remember when proper ladies wore bathing caps into the water?

Young females, skimpily covered, still welcome the burning sun to their bodies as the love of their lives. Young men are strolling the beach in pairs or more, flexing the same muscles that once resided within and on the fringes of my body but have long ago moved outta town, evicted by a Whopper, a big Mac and Dottie's cheese steaks. These jocks have not yet reached the age of sucking up an inflated abdomen as a pretty girl passes by. That will come much later in their lives, but sooner than they think. Then you come to me and my sixty-five-and-older heart throbs. When we are approached by an attractive female, we still remember how to suck up that gut that conceals our feet from our line of sight. Trouble is, as the inflated tummy rises to our chest it also raises our pants, which is why so many of us are observed with our belts much nearer our breasts than our belly buttons.

Little boys still enjoy digging in the sand, and with much perseverance may completely disappear into their excavated quarry. A few older boys also seem to enjoy playing in the sand, oblivious to the fact that they appear to be almost as old as I am. Macho dad and macho mom appear with two semi-macho little girls. Macho mom in her black bikini, still proud of her figure and tan, makes sure all nearby notice her before she is seated on her monogrammed beach chair. Her countenance and appearance promote her confidence, that she truly has it all. Macho dad, in trunks and shades, also proudly displays a body that most likely visits the gym daily. Unlike me, all of his limbs are the same golden bronze. He pays no attention to macho mom or the two little girls as he reads the Wall Street Journal and talks frequently on his cell phone. They neither seem to get or expect his awareness or consideration. Maybe macho mom doesn't have it all after all and the reason for flaunting herself is simply a cry for attention and from being ignored. As you can see, I not only observe and listen to people but also am engaged and licensed in the practice of generic psychoanalysis.

Three baby boomer moms, my age, arrive and stake out their area directly behind us, with most of their conversations made available for publication. They evidently have come to this beach every summer for all their summers. They seem to still relive their high school memories, and each one attempts to out do the other in complaining about their children. They all appear to be disappointed with their lot in life and with the fact they cannot relive their youth. All appear to be enthralled with nearby macho dad, as their conversation frequency continues but lowers a couple of octaves, making very few words audible to me. Although this girl talk concerning macho dad would most likely be appreciated by him, I soon lose interest as they punctuate their sentences with sighs and giggles. Alas, once again they are teenagers.

A couple my age is observed walking together hand in hand along the water, smiling, laughing and conversing. I'm thinking they may have found the secret to life and are the ones on the beach who truly have it all. An old guy is chugging along the water, leaning into the breeze and with short, pronounced steps still leaning into life and whatever it has in store for him. The sun and the cool breeze are never absent this day. Baby carriages on the beach have changed, as have other means of transportation over the years and are unrecognized as such. Kids can still be kids at the beach and memories are still made for a lifetime and for generations.

There are still a lot of overweight and obese folks in this world but not nearly as many proportionally at the shore, on the beach or in the water. Like smokers, they still exist but tend to remain in areas where they evidently feel more comfortable. Another small plane, advertising crab cakes at a local restaurant, flies along the beach. I would love to hire one of these planes to occasionally fly over the hills and fields of Southern Lancaster County advertising, today only, free feed at Powl's Mill, free gas at Musser's Market and, at Beiler's Blacksmith Shop, shoe one horse and have the second one shod for half price. I would be especially interested in the response, and in particular that of the Amish. A backup of cars, trucks, scooters and buggies would surely clog and snarl all existing local traffic. Not sure how the local business folks would respond to this old farmer's fantasy.

Walking by is a seventy-five year old man, who from his physique is obviously still in shape. Much to my displeasure, this reminds me I am not. I wonder if he, like me, once discretely tore a Charles Atlas ad from a magazine in his local barbershop. Very few photos are taken at the beach any more. A twenty-something young man runs full speed ahead into the ocean, diving under the first large wave and surfacing ahead of the next. Doesn't he know the water is freezing? That water is so cold that when I made my once—every-five-year ritual into the shoulder high waves to pee in the ocean, by the time I got situated I forgot why I was there.

I can actually remember when I had a full head of hair and was considered thin. I no longer turn any heads on the beach except a close-at-hand seagull. The only reason it even looks my way are the occasional pieces of pretzel I slip to it unnoticed by all but the gull. Nearby sun worshipers complain at the closeness of my affectionate admirer so I eat the remaining pretzels and ignore the gull that stands at my feet staring at me. I have a feeling other eyes on the beach are also staring at me, but not with affection.

This evening we drove to Cape May for dinner. We hadn't truly realized how quiet and laid back Stone Harbor is until we drove through Wildwood. We had remembered that even years ago there was more activity in Wildwood at three in the morning than at three in the afternoon. Nothing has changed. Cape May, although not as quiet as Stone Harbor, is still a neat town and fun to visit. We dined at the popular Lobster House overlooking the bay and the activities of boats of all sizes. Seafood tastes so much better when the sight, sound and smell of the ocean and bay are infiltrating your senses. The return drive along the coast at twilight was beautiful, and I thought of Bill Ressler, our famous former neighbor and Chestnut Level native whose beautiful seascapes enhance many of our homes and hang in the finest stores and shops displaying fine art for sale.

Following another quiet, restful night we awake to the undisturbed, now familiar sound of the ocean's song. Scott's entire house reminds me of a giant seashell held tightly to my ear with the sound of the ever-present sea echoing and reverberating throughout. We decide to investigate this town and search for some place that serves breakfast. Ruthie has always cooked and served others, so any meal prepared by someone else is always a treat for both of us.

We find a small place along 3rd street that appears to be no more than a hole in a wall. Upon entering we walk past several tables to an unseen deck in the rear that displays a beautiful view of the bay. We are in awe that we have found this enchanted place accidentally. Although it was small we have a table by the water and our waiter soon arrives with menus.

The folks at the table beside us have finished their meal at this time and all arise from their seats and leave. In an instant, a sea gull startles us by landing on this table; it snatches a half-eaten piece of French toast and flies away. Evidently, this particular breed of gulls has a monetary system that is different from ours, because although he stole his breakfast he ignored the ten dollar bill lying beside the plate containing the French toast. In an instant two young boys appear and clear this table, much to the dismay of another gull who had evidently witnessed this short-lived, sea-shore, sea-gull, fly-through breakfast buffet.

While viewing this beautiful landscape and thoroughly enjoying our delicious breakfast, we both revert back to our tribal instincts, becoming aware of the folks seated behind us. With my back to them, I record their conversations with the tape recorder located between my ears. Ruthie, with most of their words unclear to her, is facing our subjects and immediately engages the camcorder located in her right eye. We don't know where this will lead but, without speaking, through nods and several facial contortions, we feel there is a news-worthy story seated at the table behind us. Evidently, a grandmother, a mother and three children ages approximately two, six, and eight are our subjects this morning. Without seeing them, it is quite obvious to me through their conversation that this family is extremely well off. They mention a realtor showing them a three million dollar house. They talk about their friends and other family members in such a derogatory way I can't imagine how they would speak of their enemies. Ruthie observes diamond rings that swallowed a finger on each lady. The children are not disruptive that I could hear but I knew that facial expressions from the one seated across from me indicated something was amiss. Because their table was located so close to ours I dare not turn around, but when they finally leave I cannot contain myself any longer. What I see resembles a food fight at a college dorm: Pancakes on the floor, French toast on the chairs, the basket on the table containing three-dozen containers of jelly—emptied and scattered throughout the breakfast area.

The three children had done this as the mother and grandmother engaged in a normal conversation for them. I did not hear, nor did Ruthie see, any scolding or reprimanding of the children. Mother, grandmother and kids then walked away from their table, each tramping through this strewn-about breakfast. We were both speechless, with our silence broken by an old fisherman sitting nearby who also had observed these folks. His comment to us through a scowl was this, "if you ever wanna know what the hell is wrong with our country it was all seated at that table. Will those kids grow up imitating their parents or will they someday see the light?"

Two young boys appeared to clean up this table and floor, and the three-dollar tip that was left offered little consolation to their chore. Their comments to one another, also heard by me, "Well, its not as bad as it was last week when they were here." The old fisherman scowled again saying, "Those two lads cleaning up the mess are the lucky ones, and I just hope they realize it someday." The old fisherman's final thought as we also departed, "They probably had a nanny for the children but I'm sure she's recuperating at an insane asylum." Ruthie's thoughts in two words—"No Control." My thoughts—Don't profess to me that you love and respect your children if you never discipline or correct them.

This morning we make our final pilgrimage to the beach. Although the sun and breeze are still present a haze hangs over the ocean, making it impossible to distinguish where the sea ends and the blue mist of sky begins. We know the routine by now as chairs and towels are each situated at our appropriate spot. A girl of five or six relays to her mom, "I'm bored" as I plop in my beach chair and bury my feet in the sand. An extra large middle-aged lady in a one-piece blue bathing suit repositions herself on her stretched-out chair that sinks a full six inches into the loose sand. She and all she encompasses face directly into the sun. I hope there's still enough to go around for the rest of us—sunshine that is.

Not many old folks on the beach or in the water today. Oh my God, I'm the oldest man here! A small baby cries somewhere behind us but is soon quieted. Some children who played near us in the sand all day yesterday have returned to cheerfully take up where they left off. Many young men's bathing trunks seem to have patterns and designs similar to Michelle Obama's dresses—maybe it's just me. Another observation—the older the man the more he dotes on his mate.

Young girls and attractive ladies in skimpy bikinis are constantly adjusting all areas of their front and back covering. I hadn't noticed this until Ruthie mentioned it!!! This continual tugging at their bathing attire leaves this old farmer wondering: are they trying to hide their hide or expose it. It seems rather perplexing to me that such a tiny amount of material could cause such discomfort and aggravation to the female manikin that displays it so willingly. Not since Janet Jackson's halftime performance at a recent Super Bowl has such a tiny sliver of thread caused such annoyance to the one who wears it is my final thought on ladies bathing attire. Nude beaches were evidently created for folks with no imagination.

Everyone is shaped differently is another observation on the beach by me. Could a tsunami occur along the Jersey beaches? One last dip in the frigid ocean water makes me question Al Gore and global warming. Finally, at the age of sixty-five, I have discovered I can both write and read while sitting on a chair in the sand facing the ocean. That is what I most remember as this old farmer duz Stone Harbor.

On a return journey to Stone Harbor with Scott this past summer, following a 2-year hiatus, I observed little change from previous visits. However, new lenses in old eye glasses revealed the cleavage of a few well-developed females has noticeably reached new lower levels. This was realized as I observed them briefly and then was smacked by an unnoticed wave from the rear, on the rear. I then received a few disgusted glances from the resident sand-squatters, as evidently when I turned my back to them I displayed a well-defined cleavage of my own. Boy, I hate when that happens. I'll blame it on 30-year old swimming trunks; as a conservative, Presbyterian old farmer, I can honestly say, I have never, ever mooned anyone intentionally.

As for the eye lens change, I realized last spring I was misinterpreting a few things. Driving past Eli Beiler's place along Oregon Hollow Road, I waved to him in his roadside garden at every pass. He occasionally seemed to move an arm at my passing and I thought little of his cautious response until I stopped one day to see him. Again working in his garden, I approached him from behind his house. So as not to startle him I began talking to him as I tiptoed across the peas, beans and sweet corn. I soon made an about face and hoped no one in his house or on the nearby road had observed me conversing with his look-a-like scarecrow.

Another noticeable Stone Harbor change is dogs of every breed, size, shape, religious affiliation and ethnic background appear each morning and evening on the Stone harbor sidewalks and grass walkways utilized as woof-woof porta-potties. I would say a canine that spends vacations or perhaps the entire summer in Stone Harbor lacks very little in its pampered, entertained, delightful, fleaness life. With the dog leash tethered between man's best friend and the individual accompanying it, I always speculate, who's escorting who?

It's quite obvious when petite, timid Sparky or massive boisterous Bruce stop to relieve themselves, on their terms, at their predetermined place and time, they've brought the other one along just to clean up the mess. Should aliens from outer space observe us, surely they would conclude that 4-legged creatures rule this world and are served and pampered by 2-legged slaves.

What crosses the mind and is remembered by this old dairyman is well-dressed acquaintances, family and even proper strangers arriving unannounced at the farm. I would be embarrassed and ashamed because of farm odors and cow manure somewhere on my jeans and shoes. Now all these proper, educated, well off folks are observed on hands and knees on public sidewalks with pooper-scoopers, paper towels and Kleenex removing dog feces from concrete sidewalks and/or grass. They don't appear to be the least bit embarrassed and exhibit no shame. Just once I'd love to walk a haltered Holstein down a Stone harbor sidewalk with a 3-foot barn shovel resting on my shoulder. I'm sure the conversation with the local dog walkers would be very interesting.

Till next time, that's all from the beach folks. Perhaps one day before we all return to dust we shall meet and walk barefoot on the sands of times together. For obvious reasons pets must remain in their crates!

Mooving Along

The long 18-wheeler "Polar Express" milk truck on a moonless night slithers its way along asphalt covered ancient animal trails. A couple miles away as the crow flies it appears alone across the open frozen fields in the distance this cold December night, as a slow moving outdoor Christmas display. It twists and turns, rises then lowers, as it remains firmly attached to the distinctive topography that is Southern Lancaster County. These moves most assuredly resemble and mimic those of Santa's sleigh and his reindeer on Christmas Eve.

This driver that holds the reins to this shiny, stainless steel sleigh and commands the controls of this reindeer powered engine transports this essential food at all hours day and night and in all types of weather from the "farmer in the dell" to the dairy. Only hours earlier fresh nutritious grain, hay and silage has been transformed by the dairy cow into what many have referred to as natures most nearly perfect food. In a matter of hours this fresh, cold, udder gold will again be relocated to the cool compartments of your local grocery store. It is my hope that you enjoy this product from the country and appreciate all who participate in providing it, including the dairy cow.

All who are of my generation and older that weren't dairy farmers recall the days of the milkman delivering milk to their door in glass returnable bottles. When emptied, they were washed by the housewife and placed inside a milk box outside the front door with the local dairy logo on both box and bottles. This delivery and bottle exchange usually took place early in the morning, with fresh milk available for most breakfasts.

Originally, in cities and towns, this was delivered by horse-drawn enclosed milk wagons. As motorized vehicles became more prevalent, the horse and wagon were replaced by small box shaped trucks equipped with a sliding door on either side. As more and more folks in rural areas discontinued dairy farming in the 1940s and 50s, these odd shaped trucks and their drivers—some dressed completely in white—appeared not only in large cities but also in the countryside. A few dairies I recall locally were Harner's Dairy, Drumore-Cedar

Lawn Dairy, Chestnut Level-Norwood Farm, Quarryville-Harnish Dairy, New Danville-E.W. and E.L. Huber, Marticville, and Wade Dairy, Quarryville.

A lady who will vouch for its validity and swear of its truth told the following account to me years ago. Names have been purposely omitted to avoid embarrassment to future generations of her children and grandchildren. Seems this lady had an uncle Johnnie who drove one of these old horse-drawn milk wagons in Philadelphia. Evidently this old fellow worked at this milkman job for years, never missing a day's work.

Eventually in his later years, this faithful fellow became ill and reported he was unable to attend to his milk delivery this particular day. His temporary replacement was told that the horse that pulled the milk wagon had become so familiar with the milk route and every stop that it would halt briefly at each residence. All the temporary milkman replacement had to do was walk behind the milk wagon carrying the full bottles, place them in the milk box and return the empties to the wagon.

Much to the replacement drivers surprise, the horse actually stopped at every customer—up one street and down the other—for blocks with no direction or encouragement from the unfamiliar driver. Approximately 3 hours into the new milkman's route, he was amazed how the routine of the old regular driver had taught this horse to stop briefly everywhere the driver needed to go. It was then that the old nag rounded a street corner and stopped directly in front of a bar and lay down. Needless to say the old milkman's secret was exposed forever by the loyalty of his trusty 4-legged companion who spoke not a word. Our innermost secrets and long standing habits, both good and bad, are eventually exposed by someone or something, then later observed by a person who forms an opinion of us.

As larger grocery stores were built with a much larger variety and abundance of items and local mini-markets appeared at rural crossroads in the country and on busy street corners in towns, this home delivery of milk became economically unfeasible. This occurred when today this milkman's wages would be considered below poverty level and when gas was 25-30 cents a gallon.

I recall when bread was delivered to our door 50 years ago even in our rural area. I believe Russ Gainer was our bread man. Living within a mile of Liberty Square store, we were not far from groceries when needed. I recall a couple of stores farther south of us at Wakefield and Cherry Hill where the grocer took your order of groceries over the phone and later delivered them to your door. Thinking back on that era, we country bumpkins weren't as inconvenienced as we may have thought. Most all-essential items were available to us; it was the money to pay for them that remained scarce. I understand a few trucks filled with groceries have returned and regularly stop at our Amish neighbors and, like other facets and facts from my life 50 years ago, it's dejavu all over again. I'm sure folks older than myself who indicated they could relate to and enjoy my words can add much to this chapter of yesterday. If you have the opportunity don't postpone asking them. Most have more local history inside their head than any book ever written.

Observations From Local Grocery Store Parking Lots

Occasionally I will sit in the center of Park City just to observe the array and diversity of people who pass through this epicenter of Lancaster County culture. Although there are dramatic differences between many of these folks, I never entertain a feeling of kinship with them similar to those I observe at our local grocery stores.

Smoking evidently remains socially acceptable during the sun-drenched days and the soft artificial light nights outside these stores, with those addicted relishing that last long puff before going inside and already looking forward to lighting up in the "free smoke" parking lot outside. Although not encouraged, spitting upon the black top stage is not frowned upon by owners, employees or patrons is my observation.

The purchase of lottery tickets is a given and all who play fully expect to win. To me, those who play appear to be every bit as happy, content and satisfied with their lot in life as those who annually receive, well-into-6-figure salaries and also may be part of this assembly. These folks, who appear to be more financially affluent than most in this row, don't engage in the ongoing, in line conversation with others. They almost look as embarrassed at being seen as a teenager in a liquor store or a man buying personal items at a drug store. They constantly glance and observe in all directions, hoping not to see anyone they know. While waiting in line to purchase this life changing, winning ticket most express a willingness to share their proceeds with all others waiting with them. I'm sure this feeling of sharing, although perhaps only temporary, is something many Ministers wish they could capture, replicate and convey to an unmotivated congregation on Sunday morning. Most clergy make an attempt to communicate this idea of sharing and helping others but the results are usually limited.

Sodas are evidently a cherished necessity and are purchased in large quantities depending on the size of one's vehicle and the cabbage in one's wallet. Turkey Hill iced tea runs a close second in the thirst-quenching marathon that rewards many participants with several varieties of kidney stones. These organically grown human pearls may be removed surgically or passed naturally that involves a painful process very similar to childbirth. I've given birth to a couple of these off spring, the first evidently breech, during my lifetime and am told by those in attendance of a few unflattering words surrounding the Turkey Hill logo uttered by me during my rolling stone delivery. Imagining the flint rock that slowly, painfully, passed through my innards to be the size of a golf ball with jagged edges, I contemplated having it made into a ring. Following my sweat-soaked body's difficult delivery of my very own personal birthstone I was terribly disappointed when I observed this tiny grain of sand fragment that produced all that pain and discomfort didn't even resemble me.

Blacks, Whites, Spanish, Amish, Mennonite, Red Necks, Businessmen, working Women, Farmers and girls in white uniforms all shopping together without any incident. The few who imagine themselves to be above the rest are not nearly as far removed from them as they assume. They are but a few short years from joining this congregation of ordinary folks, which they will disappointedly realize very shortly.

The skullcaps and hats worn by the male contingent crossing this parking lot vary greatly. The Amish appear in circular brimmed straw or black hats resting at different angles and positions, with the very young lads' hats residing on the very back of their heads. With their hats located in this position, an unexpected wind gust always removes their headgear and causes tiny legs to move quickly. If an Amish lad learns to walk one day, he must run the next day; otherwise, he may remain hatless for sometime unless he inherits a kind older brother. The teenage Amish boys and young men wear their hats further front, covering half their forehead, almost cocked and firmly planted. The older men's are worn in any position but always firmly attached to avoid the embarrassment of chasing one's hat that may travel at speeds faster than its owners can obtain. The Mennonites also wear black circular brimmed hats signifying their religious beliefs.

The local boys and most others wear caps of local farm related enterprises from feed to seed to farm equipment logos displayed with the bill shaped in a upside down U. Flat bills shading either ear are also prevalent in Spanish; black lads and a few others try to emulate them. Spanish folks, mainly Mexicans, have recently appeared in great numbers in Southern Lancaster County. During the 1950s many men from Puerto Rico appeared and worked as migrant workers in this area. Today these folks, mostly from Mexico, seem to work at many various jobs and may be here to stay.

A man displaying a well-groomed head of hair not hidden by a cap almost seems out of place in this community. This will change as those, not Amish or

Mennonites, but related to agriculture are slowly diminishing. However, for now those of my generation still appear regularly in dusty jeans and wearing a faded Powl's feed or John Deere cap. Their grease-stained hands are not nearly as prevalent as in decades past. These fellows, a little bent from hard work, appear to be carrying something, but it is only themselves on far from limber legs.

Hardware appears indiscriminately on any or all-facial features of a few, including their tongues. I can't help but wonder if this is done for attention or from the availability of an extraordinary supply of scrap metal. I realize one's companion could be kept close by and in check if his or her face contained all this metal work and their significant other's pocket concealed a magnet. So don't be offended when a young lady sticks her pierced tongue with attached ring out at you or raises her ringed nose heavenward similar to a German shorthaired pointer approaching a hidden pheasant. She's most likely entered a magnetic field and has absolutely no ill feeling toward you or control over her facial features punctuated with metal piercing. Many years ago I personally knew a couple good looking guys who were referred to as "girl magnets" but this had nothing to do with a piece of magnetized steel.

On the farm we put metal tags in the ears of cattle for identification. Only recently have I thought that perhaps this metal on teenagers could contain their Social Security number. I realize this could actually be beneficial with the importance today of those sometimes forgotten numbers. If someone of authority demands this identification unexpectedly you could simply stick out your tongue, wiggle your nose or uncover your naval. However, I would suggest to avoid any unsanitary embarrassment to either party involved it may prove beneficial to brush your teeth and blow your nose daily and be aware of any unwanted belly button lint that could conceal or distort a few numbers. Down on the farm we also put rings in the noses of pigs to keep them from rootin' and in the nose of a mean bull to lead him around and discourage his vicious behavior. It is for you to contemplate if these piercings in folks are related in any way to those in our farm animals.

The natural color of most women's hair is still visible in the roots clinging to and imbedded in their scalp. Most older women have their hair cut extremely short with both ears clearly visible, which improves both their appearance and hearing. Consquently it is best not to whisper an uncomplimentary remark near a shorthaired old woman unless you are very quick and sincere with an apology. During the 1950s I recall red, black and yellow coloring appearing as the unnatural shades of young ladies hair. When exactly did green, purple, pink and orange enter the hair color charts? I recently came face to face with

2 young ladies in the grocery store displaying the exact same 2-toned color scheme as Rob McSparran's 56 Ford and Denny Hess's 62 Chevy Impala.

Middle-aged men who are partially bald allow their remaining hair to grow close to shoulder length, with ponytails optional. This makes a statement to any who observe them that they can still grow lengthy hair but more in some areas than others. They have over the years progressed from the comb front to the comb over to the brush back. The Don Eagle Indian haircut from the 50s has never gone completely out of style for a few in this area and doesn't seem out of place even today. Many gentlemen, including married Amish men, support various amounts of hair on their faces. This can vary from a handle bar mustache to a beard intent on covering its host's naval to a white blob on one's chin that resembles a small dip of vanilla ice cream. Most men, as this old farmer, wear some type of hat or cap that is removed by most, but not all, only at bedtime. Those gentlemen that appear regularly in this parking lot that work, eat and sleep wearing a cap are not considered eccentric, but simply always prepared for any unexpected, immediate activity.

We capped caravan of locals sometimes display a hattitude towards the man with thick wavy hair wearing no hat. We both envy and scoff at the guy that can stand in the midst of a hurricane or ride his Harley helmet-less and never experience a bad hair day. I've experienced that flyaway hair look from just riding an escalator or elevator or someone sneezing behind me at Church and am currently looking forward to complete, absolute baldness. Ain't that just my luck. The hairstyles of over 50 years ago for we hepcats are returning and I'm well into the thralls of imminent baldness. I remember all the dips and do's, the duck tails and locks in a curl over hanging foreheads like a breaking ocean wave and all I have remaining is the barren beach with a blob of seaweed residue remaining above each ear.

Many folks in the parking lot have personalized license plates and bumper stickers on their vehicles. Some I can interpret but, perhaps due to my age, some I can't. IMAQT made an impression on me until I realized it was a man driving the car. Even I understood the bumper sticker, "Don't mess with ladies that drive a Mercedes." Just now a middle-aged lady pulled directly in front of me in the parking lot and ran hurriedly into the store. I completely forgot her until she casually returned sometime later and slowly drove away. Her license plate read **IGOTTAP**.

The guys who return the carts to the store seldom wear coats, even during the coldest weather. Ah, the exuberance of youth still warms their scantly clad, fluid bodies. I have found that every decade past the age of 40 warrants another layer of clothing during cold winter months to keep me warm and limbs mobile. Loud mufflers remain almost as prevalent on young men's vehicles as in the 1950s and are roared for all to hear and appreciate at appropriate intervals. Gas prices are of no consequence to those who believe the sound of their transportation is every bit as important as its appearance.

Local tame, wild geese fly overhead in conjunction with the community crows looking down on those of us carrying our food to awaiting vehicles. They also have been food shopping although their carryouts are in gullets and not paper or plastic. Their individual horns are periodically sounded indicating the occurrence of "Air Rage." The flight patterns of air traffic controllers followed by the geese and crows seems very erratic to say the least. I would bet that a gaunt gander and a dozing cross-legged crow, sitting atop their electric line flight control tower, would be severely reprimanded by their old buzzard supervisor at day's end.

A bearded Amish man arrives with three small children in his horse-drawn buggy. He arrives from the nearby bank where he most likely made a deposit, and while driving through this parking lot his horse makes a deposit of his own. The Amish fellow is carrying a baby that appears to be approximately 1 year old and informs the check out cashier his wife is at home with the new baby born last week. I recall observing this same Amish fellow a few years ago also in this particular store with no beard, his hair evidently styled by an English barber, wearing an Eagles jacket, sporting an earring and driving a fancy Camaro. Today as I observed the change in his appearance I couldn't help but think even his horse is an old plug and not a handsome, high stepper that most young Amish of similar age own. Marriage has evidently converted him from English youthful ways back to his ancient Amish roots.

Not all who park in the handicapped parking areas are disabled, as they dash unimpaired toward the assembly of carts. Others later are observed struggling across the parking lot stopping occasionally on their difficult journey from store to car. Groceries placed in plastic bags are double tied if they must ride in the back of a pickup truck. Surprisingly, most all infants are placed in car seats. A ring of keys hung outside of one's pants from the belt seems to be a rite of passage for both men and a few women. The way one walks is evidently practiced to achieve a certain continuous rattle. Diesel engines in pickup trucks appear to be gaining in popularity. A few are left unmanned to idle alone in the parking lot sounding similar to a half dozen operating corn shellers.

The warmth of spring brings forth the emergence of flowers of all shapes, colors and sizes. Some are newly planted while others are perennials and reappear every year. Clothed and hidden under snow, leaves, wool and corduroy these flowers and personal messages appear on our landscaped lawns and more recently on our bodies. Concealed behind shower curtains for 6 frigid months and covered by November sweaters, January jeans and March thermal underwear, they reappear as perennials or as freshly formed pen and ink posies and personal words. Displayed cautiously in April and May they all seem to burst forth and are all in full bloom by July 4th. Revealed proudly by their owners these tattoos seem to relish and thrive in the summer heat, although I have a feeling there may be a few located in places where they have never come face to face with Mr. Sun. This old farmer however can't help but wonder how the designs and words on some folk's bodies may change with age. That tiny rosebud on the thigh of a perky teenage girl may eventually become a hydrangea when she welcomes her first grandchild. The name of a sweetheart inscribed on a young man's shoulder may be altered by the lines and wrinkles of age, if not painfully by his new wife.

The sound of an old John Deere tractor is heard as a 20-something young lad starts it this sunny June morning outside Musser's Store. The cultivator attached to this faded green and yellow half century plus old machine makes me remember a time when it would have just finished cultivating weeds in a nearby field of tobacco or tomatoes. Although not hard work, it was tedious and slow as I recall. It was a task in which every local farm lad of my generation participated. Your eyes remained focused on the row you were tilling, never glancing up until you reached the end of the row. If you were working near a road and someone who knew you blew the horn while passing by, you raised your hand but never your head.

The speed of your tractor remained slow as the cultivator removed unwanted weeds and grass. The rows containing the tobacco, tomatoes or, years earlier, corn that passed between the cultivator teeth which were set precisely to not only remove the weeds but distribute loose dirt evenly on either side of the tender plants. This free flowing soil covered any small, unwanted weeds or grass sprouts and discouraged their regrowth. The amount of soil that flowed from the cultivator teeth to the base of the growing plants was regulated entirely by the speed of the tractor and the precise driving of the operator. This was all determined during the first few minutes of the cultivating procedure. Following that, your body became part of the machine as one-by-one your eyes observed each growing plant as it passed beneath you untouched by the cultivator teeth. This was one of the few menial jobs on the farm in which your mind could travel around the world as long as your hand remained on the steering wheel coordinating with your eyes, focused on the rows being cultivated.

This is what I was thinking as I glanced at that old tractor and smiled. Others also looked and observed as the loud putt-putt disrupted the normal sounds within the store parking lot. Some nearby appeared startled by the abrasive sound and a few acted disgusted as if this 50-years-ago sound had completely disrupted and ruined their day. Nevertheless, off to my left I noticed a couple old farmers in bib overalls, standing side by side, who stared emphatically, listened intently and watched proudly as the noisy putt—putt sound that had saturated the parking lot slowly faded in the distance. Perhaps they, like me, were having similar thoughts of a time when they were the boy driving that tractor, when it and they were young. With the appearance of agriculture herbicides the last several years, this particular farm activity I've just described is rarely observed.

I suppose one could say it is a good time to be a teenage boy with many of the young girls dressed so scantily. My impression and observation is that most of the lads are familiar with the present dress code and really don't seem to notice or observe young ladies nearly as much as we old baby boomers. The young Amish boys are a different story. I recently observed a young, good-looking Amish boy with his hair evidently styled by an English barber as he walked from his buggy toward the store entrance. He was purposely or unconsciously directly in the path of 2 young girls dressed in halter-tops and short shorts. As both their possibly predetermined courses crossed, neither his straw hat nor the part of his anatomy that it sat upon wavered but both pupils in his eyes completely disappeared. I have observed this "eyes pass from sight" maneuver before in a few Amish boys while conversing with them as my TV plays in the far corner of the room where it and we were located. I'm not exactly sure how they accomplish this relocation or where they situate their eyes but I would never attempt to sneak up behind an Amish man because he may be watching me from behind his ear. My good friend Liz Sinclair claims if your headlights at night are flashed upon an Amish fellow his eyes glow similar to those of a cat. As this particular Amish boy walks stoically away from the observed girls, his face now hidden from me, I notice his ears are scarlet. As I glance one last time toward the store's entrance, long flowing purple and black dresses that rest on shoulders and cover completely to shoes enter the store near the girls whose most observed bodily covering is their skin.

Sitting in our car half dozing while Ruthie shopped, I became aware of 2 perhaps 16-18 year olds, apparently a couple, who evidently had a spat inside the store. Although the boy didn't strike the girl, he abused her verbally for at least 15 minutes. The reason for his displeasure with her was unknown by me, but he went on and on loudly berating her and seemed unaware of my presence directly beside them. The only words she spoke during the ordeal were, "Let's just go home." Had he hit her, I would hope I would have confronted him. Much to my own displeasure, I was weighing this if that had happened. Finally, after he cursed her one last time, he started the vehicle. As they roared away in a worn-out car with tires screeching, I caught a tearful glance from the young girl as they narrowly missed an elderly lady crossing the parking lot. I couldn't help but wonder with what I had seen and heard in this public place what would be the consequences for that young girl at home behind closed doors?

I have found the last 25 years of a woman's life can be heard and documented if she talks on her cell phone near where I sit in the parking lot.

This all can happen in less then 30 minutes. Reared back in my seat, pretending to be sleeping and evidently invisible on this slow, people-watching day this lady both entertained, and enlightened me. This middle aged female talked continually, leading me to believe the one she was conversing with only gave 1-word replies. I sometimes had the feeling I was even more attentive to her life story than the one she was talking to. Twice, I almost interrupted and entered her one-way conversation.

A couple of men who reside permanently at a nearby, local motel enter the store. I have a feeling they visit this store at least once a day, perhaps more. Not much room for food storage in a motel room. They are not alone in their frequent grocery store rendezvous. I'm amazed at how all of us, including this old farmer, have become so dependent on the local grocery stores. Maybe it's the mini market on the corner that may contain a few items deemed necessary or that large super market complex measured in acres that contains everything imaginable. Many folks seem to frequent them almost daily and I shudder to think what could happen if all closed for any length of time for some unforeseen reason. Gone are the days when ample food for the winter was stored in the root cellar, spring house, icehouse or basement. When the local weather forecast includes the possibility of an up-coming snow flurry, most folks flock to the store to wrestle over the last loaf of bread, the last gallon of milk and last roll of toilet paper. I've often thought these local TV weathermen must also receive their extended forecast from the local grocers who are experiencing a slow day.

I have just as much respect for the guy who enters the store with dirt, grease and soil on his shirt and jeans as the one who arrives clean, perhaps more. It is difficult for me to relate to the man in a $500.00 suit displaying a $50.00 haircut, manicured fingernails driving a $50,000.00 vehicle strolling across the store parking lot. I neither resent nor envy him.

Even in this 21st century computer age, food remains one of the few basic essentials of life. Some basic foods are but a few short days from the farm to your refrigerator. I would hope you appreciate all who grow, transport and strive to provide it at an affordable cost. Have you ever been hungry, without food? Those who could least survive a food shortage are those who have always had an abundance of this necessary essential that all assume should always be provided and to which each individual is entitled. An empty belly could soon put everything in this acquiring-stuff, me-first nation into perspective. God help us all if this should ever occur.

The Party Line

In 1886, the Hensel family of Quarryville entertained the first assistant Post Master General of the United States and they were discussing the name for a new Post Office at Centerville. Centerville, as other rural hamlets, was no more than a few farms and houses located along what is now route 272 in the area just south of where River Road now intersects it running south to Goshen Mill Road. The reason for renaming this tiny village Post Office something other then Centerville was there already was a Post Office in this general district with that name. The assistant Post Master General said the name of this Post Office would be Hensel, after his Quarryville friends. The man who renamed this tiny community and Post Office was Adlai Ewing Stevenson, who later became Vice President of the United States under Grover Cleveland.

During his time as Post Master General, he fired over 40,000 Republican postal workers and replaced them with Democrats. His great grandfather was Jesse W. Fell, a prominent Quaker from Pennsylvania. He also was the namesake and grandfather of Adlai Stevenson, who twice ran unsuccessfully for President, in 1952 and 1956, against the popular Dwight D. Eisenhower. I recall listening to and watching Stevenson on TV in the early 50s and remember him as an eloquent orator and statesman.

The first phone service in our immediate area was centrally located in Hensel and our particular phone line was known as the Hensel line. I have an old telephone book of that era, from 1946-47, for the areas of Atglen, Christiana, Gap, Hensel, Kirkwood, Strasburg, Parkesburg, Oxford, Intercourse, Quarryville and nearby points. A few noted interesting facts lifted from this booklet are: "For the telephone number of the F.B.I.—call the operator. (I'm nearly 70 years old and I don't believe I've ever known anyone in my lifetime who has ever telephoned the F.B.I. Perhaps in this rural area we have led a sheltered life.) In case of an emergency call the operator and say: 'I want to report a fire' or 'I want a policeman' and give your name, address and telephone number. Reports to the fire department and police are not a part of the service for which the phone company contracts, and may be discontinued at anytime."

Party Line Service: "Party line service can be maintained only by the courtesy of the various parties on the line. Conversations should be "reasonably limited." Subscribers should answer only on their own ring, and they should, always out of courtesy to other subscribers, listen in on the line before ringing in."

As I recall, this "listening in" could last several minutes until one of those involved in the original conversation heard the click of a third party evidently still listening to the on going spoken words would mention, "there's old nosey again." This was usually followed by another muffled, concealed click as the embarrassed third party hung up.

The daughter of a local, now-deceased lady known for her listening-in expertise recently relayed this family anecdote to me. Everyone on a party line had a different ring, perhaps 2 short rings, 1 long ring followed by 1 short. You picked up the receiver when hearing your personal ring. You also soon recognized the personal ring of everyone else on your line so you knew for whom this incoming call was without lifting the receiver.

This particular lady was on the same line with a man who bought tobacco from neighboring farmers. When this man's phone would ring during tobacco buying season, our lady of perpetual, overheard, overtures would cautiously listen in. The head tobacco buyer in Lancaster would inform this online buyer what to pay today for this local, important, cash crop. Consequently, this wife's husband somehow always received the top price paid for his crop of tobacco. Evidently, listening in on the phone could be more beneficial than speaking into it.

With 7 or 8 rural families sharing a party line, one might envision constant bickering and contention between neighbors, but I don't recall that happening. There were, however, a few accusations that a couple ladies on local party lines developed a technique of silently raising the receiver on a phone and listening to most all on-going conversations. Any words spoken on a party line, whether considered strictly private or public knowledge, were rendered old news locally before sunset. Twittering and or Facebook are not considered a communications marvel to these former party line receiver boppers of 65 years ago.

With all calls coming through a central, local operator who would then ring and transfer the call to the appropriate party, there were always accusations that this operator was also listening to most all telephone conversations. A couple older local men receiving calls were known to begin every conversation stating, "You can hang up now Annie," the telephone operator's first name.

I recently mentioned my thoughts concerning party lines to a gal of my generation and she immediately recalled that her party line also had someone who was known to listen in on most conversations. This listening-in lady was known to remain very cautious, discreet and quiet when lifting the receiver. This harvester of local news evidently relished gleaning most all talk between neighbors so much that she completely forgot her canary in a cage singing in the background. I'm told locals would occasionally visit this lady, comment to her on the extraordinary voice of her bird but never gave him up or revealed him as the one implicating her as the silent third party in most phone conversations. I'm told a couple visitors to the lady thought this bird expressed a worried, concerned countenance as the visitor spoke of her yellow-plumed friend that, unknown by its master, was directly involved and a willing participant in each of her secret, wire tapping efforts. Although behind bars, this bird communicated daily to the outside world inadvertently sending secret messages to everyone on this phone line.

A local irate Scotch-Irish dairy farmer with a sick cow was said to have butted into a neighbor lady's conversation with another, following several pickups of his phone with these blunt words: "Peg, you're gonna haffta get the hell off the damn phone so I can call the Vet." Although this abrupt conversation was humorously repeated among neighbors, the participants never showed any trace of animosity toward one another the following Sunday morning in Chestnut Level Church.

Picking up the telephone receiver 60 years ago on a local party line was similar to Forest Gump's box of chocolates, you never knew what you were gonna get or gonna hear. My uncle, John Denlinger, who farmed near Chestnut Level, once raised his receiver to call for farm supplies only to hear his nearby neighbor lady who was known to possess an unrestrained, unrefined, crude vocabulary state to another phone patron, the following. "John Denlinger is the best blankity blank, blankity blank neighbor I've ever had." Uncle John and all the Denlingers always had a much-improved and the utmost wonderful opinion of this woman after hearing this chance, descriptive phone conversation. However, it was best to never imply anything derogatory about a man, his wife, his children or next of kin if that person shared a telephone party line with you. Those unflattering words, perhaps spoken in haste, always somehow made their way to the individual you referred to, then eventually retuned to your house to roost. Perhaps this was Wiki leaks 70 years ago.

The monthly cost to be a subscriber of a multi party line was $2.08, with a few local folks choosing not to acquire this modern convenience but use the one at a neighbor for free. Occasionally, a few neighborhood Amish will mimic this ancient English trait but most have phones located in small, wooden, homemade phone booths near the edge of their farm, as far from the house as possible.

They use their phone every bit as much as their English neighbors but evidently it is mandatory to make this use unhandy. The path leading to these plain, weathered Amish communication shacks is well worn and at times some are standing outside waiting for their turn. I'm not sure if a man with a sick cow has priority to the phone.

Driving past these booths on a hot day, with the door partway open, may reveal an Amish fella seated on an old lazy boy recliner or bucket seat out of a Chevy Camaro, with feet propped up similar to a Wall Street executive. Once, when an unnoticed breeze blew open their phone booth door, I noticed an embarrassed Amish lady in a similar position.

Almost immediately, the telephone was deemed a necessity and convenience for most everyone-especially in our rural world. Nevertheless, at first it was thought of as an affordable, accessible, marvel and not to be abused or over used unnecessarily. In the beginning it was mostly for dad's use to call for essential farm supplies, service, veterinarian or doctor.

Later, in most households the wives and mothers gradually enjoyed conversing with one another regularly, particularly when Dad wasn't in the house. This female chitchat seemed to fill a void in the lives of the every day housewife who at this point in time had mostly not yet worked away from home.

Then teenage children began using the phone, talking to friends and school acquaintances and usually abruptly ending this teen talk when dad came through the door. Years later, when someone we knew acquired a private, personal phone line of their own, we assumed they had to be wealthy.

I recall in our home my parents and grandparents evidently believed the louder one spoke into the receiver protruding from this wooden box attached to the wall the better reception the one at the other end would receive. My grandfather Smith once stated the following to his wife, Margie, who was talking by phone to her sister, Kit, who lived a mile over the adjacent hill, "If Kit can't hear you on the phone, just open a window."

The old phone book I'm glancing through has no yellow pages but is infested with local business advertisements. Containing less than 30 pages of subscribers, this thin publication would be dwarfed by the one of Southern Lancaster County today. The explosion of cell phone use, even among the Amish, has once again taken communication to an entirely new level. Although not possessing one personally, it appears I'm privileged to the conversations of everyone near me, known and unknown. Somehow I feel like the old neighbor lady who listened in on most party line gossip from the past. I sometimes wonder how much money is paid to working employees while they are having a personal conversation as to who is supposed to walk the dog tonight? Just a thought.

A few businesses represented in this local phone book from years ago are as follows, including their phone number, just in case anyone reading this wishes to contact them: L.E. Book Garage and Massey Harris implements at Kirkwood (9R3), Jacob Erb Lumber at Quarryville (30R21), Walter Hassel Lumber at Quarryville (93), R.A. Grubb, Gulf gas and groceries at Hensel (24R3), Ross Ulrich Field Feeds at Hensel (19R3), Charles and Roland Gochnauer, Painting and Paper Hanging at Quarryville (163), Leon Fite, Livestock at Hensel (19R51), Ferguson's Variety Shop, Women's Clothes at Quarryville (73R2), B. Maude Quigley—Say it with flowers at Quarryville (28R3), Rex Cully, Native Lumber at Quarryville (187R51) and lastly LeRoy Stumpf, Livestock Dealer and Hauling at Quarryville (115R12). With all these dealers of livestock, I'm obliged to mention Charles Lamparter, Dead Animals at Quarryville (94R6)No Horse too large—No pig too small.

The ad that appears most often in this old phone book is as follows "I'll see you at Murphy's Hotel," Quarryville, PA.—Beer, Wine and Liquors, phone 86, "Where Good Fellows Get Together." It occurs to me the farther back I glance into our local history the more prevalent these types of establishments seem to exist. They continue today. A man I knew well who seemed to be a generic scholar of the Bible and also a frequent inhabitant at a local bar, once offered the following to an elderly lady reprimanding him on his regular consumption of alcohol. He stated sternly the following to her: "Old girl, I've read through the Bible at least a half dozen times in my life and I've never found one instance of Jesus turning water into that Turkey Hill iced tea that you drink daily!" Amen.

An indication as to how far our local ladies had progressed in the mid 1940s, the largest and only full-page ad in this entire phone book is Marionette Beauty Shop owned by Marion Markle at Quarryville 165 for appointments. Our local gals are now driving automobiles, talking on the telephone, voting and regularly getting their hair done. What could be next? This regularly getting their hair done continues today for those of my Mother's generation and takes precedence and has the highest priority of most anything in their personal lives. Sixty-five years ago who would have believed this fad for ladies would continue until their passing. I've always wondered why a lady got a permanent and a few months later receive another. Perhaps a "perm" should actually be referred to as a "temp." Either way we gentleman can only say, "You've come a long way Baby."

I suppose communication will always continue between us, having been developed in unimaginable ways during my lifetime. As an old storyteller I hope this aspect of communication remains encouraged and is never lost.

The Old Farmer Duz Woodstock

I was recently reminded that this past summer of 2009 was the 40th anniversary of the gathering of thousands of my generation on a dairy farm at Bethel, New York, referred to as Woodstock. At that point in my life, 1969, I was fully involved in farming on my dairy farm—with a wife, 2 kids and a mortgage—doing what dairy farmers are supposed to do. Milking and caring for the health and well being of 100 dairy cows for 45 years eliminated all my Woodstock festivals until I sold my dairy. I never would have imagined 40-years ago that attending a music festival at a dairy farm in upstate New York would be remembered by many of my generation as a highlight of their otherwise fairly normal lives. Working on the farm for what today seems like welfare entitlement, the birth of both children was paid in full from two separate tobacco checks.

These were turbulent times and those who discuss the financial, political and social woes of today surely must have absolutely no knowledge of the 1960s. In my limited Liberty Square world, I can't remember ever knowing anyone who attended Woodstock. However, I knew several who experienced first hand the war in Viet Nam. Farming and family evidently kept me from the war although I must admit shamefully to experiencing some guilt even today when conversing with those of my generation who served. I cannot list all that transpired during the 1960s and the horrors that graphically played out in our living rooms via TV. The 1950s and this modern marvel that had brought mostly joy and entertainment into our homes now introduced us to the violence of war, assassinations and the civil rights movement. The pleasure the TV produced a decade earlier was replaced by unrest, doubt and fear.

I always assumed, right or wrong, that Woodstock was a short period of time for many young folks to drop out—temporarily for some, a lifetime for others—from all that was transpiring around them. There remain even today a few among us referred to as old hippies who still genuinely believe they can make a change in their society and a difference in their world. God love em, but their cause seems less motivated and their appearance and long hair goes mostly unnoticed while protesting a war, a Wal-Mart or a puppy mill. It is certainly normal that most young people do not wish to become exact replicas of their parents. Grudgingly, this in many instances will eventually occur later in their lives. Around Liberty Square, that's referred to as maturity.

Those who truly believed in anti-government causes must surely harbor a great deal of resentment as they now sign up for Social Security, Medicare and in a few cases previously, welfare. The generation gap of 40 years ago continues and will always and should always exist. But the difference in hair, music, clothes, politics etc. doesn't seem as noticeable to me today. The 4-decades-ago cry that it matters to be different doesn't seem to matter anymore.

We recently attended an outdoor picnic at Quarryville Presbyterian Home, where my parents are residents. The gathering of over 500 permanent residents and family was accompanied by scrumptious food and entertainment by 2 gentlemen who played and sang everything from blue grass to 50's pop, from Gershwin to protest songs from the 60s. Babs Herr, a high school classmate attending with her mother, decided this was as close to Woodstock as she and I will probably ever get even though our Quarryville crowd was only 499,500 fewer than the festival held in New York. At Woodstock there were numerous drug busts; at our gathering all drugs and medications were handed out before and during the meal to residents of the home. Following the festivities, bumper to bumper wheelchairs and walkers progressing at a snail's pace was as slow as the crowd that departed from Woodstock that I've read took days, with traffic jams exceeding 20 miles.

My closest encounter to Woodstock occurs every year at nearby Susquehannock State Park. Referred to as the Fiddlers, these folks that play and sing the old time blue grass, country and gospel music gather every year in August to revive, continue and promote this old country music.

While some may play, sing and perform to a higher professional degree than others, it matters little to the appreciative audience and me. That's exactly what I thought 60 years ago when first listening to this music. The instruments remain constant with guitar, fiddle, banjo, mandolin and bass remaining the most observed and heard. Young and mature voices may vary, but there is little change in the sound of these old stringed music makers touched lovingly by sensitive fingers, and therein lies the attraction. No matter your old age infirmities, if you can still tap your foot to the music you remain young, alive and well. If you don't and won't allow this toe tapping to occur, you best not attend and should be checked by a physician for a pulse.

As 2 who appreciate all types of music, we always make time to attend the fiddlers and 2 or 3 old time blue grass gospel concerts a year. They always strengthen our hearts, soothe and comfort our souls and greatly increase the blood flow within our bodies. It's kind of like a stress test without the machines, wires and technicians.

I'm well aware that most folks attending these blue grass concerts are my age or older. You either enjoy this type of music or you don't. Old friends Merle and Mary Ann (Tub) Farmer and Ronnie and Sandy Waltman Arbogast of similar age and background are 4 we regularly see at these functions who appreciate and enjoy this music. It may someday disappear along with us; I hope not.

While most who attend these local old time music get togethers were definitely alive in the 1960s—and a few may have even attended Woodstock—there is nothing in their appearance today linking them to that era. Dressed casually they come from all walks of life and most arrive unnoticed in cars from 2 to 10 years of age. Only a few pickup trucks appear and they also are not new.

What impresses most folks, and me, is a '58 Chevy and a '57 Ford convertible or any car from that era that appears, showroom shiny and new. The older man driving is probably retired and collecting Social Security. He's usually wearing a baseball cap with the bill shaped in an upside down U that conceals his flat top or duck-tail hair-do that has long ago gradually disappeared down the shower drain. He no longer smokes, his shirt pocket contains a pack of roll aids instead of a pack of Camels, but he still encounters regular nicotine cravings.

In the 1960s he may have worn bell-bottoms, a psychedelic tie-dyed shirt and beads, but the cars return him to the happier, uncomplicated time of his youth—the 1950s. He has reverted back to jeans and a pullover shirt unless he is 50 or more pounds overweight. If he now appears 6 months pregnant and only ever observes his boots while in a sitting position, a buttoned-in-front shirt is worn outside his jeans. His hairline has receded miles from his eyebrows, with gray the primary color appearing around the fringes of his cap. He is totally content and at ease within his own skin even though that once-youthful, handsome face now contains wrinkles that resemble the street map of Quarryville, with the dimple in his chin being the local Turkey Hill. When facing him, 4th Street runs up from this dimple on the right side of his face; Good's Store is located at his cheekbone. The line on the left side is State Street that runs past the Post Office located at his other cheekbone. These 2 wrinkles on his face continue to his forehead where they each make 90-degree turns above his eyebrows heading toward one another eventually meeting in front of Joe Strickler's Barber shop, forming Church Street. This well-defined wrinkle and well-traveled road runs parallel to 2 other lines above it that are Hess Street and Lime Street. The faces of all us old men contain a map of some place; the secret is to match the gentleman with the neighborhood. Just be careful not to use these "Mature Mugs" exclusively for your GPS because these streets and businesses may at times fluctuate when us old guys smile. You may believe you're driving into Good's Store, expecting to buy one, get one free and find yourself face to face with Joel Reynolds, our local undertaker located farther up the street.

His wife, of similar age minus her peaches and cream complexion from years past, is mainly responsible for his acceptance of growing old gracefully. She lovingly refers to him as a dapper, mature teenager. They have arrived together in their red and white '57 Ford convertible, their bodies positioned side by side with plenty of room for 2 more adults in the front seat with them. They both depart from their 50s time capsule by way of the same door. Once outside the convertible, their every move and appearance coincides with their regression back in time that they remember and refuse to relinquish. They probably have children and grandchildren. I'm sure they've had heartaches and encountered the storms of life that all of us have faced. But she still wears her hair in a ponytail, and he, when driving, still rests his left arm on the car door, elbow pointed out, with his right hand visible on the top of the steering wheel. From a short distance away, both of them and the '57 Ford appear young. Her blouse and flowing poodle skirt are vintage 1950s, and with a sincere smile that when flashed conceals her crow's-foot countenance and all troubles and trials that have occurred in her life. Seated in lawn chairs listening to the music their feet tap together and mimic mine.

The music played and sung is the old traditional sound that resonated 75 years ago from the Carolina, Kentucky, and Virginia hills. Folks migrating north in search of work and a better life carried it to this area on the instrumental strings of continuous warm southern breezes that continue to echo this music locally. Many settled in these rolling hills permanently, finding jobs and developing skills in factories, construction and in farming opportunities. They were and continue to be a genuine asset to this community that is now theirs. Living among the Amish, Mennonites, Presbyterians, Catholics, Quakers and Baptists and all the diverse religious sects sprinkled abundantly across hill and dale, causes me to believe freedom of religion certainly exists profusely and prospers without provocation in Southern Lancaster County.

The melodies played by our local musicians are uncomplicated, repetitive tunes that heard once invite and encourage audience participation for even those who carry their tune in a bucket that occasionally spills off-key phrases. The simple, unedited words are of joy and heartaches, of love gained, then lost, and of God and his promises. They are simply about this life and the perception of the next, structured in a pure uncomplicated form that is to be both heard and felt.

When the crowd slowly disperses at the end of the day, our fiddlers gradually discontinue their playing and singing. Entertaining just for the joy of it, with the collection taken given to the Blind Association, our performers seem reluctant to stop until the crowd is reduced to a couple of dozen. Some of the older entertainers wear matching suits and cowboy hats from the 50s that cling to weathered bodies and identify them as belonging to my generation. Others that are younger, without matching attire, have apparently stopped to participate in the singing and playing on their way home from work. All are accepted and enjoyed. Our couple from the 50s also exit and enter their vehicle through the driver's side door. This gets me thinking about seat belts-do they have them and can they both use them? The most distinguishable attribute of a car from the 50s now occurs as our driver starts his engine. That sound from over 50 years ago, filtered and forced through glass-packed mufflers and dual exhausts was every bit as important to car and driver as its appearance. There most assuredly wasn't 800 horsepower under the hood of those 1950s rods, it only sounded that way. As our golden couple glides away, cap, convertible and ponytail slicing through the breeze, I'll look forward to their appearance following another year, although for them next year will continue to be 1958.

Ruthie had dropped me off at the Fiddlers, near the conclusion of their program, then ran some errands. I had been seated on my lawn chair surrounded by the green, green grass of summer with my mind and soul foraging on the music as my body devoured the appreciative cool breeze beneath old shade. I watched as the last of the players packed stringed instruments in cases and placed speakers in vans. Deb Maule, a local hard-working gal, had provided food and drink from her kitchenette on wheels, powered by a generator in the back of a pickup truck. Her well-organized work, with family help, had been a joy to observe as they precisely repacked everything and drove cautiously away.

Nearly alone in my Woodstock meadow with tall trees, I was totally at peace with my surroundings and myself. Five ladies older than I, the last of the spectators, slowly shuffled past me on their way to the only remaining vehicle in the parking lot. They spoke to me cordially as they approached, and at that instant I realized I was the only one remaining at my Woodstock festival. I remained seated as one said, "Can we give you a ride, mister?" Regretfully I said, "No thanks, my ride will be here shortly and I just live **OVER THE HILL**."

"Don't we all," one lady replied woefully under her breath.

This prompted another old girl, at least 80, to say, "Well, if you don't get a way home at least you'll be the first one here next year!"

As they slowly drove away in their untraded cash for clunkers auto, they all waved fondly to me, a stranger. Perhaps like me, this time we shared together was also their only Woodstock festival experience.

I remained seated among the oaks, completely alone until Ruthie finally returned. I told her she got here just in time as 5 sexy, senior, sorority sisters from the 60s had attempted to pick me up. Her unexplained, ensuing laughter continued throughout the entire 5-minute trip home and remains to this day a mystery to me. Here's hoping you've had a Woodstock experience sometime and somewhere in your life. PEACE!

PART FOUR

BEAUTY, FORGOTTEN VOICES AND MEMORIES

Scalpy Hollow

Traveling in October along the tree-lined roads around Liberty Square nature always treats me to my very own personal, colorful, ticker-tape parade. This may occur during a relaxing Sunday afternoon drive or a necessary farm-related trip in my old truck along any linear presence of a trunk supported branches and leaves pathway in downtown Drumore. Either way I'm always regarded as a famous celebrity, a sports hero or a popular politician. My favorite ticker-tape parade is not up the concrete canyon of heroes on Broadway in New York City but down Scalpy Hollow from route 272 all the way to the Susquehanna River following the bends and twists of a meandering stream known as Fishing Creek. Scalpy Hollow, the tree lined area surrounding this stream can be reached by turning West on Oregon Hollow Road from 272 approximately 3 miles South of the Buck then taking the first left. Scalpy Hollow supposedly received its name when a scalp or skull was found in this area nearly 2 centuries ago.

If you care to ride along with me in my old dusty, rusty farm truck I will gladly relocate all tools, wrenches and grease guns to the back and even wipe the accumulated dirt and dust from the windows using one of my old shirts rumpled together on the front seat. For me this scenery is ever changing and I always notice something unseen on past trips. I shall point out a few old dwellings and historical facts that hopefully may convey to you a tiny glimpse of the character of this area. Climb in my friend. What's that you say—NO, NO, NO, that is an old hydraulic hose peering out from under the seat and not a black snake although on rare occasions your first assessment might be correct.

This pristine stream flows through mostly woodland, occasionally meandering into open meadows and welcome sunshine, all the while accepting and acquiring spring—fed tributaries along its joyful journey to the Susquehanna. Bubbling, swirling pools containing native trout regretfully relinquish their temporary hold on the cold rushing water, allowing it to pass through rocks and again regain speed on an unstoppable, purposeful, gravity-spurted, marathon race to the river. The cold temperature of this water, maintained by the shaded forest thermostat, is absolutely necessary for the survival of this native fish.

In mid-summer the sunshine almost seems to need reservations to appear briefly in only certain areas and at only certain intervals within the dense forest before relocating with glorious streams of light elsewhere. We have driven through Scalpy on an October evening with twilight approaching all the area along the creek while the treetops remain bathed by the slowly receding sun. Looking skyward reveals all the majestic colors that shine in a fiery glow that resembles the stained glass ceiling of a giant Cathedral with all shades of colors ablaze.

Standing in the breezy autumn air the congregated crowds that reside in the soil sidewalks along my route both applaud and wave with partially naked limbs as I slowly pass and nod my head in appreciation. Those much younger, absent of protruding branches, wearing only colorful attire on their heads appear to bow in admiration. Those appearing to be more mature, standing stoically, seem not to notice or disapprove of the fall breezes that are gently, methodically disrobing each. My path is completely covered with the colorful garments that once adorned the bodies of my admiring congregation. Later the strong, brisk winds of November arrive to serve as street cleaners as they remove nature's generic confetti that had carpeted my way over the road.

Every season brings something special and unique to this tiny, remote slice of local natural beauty. Usually this quilt of confetti in vivid detail and assortment of shades of colors that nature composts is eventually covered under a blanket of fresh fallen snow protecting plants and mammals from harsh, winter cold. This snow that remains pure and white compared to that which soon appears gray and dirty in cities and towns is distributed proportionately in equal amounts throughout the forest. Shaded by shadows cast by the multitude of inhabitants, this snow will be the last to melt locally.

The narrow turnpike that mimics its name with similar twists and turns as the stream it parallels never encounters snow drifts as do those swirling, wind swept, country roads along unrestrictive open fields. Many times over the years I have driven down Scalpy and made the first track through this new fallen, virgin snow. I envy our local Amish neighbors who journey on this rural pathway located amidst their community in transportation similar to my ancestors 2 centuries earlier. During winter they travel wrapped in December blankets with only stinging, ruddy cheeks on the women and facial hair on the men observed. The horse, pulling the rattling carriage and enjoying the excursion every bit as much as those riding inside, blows methodical streams of steam with every exhale of lung heated breath.

With the welcome spring sunshine that slices through the naked forest, life begins anew. The color green, almost totally absent at this time, emerges so slowly that it is hardly ever noticed until it completely covers everything except the narrow road and the limitless springs that fill this stream to capacity following April showers. Once all the trees and shrubs are completely dressed and growing green, as they have for centuries, this canopy restricts the warm sunshine providing God's cathedral with nature's central air.

This same scenario played out years earlier in my life as I rode horseback within this same area and also through the dense areas along Muddy Run Creek and amidst the laurel, rhododendron and undisturbed woodland that later would become Susquehannock State Park. During this era, it seemed that only a few of us knew of and appreciated these remote areas that invoked both beauty and inspiration simultaneously.

Observing few signs of civilization for 2 or 3 hours, it took very little imagination to transfer those precious moments to a time much earlier in our local history. For short, brief, imaginative intervals I was transformed into a hunter, trapper or scout exploring areas west of pioneer settlements to the east. Straddled atop my 4-legged, sorrel, time—capsule, we moved as one along the ancient trails of animals that freely roamed these places centuries before my intervention.

Both the Muddy Run and State Park areas once thick with native plants and trees changed dramatically in the last 50 years. The park now contains picnic areas, ball fields, numerous trails and modern bathroom facilities while the Muddy Run Creek and entire basin surrounding it has been flooded with water that at places is over 200 feet in depth. Scalpy Hollow remains serene, unruffled and unchanged. Although all these areas are now accessible by vehicles to drive around or through, when doing this I no longer conjure up thoughts of Daniel Boone and myself exploring uncharted wilderness.

Thankfully, much of this natural beauty has remained undisturbed for centuries along this Scalpy Hollow trail. A couple of 200-year-old native stone farm houses and 2 grist mills, one that I visited regularly with my father until approximately 1950 still stand. They remain, stoically planted nearly 2 centuries earlier by stouthearted men whose time and purpose have passed.

The first old stone farm house encountered is situated on the west side of the road after you cross River Road following your drive down Scalpy from 272. Dick and Esther Warfel owned this house during much of my lifetime. It is located near the tiny bridge dedicated to Wilmer "Bill" Bolton, a local Drumore Township Supervisor for many years. It is presently owned by Ezra Beiler and at this writing the house, small barn and adjoining meadow are all for sale. During the completion of this writing it was sold to Quarryville businessman, Robert Landis Jr. Previously the Penrose family, who built the house in 1868 and operated the nearby mill at the corner of Scalpy and Furniss Road, had owned it. I presently do not know of any who carry the last name of these Penrose Quakers but a few still have this forgotten surname as a middle name in their identification. Not only have these prevalent, local folks with a familiar name more than 100 years ago disappeared but in many cases their family name also vanished with them from the area. This fact has been recently reaffirmed as Kate Bolton Tassmer with husband Pete and family have moved from Drumore, relocating locally as this was being written. This ends the nearly 200 years of existence of the Boltons residing in Drumore and also the Bolton name as Kate's father Bill had no sons. Bill's other daughter Anita is a Catholic Nun living near Philadelphia.

With most of this immediate Scalpy Hollow area owned and preserved by our local Conservancy, hopefully this natural, native forest will remain unspoiled to be appreciated by others in the future. Recently a group of local folks have formed, "Friends of Fishing Creek," to care for and have this stream designated as a pristine waterway.

Ankrum Homestead, house built in 1765, home of Archibald Ankrum, his son, Dr. Jimmy Ankrum practiced medicine from this house.

We turn left onto Furniss Road, which was named for Gardner Furniss who settled in Drumore Township in the late 1700s. The Furniss family was originally from Scotland, near Furniss Castle, hence the name Furniss. It is also interesting that Gardner Furniss and his wife deeded in 1835 a plot of ground to the trustees for the yet to be built Mount Zion Methodist Church. A store and also a Post Office named Furniss was located on the corner of Furniss Road and Slate Hill Road, established in 1889 and discontinued in 1935. The Postmasters were Elwood Stubbs 1880, Gardner Furniss 1889, David Weidley 1894, William McSparran 1930, Ira Wentz, John Pearthree, and lastly Verle Booth 1935. Most also owned and ran this general merchandise store.

Continuing a short distance on Furniss is the present home of the Valley Lea Riding Club. Containing nearly 350 members this mixed group of horse lovers and trail riders was established in the 1950s in Quarryville with my father and I and approximately 60 other locals as founding members. Later the present grounds were purchased from John O'Donnell for its headquarters and have many members within and outside our local area. The area described in this chapter containing miles of woodland trails is what draws both horse and rider to this area. I have been fortunate to have ridden most of these trails 50 years ago. Later, full time work with dairy cows interfered with my stimulating saddle setting and my riding has grown completely stagnant from impaired knees, hips and the absence of a horse.

Traveling a short distance further to the top of the hill is our Drumore Township building that houses all of our township equipment and where all local township meetings and squabblings are held. A small area has been set aside behind this building known as Drumore Park. I urge you to also visit this quiet place along the rippling spring waters of Fishing Creek. Walking along the peaceful stream a hundred yards north in the park reminds me of the Canadian Rockies with rushing water running rampant through resistant rocks. Although this scene appears on a much smaller scale than the remote Northwest wilderness, the feeling it generates inside me remains similar. Our majestic snow capped mountains are only tree and green coverlet covered rolling hills, our roar of the wild rushing water is but a restrained whisper, and the force of its powerful current does not take your breath away. But a large, boisterous man is no more remembered or impressive than a small, quiet guy with character who speaks softly. Two picnic pavilions have been built in memory of Mart Eshleman and Bill Douts, who were instrumental in the establishment and construction of this tiny peaceful Park.

Continuing south on Furniss before descending the hill are 2 recently built homes, where new is occasionally sprinkled among the old. My friends Bob and Betty Herr Adams built a beautiful home surrounded by pasture to the west of Furniss and old school mate Bob Herr and wife Wendy constructed a house with a corrugated, schnittshear roofline visible opposite the Adam's to the east.

Home of Gardner Furniss, Post Office and store–early 1800s.

Approximately 1 mile further along Furniss on the north side of the road is the old stone house, still standing at this writing, known as the Ankrum homestead. This deserted house is located among the buildings and on the farm owned during much of my life by Ben and Lib Herr. Years earlier it was the home of Archibald Ankrum then later the residence of Dr. Jimmy Ankrum, a doctor during the Civil War. This old house, with a beehive oven close by and once a beehive of activity within its walls, is now deemed unsafe to enter. The Ankrum name, once very prevalent in this area and particularly at Chestnut Level Presbyterian Church still persists, locally but not nearly as great in numbers as when I was young. Walking through Chestnut Level Cemetery one views this once abundant local common name etched in the granite stones of years past.

A short distance from the Ankrum homestead you will again cross the vast, mighty waters of Fishing Creek and one of Drumore's largest and highest bridges, approximately 4 car lengths long. You will need neither cash nor Ezpass to cross this span, as tolls have not yet gained acceptance on our asphalt cow paths and creek crossings. Upon descending from the clouds, "on a foggy morning," from this locally designed and constructed architectural concrete wonder; take the first road, unpaved, to the right to continue your journey. This highway is presently known as Fishing Creek Hollow Road. This 2-century earlier, well-traveled by-pass will once again take you along, across and in some cases through the waters of Fishing Creek. Wearing life jackets, at this writing remains optional for this excursion.

This unpaved road contains no guardrails, tollbooths, traffic lights or even a yellow painted line on its gravel center. But years ago it was the highway used by all folks transporting goods to and from Chestnut Level and the areas surrounding it, to and from the river port at Fishing Creek. It was the pathway of choice because on this turnpike you encountered no steep hills. During this thrice crossing of Fishing Creek in this remote area you may experience the same feeling as those from 2 centuries past. Further down this local autobahn you will encounter a fork in the road also heading north. This was the by-pass taken from Fishing Creek if you were headed in the general direction of Liberty Square. Later, when roads were paved and climbing hills became much easier with rubber tires turned by internal combustion engines instead of wooden steel rimmed wheels powered by steel rimmed hooves the large steep hill at the former Cutler homestead became and remains the popular way in and out of Fishing Creek to the north.

Fern Glen home, store and Post Office.
Residence of Thomas B. Hambleton, destroyed by fire in 1903.

Taking the aforementioned fork of Fishing Creek road and turning north on Fern Glen Road toward Liberty Square, there was once located another store and Post Office named Fern Glen. This was the home of Thomas Hambleton and his wife Elizabeth Lamborn Hambleton. Open only for 13 years, it was established in 1890 and discontinued in 1903 when it burnt to the ground. It was located at the corner of Fern Glen and Park Drive. Thomas Hambleton taught school in the 1850s, and then enlisted as a volunteer in the Civil War in 1861. He later resumed teaching, became a farmer, general storekeeper and the only postmaster to serve here. Only the foundation remains today and is partially visible during the dead of winter. At this writing it has a real estate sign indicating a lot for sale. The locals including the blacks that lived along the hollow road regularly used this store and post office. The remembrance and story of these black folks of Fishing Creek Hollow continues within my next chapter.

Well, my friend, this concludes our pilgrimage through this tiny, sacred section of downtown Drumore. I hope you can appreciate the character of this still rural area and the lives of those folks, who lived, loved and expired within these rolling river hills. My own personal wish is to "Kick the Bucket" in the same locality where during an abundant life I filled, spilled, refilled and carried it. I hope you didn't experience any ill affects of motion sickness proceeding down our turning, twisting, rural roads at speeds upwards to 10 miles an hour. Thank-you for accompanying me on this pleasant jaunt along Fishing Creek, perhaps we shall one day joyfully meet again in your world or along this ancient forest and stream that is mine. Oh and yes, you were correct when you first entered my old truck, that is a black snake under your seat and not a hydraulic hose. It lives there!

The Blacks Of Fishing Creek Hollow

In 1760 William Ritchie deeded the grounds on which the present Chestnut Level Church building stands to the trustees of this Presbyterian Church with a stipulation that a gallery be provided in the church for his slaves. In the first and second census in 1790 and 1800, Drumore Township had more slaves than any other municipality or Township in Lancaster County including 76 in 1790 and 57 in 1800. After 1800 slavery greatly diminished.

The last slave holders in Drumore Township were Dr. Long, who had a female slave, Judy Rodney. Colonel Long owned James Rodney. The Morrisons had a female slave, Sall Whipper. Colonel Sam Morrison's slave, Ebenezer Jackson, was freed by law at 23 years of age. William Ankrim, father of Martin Ankrim, had a slave purchased at his father's sale. Dr. James Ankrim owned a female slave, Mint. Elijah Mackintyre held many slaves. The last living slave in Drumore was owned by the afore mentioned William Ritchie. Her name was Phillis Bush. She was described in the 1872 history of Lancaster County as a light-colored mustee, with straight hair, and long known as "Aunt Phillis." Her husband was Ceasar Augustus. At her death involuntary servitude ceased. Many of the slaves were buried in a colored graveyard on the ridge east of Chestnut Level Church, on the Rogers farm.

It is possible some of these last blacks of Fishing Creek Hollow of which I shall now write and recall are direct descendants of these local former slaves. Perhaps they remained in this area following their northward trek to freedom. Their origin and reason for settling in this area remains pure speculation on my part.

In reading this documentary of the Blacks of Fishing Creek Hollow, keep in mind that I live only 15 minutes from the Mason Dixon line. There were evidently a few pacifist Quakers south of the border who participated in the Underground Railroad delivering blacks across the Susquehanna into Southern Lancaster County. There were numerous stations as they flocked to this area, one being at the Joseph Smith farm, later Sinclairs. This farm is located less than one-half mile from where I live.

But there were also folks who later migrated to this area from the South before, during and following the depression that carried their prejudices along with their entire belongings into this area. In my lifetime, I never observed blacks being physically mistreated. But most were treated as second-class citizens is my observation.

My great-great-grandfather, Rev. Lindley Rutter, Minister at Chestnut Level Presbyterian Church from 1835 to 1875, was supposedly one of the few in this area, other than the Quakers, to speak out both publicly and privately against slavery within his congregation and outside it. This causes me to believe there were white folks living in this area before, during and following the Civil War who also harbored their own prejudices long before those arriving from the south. Some older folks have stated to me that they didn't hate or even dislike the blacks but just considered them different from us.

The Blacks that worked locally ate in the white family's homes but in a separate room. Rosie Carrigan Dommell told me that at mealtime her mother always put a clean tablecloth on the kitchen table where the blacks ate separately. All enjoyed the same food as the white family that ate in the dining room. A few older ladies stated that most blacks would have been very uncomfortable seated with the white folks and seemed to prefer eating separately as was the custom.

As a youngster I listened to stories told by a few old, long since deceased men ripe with bias, bigotry and preconceived notions that all black men were lazy and the women worse. Prejudice dies a slow death, as those who carried this torch to their grave relinquished it to offspring that accepted it armed with a clenched fist. Prejudice can eventually be killed but sometimes it takes a long time for it to die.

Having written the stories of a few local blacks of a century earlier and observed the race riots of the 1960s, who would have thought racial hatred would no longer be in season or politically correct in my lifetime. I believe this is what has happened, as the vast majority of folks are ashamed and unwilling to carry the torch of racial hatred any longer. Now with a black man as President of the United States I certainly have witnessed these feelings of years past almost completely disappear in this area. Discrimination in most folks I observe today is dawdling to decay.

During a short conversation with an over 80 white lady in an elevator at the Quarryville Presbyterian Home, she shared the following with me before the last Presidential election. When asked by her which candidate I was supporting I stated I hadn't made up my mind who I was voting for. "How about you," I countered. Her immediate response was, "I think it's our time to ride in the back of the bus."

James Sinclair and his wife, Mary, lived on a farm in York County at the beginning of the 20th century owned by an attorney named Bair. He was related to Dr. Bair of Quarryville fame. During this era their large frame farmhouse burnt completely to the ground. The only thing remaining the following day, according to stories, was an enclosed space full of potatoes stored in a large bin in the cellar. Neighbors that helped during the fire came the next day and were evidently given bushels of already baked potatoes.

The Sinclairs heard through a lime salesman named Taylor of a farm for sale on the Lancaster County side of the river between Liberty Square and Fishing Creek. They eventually bought it for $6500.00 in 1906. They arrived with a few farm items, their livestock, a few personal items and 2 sons, named Carl and Paul. The other children later born to them on this farm were Luther, Joe, Bob, Ruth and Ellen.

There were black folks living in Fishing Creek hollow at this time and Jim Sinclair persuaded Jim Milburn and a couple other blacks to help him move what few items he had left and his livestock. They drove the animals to McCalls Ferry, where they floated them across the Susquehanna. Then they coaxed the livestock south on unpaved roads to their new home. While Joe, one of James and Mary's sons, was relating all this to me, I couldn't comprehend driving frightened, stubborn livestock onto a ferry, then along rural roads in unfamiliar areas. He stated at this point in time this was commonplace and was the normal mode of transferring them from one place to another. Mart Eshleman, another Fishing Creek neighbor a couple years older than Joe, had told the story of driving cattle from the Buck to Lancaster Stockyards. He laughed as he related how as the small herd approached, all the old women in Willow Street came flying and frowning out their front doors with brooms to keep the cattle off their yards. This must be a female thing as my mother, when our cows got out, always helped round them up with broom in hand.

Joe, my friend and neighbor for 67 years, relates much of the following information on the blacks of Fishing Creek. He eventually purchased the home farm of his parents and continues to own it as this is written. He and his wife, Betty, raised a family of 7 children of their own at this place and Joe is 88 years young.

James R. Milburn lived in a little stone house along Fern Glen road that also contained a barn and 2 or 3 acres. He also at one time owned land at the corner of Fern Glen and Park Road that once was the site of Fern Glen store and Post Office. It had burned very early in the 20th century and was never rebuilt. James R. is remembered as a kind and nice old man. His wife, Mary, died young leaving 5 small children. Joe stated convincingly that James R. and Joe's father were as close as brothers. Every April 1st Milburn got one of the Sinclairs to take him to the Farmers Bank in Quarryville to get his interest money. When younger he worked with dynamite at the slate quarries at Peach Bottom. Joe, with lots of fond memories of James R., stated that he and his dad would walk down the hollow and visit him on Sundays. He helped the Sinclairs cut and husk corn, haul manure, cut and split wood and many other jobs around the farm, including repairing fences.

Joe also recalls, as a boy, that a large flint stone was located in one of their fields that obstructed the tilling of this area. Following Joe's dad's request James R. came and dug all the dirt away surrounding this giant flint. He placed a couple sticks of dynamite under it, lit the fuse and ran away as fast as He could travel. **KA BOOM**, out rolled the stone. They then poured 5 or 6 cans of cold water on it and began beating it with sledgehammers. It soon was reduced, according to Joe, into a thousand pieces. He again stated emphatically: "It was a big stone."

Milburn had a large garden that he shared with the Sinclairs. Joe said, "He would bring vegetables and fruit to my Mom." When Joe was a small boy some 80 years ago James R. brought and planted a rose bush that still grows and blooms along the walk leading to the Sinclair home. Every summer Joe and his dad would help Milburn with his hay. James R. occasionally butchered an old cow or hog. Most all the other black folks, especially the Wilsons, got very friendly with Misser Milburn on butchering day.

Years later one of James R.'s sons lived along the road from Tom Ankrum's lane to Mike Murphy's present house. One sad day this son shot and killed his wife and then himself in front of their 5 children. Supposedly, a few hours earlier as Tom Ankrum returned from delivering his milk and passed by, Milburn told him of his intentions but Ankrum dismissed it.

George Milburn, another descendant of James R., was nicknamed Monk while others referred to him as Pinhead. His wife was Mercy, who chewed Red Man tobacco that she kept in her stocking near the top. Neighbors in describing the family of Monk and Mercy stated there were his kids, her kids, their kids and someone else's kids. They had twin sons named Amos and Andy, who would dance if the white boys would throw them pennies. Due to the diet deficiency of the boys or their mother, one boy had teeth by school age, one didn't. I'm not sure if Red Man and or cheap wine played a part in their child's lack of dental development. I've been told the one with the teeth would chew on a piece of tough meat then hand it to his toothless brother. The twins were often caught stealing food from their classmates' lunch boxes their first couple of years at Mt. Holly School. Joe Sinclair would recall years later, the poor little devils were starving. The locals would say they never knew of any black folks who starved to death but they were not sure of what all they ate to survive. One family supposedly lived over the 3 winter months on mostly potatoes.

Monk and Mercy had rain barrels to catch their water and walked daily to get drinking water on a well-worn, up-and-down, half-mile path to Fishing Creek. It was said they would eat whatever wouldn't eat them. Wild game that wasn't always available was preferred, including possum, coon, squirrel, rabbit, and groundhog. It was said that nothing on 4 legs was observed in the hollow for years after the blacks departed. Mrs. Sinclair saved her frying grease for them, and when the local farmers butchered Monk would gladly take whatever parts of the animal carcass that were left over: ears, tails, feet etc. One day 2 of these half brothers belonging to Monk's family, one being Clyde Tigert, had a dispute and one chased the other to the home of Horace and Jim Long's farm, now Mart Eshleman's. The one doing the chasing carried a loaded gun that was discharged during the pursuit. Evidently nobody was shot and the Longs resolved the difference of opinion between the 2 young black men.

Gilbert Milburn, grandson of James R., was born in Marietta and raised by his grandmother. He later came to Lancaster City and got heavily into alcohol and became a street person. When winter and cold weather approached he would commit some minor infraction that usually began by throwing a rock through the window of a business or someone's home. Most times these violations never escalated beyond these damages, and almost always coincided with the severity of the winter and the predicted future forecast. These offenses landed Gilbert in jail regularly during the bitter cold months and provided him with hot, regular meals and welcome heat.

In the spring of the year, Gilbert would head down Fishing Creek way to hang out with relatives and folks he knew. He would stop at a couple local farms, and whatever work he did provided him with money for cigarettes and cheap wine. He could work when motivated and in the mood is how the farmers described Gilbert, but he was not dependable and never returned until his booze was exhausted. Gilbert would walk the roads looking for cigarette or cigar butts. The Sinclairs allowed him to sleep in the very barn that many years earlier had been a stop on the Underground Railroad, having been owned by Joseph Smith, a pacifist Quaker known as, "The Slave Turner."

One spring during a nasty, cold, rainy spell the old original house in the meadow on the farm at Sinclairs became vacant so they allowed Gilbert to stay there for a short spell. He stayed 20 years and the Sinclair women would provide leftover food for him. They would glance down over the meadow hill daily during the winter checking for smoke rising from his old chimney. This indicated he was alive and well. During the summer, he could occasionally be seen puttering around and would walk up the hill to ask for a handout. One day, years later, when no sign of Gilbert was seen and with no smoke rising from his chimney, Joe's son Ed was sent to check on him. Ed returned stating, "I think Gilbert is dead." Another neighbor, Raymond Smoker, an Amish man with English ways, was dispatched to verify this death. Upon arrival, Smoker stuck a hatpin into Gilbert's body at various locations and officially pronounced him D O A, Death Overseen by an Amish man. The Sinclairs summoned the local undertaker.

Gilbert is remembered by the locals as never causing any trouble, a good worker and when intoxicated he would go home and sleep it off. He also was a great reader and speller. His funeral was held at Ivan Dewalds in Quarryville. There were only a few relatives and a couple of neighbors in attendance. At the close of the service, Ivan the undertaker asked if any present would care to view one last time. Dewald later told me that Mart Eshleman, seated near the rear, was heard to say, "No thanks, we've seen enough of him."

Remnants of last home of the black folks in Fishing Creek Hollow.

Leon Harris, another black man, lived where Fern Glen and Fishing Creek Road meet. These 2 roads that remain gravel today would have been located at the intersection of the black community deep within Fishing Creek Hollow. There was a graveyard supposedly located on this Harris property, but no one today can pinpoint the location. The African School, identified on old Drumore Township maps, was located at this intersection beside the Harris residence. I'm not sure how long this school for black children only was open or exactly when it closed. There is a record of several black children attending the local one-room Mt. Holly School for the community in approximately 1920. This school remains standing today at the entrance to Susquehannock State Park and has been renovated into a dwelling.

Black folks would visit Harris over the summer and buy eggs and chickens from the Sinclairs. These folks, presumed from Philadelphia, drove big cars and dressed much better than the white locals. Harris worked at the Bainbridge Naval Training Center before and during World War II. A woman named Mamie, a mulatto referred to as a high yellow, lived with him but none could confirm if she was his wife, a relative or just an acquaintance. They had a herd of goats that lived periodically in the neighbor's fields. This caused much neighborhood contention, particularly with Wade Phillips, who lived and farmed nearby. This place is now referred to as the back place of Gibson's and is now owned and the home of Doug and Gail Gibson.

The goats would eat and climb the steep hill behind their Harris headquarters, eventually entering Phillips's fields. This regular occurrence always prompted uncomplimentary remarks hurled by Wade at the goats before his gunfire, but the 2 always happened in unbroken succession. Leon was known to lose a goat or two and a few returned home partially disabled. This over-the-hill gunfire alerted Leon's woman Mamie, wearing men's work shoes and carrying a big stick, to the straying of the goats and she would locate and then herd them home down their dirt road.

When Leon Harris got a pack of cigarettes he always emptied the smokes into a dark green jar with a lid that he hid on a shelf. He put the empty pack in his shirt pocket that he pulled out to show the Wilson boys, who he referred to as "ol thing a mees" when they stopped to bum a cigarette. "Just smoked my last one," was his regretful reply to the cigarette inquiry. I wonder if the Wilsons ever questioned why he always kept the empty pack? Harris was also known to have a bucket seated beside him in his automobile to regularly spit into. Not sure how often it was emptied, but his passengers supposedly kept their distance from the bucket and upwind from the driver. Following a couple fender benders, Leon seemed relieved his bucket, although upset, was not dinged similar to his car. Later, Joe Sinclair delivered Leon's mail. Taking a cue from the Wilsons, Leon always tried to bum a cigarette from the mailman. "Just smoked my last one," was Joe's regretful reply, displaying an empty pack.

The Harris house was full of all kinds of things imaginable and tons of old newspapers. Their house got so full Leon started to build a log cabin because he could no longer enter his, but he died before it was completed. They killed and ate anything on 4 legs until most went completely extinct. He drove a Ford car and had a still for making home brew that he sold. Following his death, it was discovered that his still was located under his front porch. The still had a copper wash boiler located beside it which led local folks to ponder how much copper was in the home brew of Leon Harris.

Walt Waters also lived in the old stone house, now gone, at the lower end of Joe Sinclair's meadow that was probably one of the oldest houses in the area. Waters had 2 wood stoves and a big fireplace in the downstairs and kept it hot! Waters worked for Harry Carrigan and did most of Carrigan's farming for a few years when Carrigan had a hardware store in Quarryville. Joe Sinclair's 2 older brothers took their dad's Overland car and Walt Waters to get a motorcycle he had purchased in York County. They took with them a rope 15 to 20 feet in length to pull the cycle that wasn't running at the time home. Walt steered, while seated on the 2-wheeled machine. The young mischievous Sinclair boys soon realized part way home that if they took the corners and turns on the highway a little sharper, it was similar to a line of skaters cracking the whip with the one on the very end, the motorcycle, nearly passing the Overland auto that was towing it. The fact that Waters was hollering and cussing simultaneously only added to the situation as the Sinclairs looked ahead for the next curve in the road coaxing them to turn into it sharply and the nervous Waters to lean hard. Although the engine wasn't running, Walt later confided that was the wildest ride he ever took on that machine.

A few years later Walt Waters had sent another local, young black man, Clyde Tigert, nicknamed "Tiger" who was a member of Monk and Mercy's extended family, to transport Walt's daughter home from Lancaster to Fishing Creek. Tiger supposedly during the trip south made some advances to the daughter that may or may not have been welcomed. Although not a golfer, this Tiger evidently possessed a few of the characteristics of our present 21st century Tiger. When these 2 young folks finally returned and Waters learned of this liaison things turned ugly.

Walt Waters got his gun and a handful of slugs and headed down the hollow in search of Clyde Tigert. He caught a glimpse of him and-full of rage-hurriedly left a couple bullets fly as Tiger raced toward the river. Waters kept up the pursuit and saw Tiger, gasping for breath, on the railroad tracks. This time Walt took his time to aim, and if Clyde had assumed Waters was simply trying to scare him he soon dismissed that thought as this next well-intended bullet was not quite true but still removed half his ear. The ear of the Tiger. Another shot fired in haste left Waters out of ammunition and bleeding Tiger setting a Fishing Creek land speed record down the railroad tracks. Waters evidently was the proprietor of a temper that was not short-lived as he then walked the 4 or 5 miles to Dick Henry's Chestnut Level store for more ammo, which he got. During all this turmoil and volley of shots, someone locally called the cops, who located Waters heading down Brown's hill, now Weilers, to Fishing Creek with a loaded gun in hand and a pocketful of bullets. This particular story ends here, for now, as Walt Waters heads for jail.

Sometime later Waters fell out with a black neighbor, Orville Wilson. Waters was observed by white neighbors plowing for Harry Carrigan with a walking plow, pulled by 2 horses, and a supposedly loaded shot gun tied to the handle of the old plow. Walt's passion for solving any argument or dispute, regardless of its intensity, with a gun eventually caught up with him as he later went back to jail for killing someone. I do not know the particulars of this crime other than the other man involved was most assuredly dead. A few years after this incident, a nearby large land owner, Joe Cutler, somehow got Waters released from prison. He supposedly then worked for Cutler for several years, receiving no pay, and then was eventually freed from his service. Years later, Waters died in jail.

My great grandfather Gilbert Smith would journey down to the black settlement in Fishing Creek Hollow with horse and wagon bringing black men back to help with the farm work. This local farm work is how most of the black men earned a meager living and most all the local farmers in this area employed them seasonally. My grandfather Horace Smith also followed this routine but not to the extent of his father. Lack of money to pay them during the depression was the deterrent. One of the men my father remembers helping on our farm was Hugh Waters. He surely was a relative, possibly a brother of the infamous Walt. Pop remembers Hugh Waters later visiting our farm and recalls with pleasure his wide smile and his infectious laugh. All of these folks are now gone, and a few that requested are buried in the nearby North East corner of the Drumore Quaker Cemetery. The majority that died while living in Fishing Creek Hollow now find eternal rest at Mt. Sinai Cemetery located South West of Wakefield.

Orville and Lizzie Wilson, who was Jim Milburn's daughter, lived down a hollow halfway between Susquehannock Drive of today and the river area years past known as Fite's Eddy. This area today is located approximately one-half mile south of the Park entrance continuing south past the lane of Mart Eshleman's farm, then looking to the right down the deep valley. They probably purchased this house from the Cutlers who owned much of the ground around this place. Orville and Lizzie had 3 boys and 2 girls: Gerald, Jim, Henry, Mary and Pearl and a baby that died very young. The death of this child occurred when Joe Sinclair was in first grade at nearby Mt. Holly School. All the pupils attending this one room school walked the mile down the hollow to view this deceased child, who was in a small wooden box placed on a table. Joe relates and recalls this somber event that made a great impression on all the school children as if it happened yesterday.

Mt. Holly School 1928–top row, L to R, Earl Campbell, Eugene Carrigan, Evans Ankrum, unknown. Second row, L to R, Alice Schofield, Violet Smith, Henry Wilson, Celia Glasgow, Vaux Campbell, Paul Campbell, Becky Milburn, Milford Campbell. Third row, L to R, Hughes Smith, Alice DuBree, Joe Sinclair, Pearl Wilson, Louise Jackson, Ruth Cutler, Anna Jackson. Crawford Smith. Bottom row: L to R Lester Miles, Mary Wilson, Elizabeth Miles, Elmer Jackson and teacher Florella Duffy.

Joe Sinclair's father drove the first school bus in this area, an old converted bread truck pulled by 2 horses. He mostly hauled kids from down in Fishing Creek to Mt. Holly School. A few scholars recalled that he transported were Les Shoff, Alice DuBree, the Campbell kids, including Earl, Vaux, Paul and Mel, and Violet, Hughs and Crawford Smith, Elmer, Anna and Louise Jackson and Ruth Cutler. Sinclair was paid $60.00 a month, which at that time was considered good pay. The following year he was underbid by Elmer Dickson, another local farmer who hauled the students for $35.00 a month. Free enterprise was evidently already alive and well at this time.

Mt. Holly School–1926, first row, L to R, Eugene Carrigan, Milford Campbell, Luther Sinclair, Cecil Jackson, Hugh Smith, Vaux Campbell. Second row, L to R, Elmer Jackson, Henry Wilson, Mary or Pearl Wilson, Sarah or Gertrude Glascow, Elvina Glascow, Becky Milburn, Esther Cutler, Julie Cutler, Louise Jackson. Third row, L to R, Violet Smith, Oleta Jackson, Sarah Smith, Teacher, Miss Helen Harner, Crawford Smith, Alice DuBree.

Henry Wilson, one of Orville's sons, attended Mt. Holly School with Joe Sinclair. Hen, a little older than Joe, was full of mischief and very disruptive for the teacher, Florella Duffy. One day Henry Wilson did something to again provoke Florella, who removed the red-hot stove poker from the stove and held it above Hen's head, telling him to "shut up." Sinclair would later recall that the hot, fire-red poker made a memorable impression on Hen, and Joe stated, "scared me to death." Joe also stated Florella Duffy only taught 1 year at Mt. Holly, then left claiming she'd had enough.

Orville Wilson worked for local farmers and one winter made a deal with Joe's father. Orville would husk the Sinclair's corn for free if Sinclair would give Wilson the fodder. Following the completion of the agreement and the corn all husked, Sinclair hauled the discarded fodder down to Orville. When he returned he stated, "There was an awful lot of corn ears remaining in Mr. Wilson's fodder when unloaded." Mr. Sinclair, although disgusted, stated, "Mr. Wilson's livestock looked pleased."

Orville had an old car with a rumble seat in the rear. Joe hired Wilson to set some fence posts around his meadow one fall. Weeks later, when Orville came for his money, Joe noticed several 12-inch blocks of wood in the rear of Wilson's car. Orville evidently soon realized when digging postholes by hand that if he cut a foot from the end of the post, the hole dug wouldn't need to be nearly as deep and no one would realize the difference. This was translated into much less digging and free wood to burn for Wilson and for Sinclair a fence that was leaning by spring.

Orville through means unknown always had an automobile. The one Joe Sinclair recalls was a "Star" and for some reason, perhaps only known to Orville, it always stalled on the steep grade beside Joe's house. Orville bragged his auto was "self-enclosed" and contained a "self-commencer" which translated meant it had a roof and a starter. With the stalled vehicle sitting dangerously halfway up the hill and in the middle of the road, Orville would race into Sinclairs asking for some gas. Joe later assumed the car hadn't stalled at all, but gave Orville an excuse to get a little free gas. During one of these episodes, with Orville under the hood, evidently a few of the movable parts that regulated different functions of the motor began moving as Wilson was cautiously pouring gas into a gas line around a hot motor. He could be heard hollerin' to his wife seated inside, "Lizzie, keep ya dam fingas off them levers."

It evidently took very little to get Orville Wilson worked up, which was known by all the locals, black and white. If the local boys wanted a little excitement on a Sunday afternoon, they would think up something to get Orville going. One favorite prank was to walk down to Wilson's house, find a good hiding place and then throw a stone onto his tin roof that when it landed and rolled across his roof sounded like gunfire. Joe Sinclair said, "It brought folks young and old running out through doors and jumpin' out windows like an aroused, stirred-up nest of bumblebees." I've not been able to verify Joe's participation in this Sunday ceremony, but he seemed to describe it in great detail for one who never observed it. When asked directly, he stated it was probably gangs from Fishing Creek or Liberty Square that were involved in this particular devilment.

Hen Wilson sold the "Grit" newspaper and walked for miles in this rural area delivering it every Saturday. Joe as a young lad occasionally walked with Hen on his paper route. Joe thought Hen might have received $1.00 a week and periodically a prize depending on his sales. He looked forward to the prize, which was some sort of knick-knack. Joe thought Hen's wages per mile were mighty slim. Later Hen acquired an old wreck of a car and graduated from walking to driving and delivering his paper. Even though Wilson now had to buy gas for his machine, he still had earnings left. I suppose this newfound wealth eventually went to Hen's head, as it does many times to others. He continued purchasing gas for his automobile but also alcohol for himself, evidently unable to handle the pressures of prosperity. A short time later, he drove through a neighbor's fence and demolished his car on his paper route. Having hit the fence and the trifecta of drinking, driving while delivering the "Grit," Hen joined the noble ranks of the unemployed. True "Grit" always comes with a price. Many years later Henry Wilson died in jail. There were insinuations he committed suicide.

Hen's sisters, Mary and Pearl, stayed home when their dad had a little money. When the money was all, one or both would hitch a ride on the mail truck on its delivery to and from Post Offices at Holtwood, Peach Bottom and Drumore-located in Fishing Creek. I believe Rex Cully originally drove this mail truck and, following his death, his wife, Esta, took over. Later this mail route, referred to as the Star route, was taken over by Dick Lefever, who drove the morning route and his wife, Doris, Rex Cully's daughter, who drove in the evening. Mary and Pearl eventually moved from this area. The Lefevers didn't recall exactly how their transport of a couple black passengers, known to be illegal, got started but it continued regularly during their time carrying the mail in the 40s and 50s. These passengers, mostly the Wilsons, would be standing along the mail route leading to Fishing Creek and near their home. They would be dressed to the hilt, as if going to a wedding or funeral, then ride to Quarryville, the final stop on this long ago mail route. Later they rode the regular bus going from Quarryville to Lancaster.

Jim Wilson last black man to live in this area. 1910-1992.

Jim Wilson lived in the same area as his parents, Orville and Lizzie, although he was a little closer to Susquehannock Drive and civilization. Not far from Mart Eshleman's driveway he lived partway down the hollow on the opposite side of the road from Mart. I believe this ground of Jim's in now owned by Ron and Sib Eshleman Crawford. Years ago Mart gave and transported an old hog pen from the DuBree place to Jim's lot that Wilson resurrected into his house. Mart Eshleman, who acquired it when he bought the DuBree farm in the early 1950s, owned this small wooded lot. Wilson's rent paid to Mart was $5.00 a month. He always had his home full of all kinds of stuff, from guns to watches and trinkets, that left very limited space for Jim. Wilson had more than a couple cars during his lifetime but never a driver's license. When younger, Jim worked on the railroad; later he would earn a little money working on local farms. Occasionally he would hop a southbound freight train at Fishing Creek and ride it down to Cokesbury, Maryland, a black community at the southern tip of Port Deposit, near MT. Ararat Farm, where he was acquainted. He was made to feel welcome with cheap wine, gambling at cards and by a few of the local ladies. I'm not sure if Jim was as welcome as the cash in his pocket so I'll just say a good time was had by all and what happened in Cokesbury stayed in Cokesburry.

One time during these occasional excursions to Wilson's local Las Vegas, he hopped on the moving train between cars, as usual, at Fishing Creek. Somehow his foot got caught in the coupling between train cars where they hooked together. Trying desperately to free himself and screaming in pain he continued this fateful ride as an intricate, unwilling participant on their joined-at the-foot journey down the tracks. Jim later recalled that although he screamed for help as he passed through every tiny town the train whistle muffled his frantic cries; his desperate arm waving to folks was evidently misinterpreted, as all waved back. Somewhere within Port Deposit he somehow freed himself from the steel captivity that miraculously released its hostage. I'm not sure if medical assistance was rendered or if the wine, gambling and ladies welcomed him as usual with all of his anatomy obviously still intact. Joe Sinclair saw him weeks later and observed an awful looking foot.

One winter following a snowstorm, Jim walked to Sinclairs. Later, Joe's son, Ed, offered to take Wilson home on their mid-size farm tractor. Somewhere along the snowy way, Jim fell off the 1490 Case and was run over by the big back wheel of the machine, leaving Wilson lying prone beside the tractor. Ed came running home frantically out of breath hollering, "I've killed Jim Wilson, I've killed Jim Wilson." Finally, when Joe got Ed calmed down, they returned to the tragic accident that revealed Jim Wilson standing beside the tractor smiling, smokin' a cigarette. Evidently the snowdrift that had caused Jim to be thrown from the tractor cushioned his body as the heavy large tire rolled over him. Wilson, although he had the wind knocked out of him, was now fine. Ed probably lost more oxygen than Jim, and to this day shakes his head when relating this snowdrift anecdote.

Mart Eshleman lived closer to Jim Wilson than anyone and may have done more for him than any other neighbor. Despite Mart continually teasing him, as Mart did everyone he liked, Jim Wilson had great respect for both Mart and his wife, Nina. Locals would comment on Mart's torment of Wilson as good-natured fun that Wilson expected and most times enjoyed. Mart was probably Jim Wilson's closest friend and ally through good times and bad. Wilson overlooked Mart's teasing because Mart overlooked Wilson when he appeared at the Eshleman home incapacitated within the clutches of a drunken stupor. Wilson worked part time for Mart and always had a friendly, kind word for Nina, who was from the South and the old school of farmer's wives. Although they raised 7 children, Nina always had a large, well-tended garden that she referred to as her truck patch. She was always cooking and baking, helped with the dairy and was sole proprietor of a hen house that provided an unending endowment of fresh eggs. Knowing Nina, I'm sure she regularly gave Wilson food that evidently caused Mart to believe Jim was more indebted to him than vice-versa.

Around midnight sometime later, Jim's chimney caught afire. Having no phone, he raced the half-mile to Marts and franticly pounded on his doors and windows.

> Sound asleep in his bed, Mart heard all the clatter
> He raised up his window, to see what was the matter
> He peered through the darkness, and light that was dim
> Revealing a Wilson, that sounded like Jim
> Breathless Jim between gasps, voiced chaotic concern
> But as Mart shut the window, He said, "Let her burn."

Irritated, grumbling to himself uncomplimentary words directed toward the vision of the countenance he just observed inside a closed window, Wilson headed for Sinclairs. With the view over his shoulder of flames shooting into the black of night, he arrived and roused Joe from slumber. Joe's wife, Betty, immediately called the fire engine. Evidently Mart couldn't get back to sleep and, feeling guilty, also summoned the engine because till charred, exhausted Jim Wilson returned home the fire company had extinguished his flames. Jim later purchased a small trailer to replace his ruined home.

If Jim needed to go somewhere for supplies, good-natured Mart would haul him if Mart wasn't busy. I have seen this scenario play out many times during my lifetime: Jim returns to Mart's vehicle with whatever he needed in hand as dozing Mart starts his car. Just as Jim reaches for the door, Mart pulls ahead a couple of feet. Depending on the number of onlookers, Mart would continue this until Jim would get mad. At one incident at Liberty Square Store, with a laughing audience seated on the porch, Jim was climbing the knoll beside the store, part way home, before Mart allowed him to enter his vehicle. I always wished I could have overheard the conversation between Mart and Jim inside the car after Jim was seated and doors were closed. Perhaps not!

The story is told of Mart's wife, Nina giving Jim Wilson a full flat of day-old eggs. As Wilson walks out Eshleman's long lane smiling with pride, he encounters Mart on his tractor plowing. Jim stops Mart along the lane for some neighborly conversation and rests the flat of eggs on the back tire of Mart's motionless tractor. After a while, Mart evidently thinks this chitchat has continued about long enough, but Wilson doesn't concur and won't leave. Mart simply puts the tractor in gear and drives away, which startles Wilson and breaks most of the eggs. I'm told Jim fired the remaining unbroken eggs at Mart as he plowed off. I'm also told Mart never looked back to check the depth of the plow until he was well out of egg range and the rain of double yokers that splattered Mart and his tractor. Knowing Mart, I'm sure he was laughing.

Years ago Reber Testerman drove the large Township loader with a V-plow on the front to open our snowfilled country roads. On a pass opening deep, drifted roads down Fern Glen Road near John Gibson's lane, he spotted a piece of black plastic as he approached an extra deep drift. The normal thing to do when encountering this mountain of snow is to pull back the throttle, increasing the speed of the powerful 4-wheel drive machine to break through nature's roadblock dead ahead. Opening snow-filled Drumore roads is not for the timid or faint hearted. As Reber headed full steam ahead through blowing snow, the approached black form slowly moved. Reber stopped his powerful machine a few feet from the by-then thrashing figure and dismounted. He discovered it was none other than Jim Wilson lying in the snowdrift, evidently temporarily impaired by an overabundance of alcohol in his radiator. Reber radioed for the Township truck to come load up Jim and take him home. Testerman later recalled if the form in the snowdrift had been any color but black he most assuredly would have plowed him over.

Rick and Linda Powl always visited Jim Wilson following our Christmas Eve services at Church. This tradition began even before they were married and always involved a new shirt given to Jim. After a few years and the Powls not paying attention to the color of the shirt they once again handed him his Christmas gift. Jim's comment, given through a giggle, before opening his present was, "I's bets it's a shirt, I's hopes it ain't red again." It Was! As they left his 100-degree hothouse, Jim asked if they would bring a bottle next Christmas.

When next Christmas arrived, Rick and Linda remembered the past shirts, all red, they had given him and the bottle of whiskey he had requested. When Jim opened his Christmas gift revealing a green shirt Wilson exclaimed with disappointment, "Oh Ricky, I's don't look good in green." It was then that Jim spied the brown paper bag behind Rick's back. Rick later would confess, "I knew when I saw his eyes open to twice their normal size we had made a mistake." The Powls later turned to leave Jim and his clutter as he clutched the open bottle already sampled and providing him with liquid Christmas cheer. Rick said, "We knew we had started a tradition that had to be discontinued." It was.

Years ago, Wilson went to a dentist and had 2 gold teeth installed. Sometime later, he got into a fight and got hit with something that knocked them both out. I suppose his opponent in this free for all found one of Wilson's teeth and kept it. Jim had unknowingly swallowed the other that resurfaced the next day following breakfast. Sometime later it was re-installed and reappeared shinning within Jim's smile. He also lost a set of teeth much later in life somewhere in a local field. He searched for them for days but without success.

During Jim's last few years, he acquired an old John Deere putt-putt tractor that transported him everywhere while pulling a small rubber tired 2—wheel trailer that carried his necessary items. His green John Deere was observed at local grocery stores in Chestnut Level, The Buck and occasionally in Quarryville. The trip to Quarryville usually involved the acquisition of any liquid, other than anti-freeze, that contained alcohol. When driving his green machine, Wilson always kept both hands on the steering wheel and looked straight ahead.

Charlotte Boohar ran the Chestnut Level store for many years alone following the untimely death of her husband, Walt, at age 42 in the early 60s. If low on fuel this was the closest stop for Jim to get gas, although it was a few cents higher than at the Buck because of a larger volume sold there. When Wilson was asked by Charlotte, who had to leave the confines of her store, go outside in all kinds of weather to pump the gas, how many gallons he wished to purchase, he would always sheepishly reply, "Oh misses, I's just needs enough to gets me to The Buck where it's cheaper."

The speed at which he traveled was a little slower than a normal Amish horse and buggy. As far as is known he was never involved in an accident while driving his slow—moving John Deere. Years earlier most meadow fences in our area had a couple posts and several feet of wire regularly removed by vehicles owned or operated by Jim or his brother Hen. Evidently 50-60 years ago drinking and driving went together and was not frowned upon. Pop recalls seeing the Wilson boys gliding through Liberty Square at night when they had a vehicle. He said he could tell they were enjoying themselves as they passed by waving, smilin' and laughin' because they always had the dome light on inside their automobile.

Jim Wilson died September 16, 1992 at age 82. His obituary mentions 2 sisters, Mary and Pearl, and that he was a retired employee of the Pennsylvania Railroad. He also helped construct the Bainbridge Naval Base and the French Creek and Susquehannock State Parks and worked on local farms. Jim Wilson died peacefully in his sleep, in his bed, in his tiny cluttered home. It was reported his transistor radio was playing; he had some cash in his wallet and a drink beside his bed. In hearing of this I remember thinking, good for you, Jimmy Wilson, you left this world surrounded by the essentials of your life. Has any King or great man died with more? At the end of the day isn't this what most of us wish for, to die quietly in our own bed in our own home, encircled by that and those we love? Then following our death to be welcomed into our next life with open arms by the ones who loved us.

Mart Eshleman, who enjoyed tormenting Jim, spoke often of him during the twilight of Mart's life before his subsequent death in 2010. "Jim was what he was but he would never take anything from me that wasn't his. I think of him often and miss his presence. Although a black man he was considered one of us."

Black Bill Boynes and his wife also lived in the old stone house in Sinclair's meadow for some time. They were there during the depression in 1930 and Black Bill later worked for the W.P.A. government project under the F.D.R. administration. One day Black Bill was sitting on his porch as school was dismissed at near by Mt. Holly. One of the white boys, Dan Lynn, a close friend and schoolmate of Joe Sinclair, hollered a racial slur at Boynes as he passed by. Black Bill ran down the lane from his home, jumped the fence and supposedly was gaining on the boy as he raced home and locked the door behind him. I'm told that was the last racial slur to be hurled in Black Bill Boyne's direction. I suppose at this point in this story I should also mention that of all who had lived in the old original stone house owned by the Sinclairs in their meadow, none ever paid any rent to the owners.

The following story is taken from the booklet, "My childhood as the daughter of the Village Storekeeper," written by Velma Aument. Written nearly 30 years ago Velma, a family friend writes of her life early in the 20th century the following account that seemed appropriate to inhabit this chapter.

"Our school group was made up of village children, children from neighboring farms, children's aid children who were usually always a discipline problem because they were shifted from home to home and often made to work too hard, the sad little children from Mrs. Reese's home, and usually several black children. One big retarded black girl was one of my best friends.

Her name was Edith Boynes. She was 14 and I was 7 so our mentalities were about the same. She was big and strong and could do many things I couldn't do so we had lots of fun.

"One day Edith wanted me to go with her to her home. We walked quite a distance down a country lane to a very small house filled with little black children. The mother was expecting another baby. We played around a while and then Edith walked me halfway home. When the black baby was born they named her Velma for me.

"There is a sequel to this story. A long time afterward a black choir from Philadelphia came to sing at Little Britain Church. They really shook the rafters with their singing. There was a cute little black girl playing the piano and she made it jump. After it was over the people mingled with them to make them welcome. I talked to the girl who played the piano and she told me she had lived near here at one time. I asked her what her name was and she said, "Velma Boynes."

While I'm writing about the old house at Sinclairs I should also mention another Southern end character that I remember. Perry Drum, a white man lived alone in this same house for a couple of years. Evidently Perry spent much of his time drinking moonshine and walking the roads. This story also comes from Joe Sinclair, who swears of its content. Seems one fine day Perry Drum knocked on the door at the Sinclair farmhouse totally drunk. Joe's mother, who Joe described as being "Tuff" answered the door and shortly into this drunken, open door conversation, hit Perry with her fist, knocking him down. As she slammed the door, he was later seen staggering out the walk. Near the road Perry met Joe's brother, Luther, and related what had happened. Luther evidently thought his mother must have had a good reason to punch Perry so Luther also corked him for good measure. Joe related it was a long time later before we saw Perry Drum. He later moved to a fallin' down old house on the Bolton farm along Penny Road. During my lifetime, Perry walked the roads bundled up in July as he would in January. The old folks would claim his blood was 50 per cent alcohol. There were more than a few men living in this area similar to Perry Drum including a relative of mine, Ed Smith.

Another black family remembered is that of George Lincoln Elassis Glasgo and his wife Lena who lived in a leaning old log house with 2 bedrooms and one large room downstairs. At least 7 people lived there. There was a walled up little springhouse and they always had a garden. A few names remembered of their children were Celia, who attended school with Joe Sinclair, Sarah, Mose, and Jeff. Lena did house work and odd jobs for local farm owners wives. She came on Mondays and helped Joe's mother with the clothes washing. Joe remembers as a young lad turning the big wheel on the washer equipped with a handle. Lena also worked for Peg Long, and is fondly remembered by Peg's daughter, Betty.

George L. E. Glasgo was a man who took life easy. When he died, dozens of empty whiskey bottles were found in his cellar. He kept the old wood stove burning continuously in his house during cold weather and the inside was always hot. Joe remembers being sent by his mother along with his brother, Carl, to the Glasgo home to see if Lena could come and help their mom with a few chores. When Carl asked this question to the head of the household, Glasgo replied, "Mother goose is not at home but I will tell her she is needed when she gets back." It would seem George Glasgo's lot in life was to keep Lena busy. Harry Carrigan ran the boarding house at Rawlinsville Camp Meeting for a few years, and Lena Glasgo worked for him in the kitchen. Larry and Sherry Sinclair now live on the property where George Lincoln Elassis Glasgo and his wife Lena and family once lived. This property is located about halfway down Fern Glen Road on the left.

Ralph Murray lived for some time at the back place now referred to as Doug Gibson's. He also farmed some of the land located there, and Joe Sinclair remembers several of the neighbors helping him with his farm work when needed. Joe recalls being there with several neighbors one hot day and all of them going into the Murray home for lunch, except Ed DuBree, who remained outside seated under a tree. Ed would labor all day beside this black man, helping him whenever possible, but thought it inappropriate to eat with him in Murray's home.

Another black man, Bob Bones, worked for Kersey Bradley. He also did odd jobs associated with farming and lived in a room in Bradley's garage that contained a stove and a bed. Unlike others of this era, he ate all meals at the Bradley table with the family. He is remembered as a kind, gentle, agreeable older man. He was small framed and had gray hair.

Walt Batters, another black man worked for Billy Brown, who owned the farm that during my life was owned by the Weiler family. Brown also at one time owned the warehouse at Fishing Creek that jutted out into the river before the Conowingo Dam was built and flooded this area. Billy Brown is also remembered as the last man in this area to farm with oxen. I'm sure Walt Batters worked with these oxen many times. Batters lived in the old school house that was located across the road near Cecil Jackson's home. Walt Batters also enjoyed liquid refreshment and with friends would later drive on weekends across the Conowingo Dam then make an immediate left, down along the river to purchase his booze. When he asked Joe Sinclair to go along with them, and Joe refused, Batters stated, "You ought to go along Joe boy, you'll see all your Quarryville school friends." This was before Johnson's liquors opened much closer to the Pennsylvania border saving our Lancaster County residents thousands of gallons of gas and much wear and tear on their vehicles and horses today.

Most of the preceding folks attended the Rigby celebration, the Mount Sinai Union African Methodist Episcopal Church and are buried in this adjoining cemetery. The following is a brief history of these places.

Visiting black preachers were sent out from the First Independent Church of Negroes in Wilmington Delaware in 1832, one being Lewis P. Hood. This preacher visited homes in the Southwestern part of Fulton Township, Lancaster County, Pennsylvania and among those he visited was Jarrett Rigby. Religious meetings were held under the roof of his humble dwelling, which, according to an inscribed stone in the old Rigby house, was built in 1807. Jarrett Rigby in 1834 deeded a half-acre of his land to a Union Church of Africans and a meetinghouse was built here, later named Rigby's Meeting House.

Between 1834 and 1870 a yearly quarterly meeting was started, to be held always on the second Sunday of every August. Rigby quarterly meeting was the attraction for many people; large crowds gathered from many miles around including most everyone from the nearby Fishing Creek settlement. At one of the Rigby meeting mornings there were 55 members, 5 probationers, 30 Sunday school children and 50-day school scholars in attendance.

Following the death of Jarrett Rigby in 1870 Gilbert James, a trustee in the older Church, donated land for a new Church. Located at the corner of Cherry Hill and Rigby Road in Arcadia, Fulton Township this property was ½ mile away from Rigby's. Both Ruthie and I plan to accept an invitation from Janet Milburn Jones to attend Church services at this Church in the near future. She confided to me that the membership of this congregation has slowly dwindled to a handful of faithful folks. I think they should be commended for continuing this worship service and believe they deserve the support of this community. The faith of those of us fortunate enough to sit every Sunday at a crowded Church service surely wanes in comparison to these people.

Although the old Church was replaced by a new one, the Old Rigby Burying Grounds was still used until 1918, when the ground close to the newer Church had been purchased for burial purpose. Buried in the old cemetery are some of the charter members and their families of the original congregation. The oldest name carved on a slate was Ellen P. Milburn, who died in 1845 at the age of 84 years. There is also the tombstone of Jarrett Rigby's daughter, Sarah Rigby Milburn. She is remembered for her faithful work in the Mount Sinai Church, as she was the "founder" of that Church.

With the present Church being built at its new location, Rigby quarterly meeting drew even larger crowds. Arcadia was a stopping place for a Narrow Gauge train named the Lancaster Oxford and Southern Railroad, also called "Peachy" because it ran between Oxford and Peach Bottom. With extra coaches added on the day before and on Rigby Day, it brought many more folks that could not have attended otherwise. This continued for many years until 1919 when the train was discontinued. Older folks I have talked with, remember the large contingent of automobiles on Southern End roads to and from Rigby during the middle of this past century. An old farmer neighbor of mine always transported Jim Wilson to Rigby. Jim would caution this friend of his to make sure he arrived on Rigby day before dark to take him home. I suppose I will say that all who attended had a good time and what happened near the conclusion of Rigby Day remained at Rigby.

Rigby Quarterly Meeting, although it is still held on the same date as always, it is not as well attended as in former years, with always the hope that it can become the Meeting that it once was. Due to lack of employment in this area many black families have in years past moved elsewhere to secure their livelihood and a better life for their families.

My Mother recalls 75-80 years ago when the Arcadia area was abundant with black folks. Most worked locally with several employed by William P. King, owner of King's Cannery then later his son Edgar. The Kings built and lived in the present home of Dr. Mary Kirk, our local small animal veterinarian. The King's son Edgar was married to Ethel Shoemaker, my mom's aunt. Mom recalls the cannery and the black folks working for William P. and his wife. Names remembered are Boyer, Green, Johnson, Murrary, and at the King's residence Banks.

There remain a few black folks living in the general Arcadia area but Jim Wilson, the last of the black residents of Fishing Creek and our neighbor, died in 1992. All gone but hopefully not forgotten. Many of the Fishing Creek folks who passed during and before my lifetime find eternal rest in this present Mt. Sinai Cemetery. This tree encircled, sunny hillside, welcoming glorious streams of heavenly light has accepted many familiar names from the Fishing Creek area including Milburn, Boynes, Harris, Bones, Waters and Wilson over the past century. I also believe the tiny Cemetery along 272 South of Powls Feed to the East named Eldora also contains the earthly remains of a few Black Pilgrims. Blacks, who served in the Civil War, fought in subsequent Wars this past century and Black Marines from World War II lie side by side in this tiny graveyard that goes mostly unnoticed by those driving past. May they rest in Peace.

In writing of the Blacks in Fishing Creek Hollow I've mentioned the abuse of alcohol, the violence that occurred between them, the lack of motivation of some to work and other human and moral frailties. I wrote of these things told to me by Joe Sinclair who knew them well and remembered names and details of stories that would soon have been forgotten forever. There were a few others of his generation that supplied information documenting his truths. The total number of black folks residing at any one time in Fishing Creek Hollow is undocumented. However before the turn of the 20th century they had their own school in the center of their settlement referred to as African School on old Drumore maps. During that era the location of this school was referred to locally as Murphys Loop. This era of blacks in Fishing Creek lasted approximately 100 years from times following the Civil War to the death in 1992 of Jim Wilson, the last black man to remain in this area. There were many good qualities that obviously existed within the make-up of these folks that should have been written of and remembered in greater detail. Locating next of kin has been nearly impossible to add a black voice to this story. Hopefully someone will read this and come forward to offer a remembered voice to this forgotten history.

Unfortunately the recalled stories today dwell more on their misfortunes than their triumphs. This makes the old farmer wonder how we will be remembered and what stories will be told of us, 100 years from now. Anyone who assumes that what I have recorded concerning The Blacks of Fishing Creek Hollow of that era, in that place only applied to them is sadly mistaken. Every human experience they encountered, observed and shared also occurred within the local white community. The blacks may have been considered different but our similarities greatly out numbered our differences are a final thought of mine.

In reading of these folks the most important thing to remember is not what is written but what is not written. There is absolutely no inkling of anything done by these black folks in retribution or retaliation in any way, shape or form toward their white neighbors. There is not one act of violence, of stealing or harassment toward the white community remembered by those who lived here. If one act had occurred it would probably have been recalled more than any other. There wasn't.

Jim Wilson once told my father, seated with him on a bench inside Musser's store at the Buck that a man never becomes anything more than what's expected of him. Little was expected of the blacks that lived in Fishing Creek Hollow following the Civil War and ensuing years and sadly some delivered exactly what was anticipated and presumed. Thankfully times have changed.

Fishing Creek

The following historical account of Fishing Creek is from the writings of Robert Neuhauser. I am greatly indebted to him for granting me permission to include this piece in my publication. I hope all who read this appreciate his research and recollections of Fishing Creek.

General store at Fishing Creek more than a century ago.

To habituates of Southern Lancaster County, the name Fishing Creek evokes two memories. One is of the pristine mountain stream meandering down the Fishing Creek Valley, the trout stream of memories laced with its winding road that crosses the stream many times and dotted with trout pools under the forest canopy. For many years, rickety bridges that eventually gave way to paved river fords constructed by Drumore Township bridged this stream. The other memory is the Fishing Creek Marina and boat launching access point on the upper Conowingo Lake of the mighty Susquehanna River.

This history and "character" sketch is of the launching site and Marina that gave access to the Susquehanna Lake, the biggest Lake in the Susquehanna River system. This account takes in the valley between where Susquehannock Drive crosses Fishing Creek and the Susquehanna River.

There is very little habitation in this valley. What habitation and buildings it has is a remnant reminding us of its past role as a transportation center for this part of the region. This valley was of course a major avenue of travel for the Native Americans, who inhabited the region, particularly the islands below the Holtwood Dam site. Archeological evidence shows that these islands were inhabited nearly continuously for 5000 to 7000 years. These people were probably drawn there by the massive spawning runs of shad and other fish surging upstream to the entire Susquehanna river shed as well as its protection from winds and weather by the high cliffs on either side of the river. The shallows and narrow passageways in the river past these islands made life possible for the inhabitants during the annual runs of fish to their spawning grounds. Passage to the land on the East was difficult at most places, with precipitate 500 foot cliffs delineating the river from the "the river hills." Flat meandering valleys like the Fishing Creek Valley provide easy access to the East. It also provided easy access to the river for the settlers who pioneered homesteading in the Southern part of Lancaster County.

The river had been and still is a major transportation artery into the interior of the State. The Susquehanna and Tidewater canal in the mid 19th century provided transportation down the West side of the river. The many cascades and rapids precluded all but downstream raft travel for the early entrepreneurs of the State. The water level of the river at the Fishing Creek mouth was probably no more than 10 feet below its present level of 118 feet above sea level. The locks and canal remnants on the York County side are still above the present water level for a mile or so below the mouth of the Fishing Creek.

The Railroad, which abruptly ended the canal venture, now occupies the East side of the river, clinging to the cliffs an average of 10 to 20 feet above the water level. It originally passed the mouth of Fishing Creek about several feet below the present water level. The remnants of the original steel railroad bridge across the creek are still evident just to the North of the creek mouth, sticking a foot or two above the average lake level.

As was the custom, railway "stations" or stops for passengers, freight and mail were incorporated along the line, and Fishing Creek Station was one of the prominent ones along the East side of river because of its easy road access. Just West of the Susquehannock Drive crossing, there stands a combination grain and sawmill and miller's house. This activities demise probably came in the 1920s as a result of the introduction of electrical power and long travel distance from the farming communities to the East beyond the major hills. Going towards the river there were two residences half way to the river on the South side of the road, and until the 1970s the Drumore Store and Post Office also on the South side of the road dominated the end of the road. Just East of the store and bridge that crosses the creek, there was an old "mill building" as described by the locals, which may have served as a warehouse or an actual mill, making use of the 10 feet or so of the fall of the creek as it dropped to the original river level. This building has since been demolished. Surrounding the creek on the North are several summer cabins built in the 1930s, and to the South there are several cabins overlooking the river from the bluff above the Store and Post Office.

The construction of the Holtwood Dam in the early 1900s and the construction of the Conowingo Dam in the mid 1920s changed the character of "Fishing Creek" and its access to the river. Prior to that the river bottom consisted of a number of islands with meandering channels of water that dropped about 110 feet on their journey to the bay. The railroad was a very low-grade line, as it progressed from the bay to Holtwood area. Rising only in the neighborhood of 100 feet in 22 miles, or only 1 foot in a thousand feet, a 0.1% grade! So it's no wonder that in spite of many railroad lines being abandoned, this easy "pulling" line is still in active service. The advent of the dams did however necessitate the railroad being raised from its original grade to be able to summit the Holtwood Dam's approximately 60 feet barrier. This necessitated the major change at Fishing Creek, where a tall arched masonry tunnel rising approximately 30 feet above the present lake level supplanted the steel railroad bridge. The creek flows through this large tunnel and the lake laps at its feet.

This change made a big difference in the character of Fishing Creek, and made it a major destination for fishermen seeking to exploit the newly created 20 square mile lake and its fishing and boating opportunities. The family of Roy Smith, (a distant relative of this book's author) ran the General Store and Post Office in this big creek-side building and established a "Marina" where a person could launch and dock a boat along the creek, could rent a fishing boat, moor his own boat at an anchorage outside the tunnel in the river and get food, gasoline, fishing equipment and bait at the store. Mrs. Smith ran the Post Office and Store, Roy Smith ran the Marina operations and eventually provided fishing tours in the lake with his "Chesapeake Oyster Boat" powered by an auto engine. Smith's mentally challenged son, Crawford, was an expert and dependable presence who rowed boaters out to their moored boat or retrieving and re-moored fishermen's boats on their moorings, which usually consisted of a major auto engine part as anchor and a barrel or keg for a mooring float.

The Smith's ventures catered to families as well. There was an extensive penny candy counter in the General Store and Mrs. Smith dished out generous ice cream cones and supplied a wide variety of soft drinks in the ice-cooled cooler.

In the 1950s a flood in the creek washed away Roy Smith's treasured boat. He spent many days out on the river trying to find and salvage it to no avail. Soon after he died of a heart attack, which the neighbors attributed to the strain of his struggle to locate his lost boat.

First Post Office at Fishing Creek 1879. James Robert Milburn stands beside the ox team owned by William Brown. Names of the oxen were Buck and Berry. Milburn worked for Jim Sinclair for one dollar a day plus meals.

Mrs. Smith continued to operate the Store and Marina for many years but eventually sold the business to Merle Murphy, whose family operated and managed the place very efficiently and began to expand the Marina. Merle figured that if people could store their boats they would be much happier than having to transport them from their homes, back down the steep ramp, and launch their boats every time they wanted to go fishing or boating. There was a low swampy area near the railroad, which was not suited for a boathouse of the conventional sort, but Murphy had other ideas.

He built a boathouse whose floor was 8 or 10 feet above the water level. From the ceiling of the boathouse he suspended a big I beam of steel that projected over the creek to a pillar on the opposite hillside. On this I beam he mounted a moving trolley with an electric winch that rotated a pipe around which were wrapped 2 cables with hooks on their ends. Boats were stored in the boathouse in two rows on 3-wheeled wooden dollies.

When a boat was to be launched, it would be trundled under the winch on the beam, hooked up to the winch cables, hoisted off the dolly and then another electric winch would pull the hoisting winch and boat out over the creek. Then the hoisting winch would lower the boat into the water. It was anticipated that this would isolate the stored boats from floods in the creek. He also built a shop on the landside of the boathouse where he and his sons would do motor repair and sell boats, motors and accessories. It was becoming a bonafide Marina!

Murphy demonstrated ingenuity. He secured a barge, drove it up the river to the larger islands, salvaged downed trees, barged them back to the landing, took them to a sawmill and had them milled into the lumber that he used to build the boathouse. He properly reckoned on the boathouse design, which isolated the boats in the boathouse from most floodwater. When Hurricane Agnus dumped a record amount of water into the Susquehanna Valley in 1972, the water level in that part of the lake raised only about 6 feet above normal high water, and the boats in the boathouse were secure, while the boats in the river mooring survived the higher water for the most part.

The highest water in that part of the Conowingo Lake occurred in the spring of 1978. Several hundred miles of foot thick ice from both branches of Susquehanna cast loose and careened down the river. A huge ice dam built up on the shallower waters of the Conowingo Lake just North of the Peach Bottom Atomic Power Plant and backed up water that rose up over the floors of the boathouse. Most of the boats did not float off of the dollies, but a few smaller boats did float out of the boathouse and were lost in the ice jam, but there was no substantial damage to the Marina buildings or facilities

However, in the spring of 1958 there was a heavy late snowstorm with about 30 inches of wet snow that caved in the top of the boathouse and partially collapsed part of the boathouse floor. Neighbors and boaters formed a "barn raising party" and helped restore it to its original shape.

An additional boathouse was built to the East and equipped with the same boat handling facilities, and an improved parking lot and boat-launching system was installed, making the Marina more appealing and usable. It was very convenient to be able to call the Marina in the afternoon, ask for your boat to be launched and be able to come down from "town" after work, step into your boat and take off for an evening on the water.

In the 1960s as the Peach Bottom Atomic Power Plant was being constructed and the new high voltage transmission lines and towers were being built across the river, Murphy supplied marine and ferry services to the contractors. Before they left, the Power Company sent a dredging barge to the mouth of Fishing Creek and dredged a deep channel from the mouth of the creek to deeper water in the Lake, making a mound of soil to the South of the new channel. Before this, the channel was filling in and the boating channel had to be periodically changed and marked with guiding stakes pounded into the mud flat to guide boats into the creek and the Marina. At some of the "low water" times, the Lake was not accessible from the creek and boaters were stranded or had to get out and wade as they pulled their boats through the shallow channel. This deepening of the channel gave a new life and desirability to the Fishing Creek landing.

The Murphy's sold the Marina to Harry Fulmer in May of 1969. The Post Office moved to Liberty Square in 1970. Fulmer and his 2 sons operated the Marina for many years and added to the refinements and to motor and boat maintenance services.

Fishing Creek as a Marina came to a rapid end in July of 1984. A storm front stalled over Eastern Pennsylvania and a thunderstorm embedded in the front deluged the river hills. The Fishing Creek Valley rapidly filled up with water. The water came up over the top of the archway under the railroad and threatened to pass over the railroad itself. In the meanwhile, the boathouses collapsed as their underpinnings were washed away by debris coming down the creek. The boats were sent adrift and ground up as the current took them and parts of the boathouses and other storm debris through the archway. The observers said that the water came out of the archway like water out of a hose. Boathouse, boat parts and motors spewed out on to the river flats. The flood deposited a barrier in and across the channel, which effectively closed the creek to boat traffic. Fishing Creek no longer existed as a Marina. The end of a delightful era! The Railroad declined to offer an extended lease or to lease an enlarged area for a new and safer envisioned marina. This effectively closed the option to rehabilitate the Marina.

Ward Evans on left–Roy Smith on right.

Now for a bit of the flavor of the place and its personalities. The Mill property was acquired by lawyer William B. Arnold, who modified one of the smaller buildings into a summer residence where he entertained guests and such organizations as the Foot and Fiddle Square Dance Club and Sierra Club as well as in the Mill building itself.

The big stone residence was rented out each summer to Dr. Ward V. Evans. Ward was a native Southern Lancaster Countain and he and his family came back every summer to enjoy the Fishing Creek Valley. Ward had an inboard launch that he kept at the dock and took his guests, his dog Minnie and his friends out cruising on the river. Doc Evans reveled in playing the eccentric "river rat" dressing in shabby dungarees, a straw hat and his inevitable cigar. His boating buddies referred to him as "Warty" (from his name as Ward V). He was quite a distinguished resident as it turned out. He was the Chairman of the Chemistry Department of Loyola University and Northwestern University and a renowned expert on explosions. For some arcane reason, he was chosen in 1954 as a Judge on the three Judge panel for the hearing that was to decide if Robert Oppenheimer, the creator of the Atomic Bomb and Director of the Manhattan project, should be removed from his position on The Atomic Energy Commission on the basis of "unreliability." The selectors of the judging panel felt that they had chosen three "Hanging Judges," but in the final vote, the only dissenter was Doc Evans who said later that the decision to evict Oppenheimer, "Will be a black mark on the escutcheons of our country. To deny him clearance now for what he was cleared in 1947, when we must know that his is less of a security risk now than he was then seems hardly the procedure to be adopted in a free country."

Cecil Jackson was one of the permanent residents of the valley. He lived in one of the homes midway between the Mill and the river. He was employed by the Railroad for inspection and maintenance work and raised his family in the Fishing Creek Valley. He eventually built a small cabin between the Railroad and the river just South of the Marina.

Before the Atomic Power Plants at York County, Peach Bottom and Muddy Run pumped storage power plants were built there were virtually no residences or cabins along the river. Cruising the river at night, there were no lights on the horizon or the water except for the feeble light from the coal-oil lantern of an occasional shore-bound fisherman. Coming back to the Marina on a dark night was difficult because of a lack of shore lights. The cold winds descending from the forest through the Fishing Creek Valley was one indicator that you were on the right track to find the big tunnel that led you to the landing. It seemed as a wilderness!

The Conowingo Lake with its unparalleled Susquehanna scenery was an excellent fishing spot. Dr. Rainey, a Cornell Ichthyologist hired by the Conowingo Power Co. to study the aquatic biology of the lake, suggested that the lake held twice as many fish as you would expect from its known sources of food and spawning grounds.

The big dome shaped mountain south of Fishing Creek was Mt. Johnson Island, one of the world's only Bald Eagle sanctuaries. A family of Eagles had been building a nest that was estimated to weigh several tons high on a big red oak tree near the summit. With the advent of DDT, most of the Eagles in the Susquehanna Valley died and this nest was abandoned. After the power company located a transmission tower on the summit, no Eagles returned to that area as the Eagle population rebounded in the 1990s.

The popularity of the Fishing Creek Marina prompted local conservationists to advocate for a park in the Fishing Creek Valley. They envisioned a park encompassing the valley and its neighboring hills and big pond midway up the Fishing Creek Valley where Furniss Road crosses the creek. A new Marina with a large parking lot and picnic areas and boat launching facility on land that would be dredged up from the river bottom on the riverside of the railroad was proposed. The Marina idea folded because of safety issues involved in crossing the railroad to get access to the new Marina. The proponents for a riverfront park eventually settled on the promontory further North that is now the Susquehannock Park operated by the State of Pa. The major proponent of this project was Robert K. Mowrer, a sportsman and "Fishing Creek" fisherman who had a "second home" on the river as an avid and successful fisherman.

Fishing was the first destination of those departing from the Marina, with rowboats and canoes and shortly later with 'cranky" outboard motors propelling worthwhile rowboats. In the early 1930s more outboard motors arrived on the scene and those mechanically inclined boaters clever enough to minister to their idiosyncrasies and failures were able to wander far and wide over the large lake. A big explosion of boating arrived with the advent of the more reliable Mercury and Martin outboards. Johnson and Evinrude quickly followed suit with more reliable and easily operated motors.

In the early days it was "wrap a starting rope around the flywheel, pull"—and hope that the engine would start with fewer than a dozen pulls and that the boat would be headed in the right direction when the motor sputtered to life. A few in-boards with automotive type engines were more reliable but were somewhat outsized by the size of the Marina and the creek. Doc. Evans and Roy Smith had the first inboards that resided at the Marina, but getting them in and out of the water was a far from routine operation. In the 1940s, Homer Newhauser mounted a small engine from a small Austin(English) car in a big redwood outboard boat and cut a hot water tank in half which he installed as a shroud around the propeller. He used it to explore the rock and stump-laden shoals around the beautiful islands and cliffs in the Northern part of the lake.

Shortly afterwards, the author found a big 33HP Elto outboard engine with a combination starter generator mounted on its top, and installed it in a derelict inboard with a missing motor and propeller. The locals were always amazed when he pointed the boat out towards the river, pushed a button on the dash and the boat started out through the tunnel without any of the fuss of rope pulling. This boat started the water skiing craze on this part of the river along with skis made from ash staves supplied by Lebzelters carriage shop on North Queen Street, boiled in water in an oil drum and then curved over a carved block of wood. They were equipped with bindings made from earthmover tire inner tubes.

Shortly afterwards, other outboards appeared with jerry-rigged starters and thereafter all of the makers of the larger engines supplied them with starters and later gearshifts. This allowed bigger boats to be powered and that presented problems with getting them in and out of the water. That led to the building of boathouses and boatlifts.

Several sailboats appeared in the Marina. The Rohrer boys, whose parents had a cabin on one of the islands, had a flat "Pumpkin Seed" boat and there was an occasional conventional sailboat moored outside the archway. One "sail boat" could actually sail directly into the wind! The owner and inventor mounted an airplane type propeller on a mast. Bevel gears and shafts to a propeller under the boat coupled this. The "wind" propeller turning in the wind propelled the boat in any direction the sailor directed it with a rudder as he also controlled the "wind" propeller so that it always faced into the wind. Sailing on this lake has always been erratic due to the high hills on each side of the river. West winds were always blowing "overtop" and only North or South winds provided exhilarating and reliable sailing.

The following are a few thoughts of Fishing Creek from this author. Please excuse any similar stories of mine that overlap or partially coincide with those of Mr. Newhauser.

During my childhood Fishing Creek, where it entered the river was a thriving, busy, tiny village. Earlier at the turn of the 20th century it boasted a fertilizer warehouse, a post office, general store and the home of Ralph DuBree, who sold McCormick Deering farm machinery and fertilizer near his home. Fertilizer at this time was transported by train to the local warehouse and was then sold to local farmers in burlap bags each weighing 162 pounds. During my farming experience I have handled hundreds of bags of fertilizer but in my lifetime none that weighed more than 80 pounds. I suppose those earlier times were referred to as back when men were men and hernias were hernias.

Ralph DuBree's son, Ralph Jr., lived in Fishing Creek as a young boy and remembers occasional floods that occurred along the Fishing Creek stream. During one, he recalls that stone railroad bridge across the Creek that contained a large arch allowing the water from Fishing Creek to disperse into the river. Following a violent thunderstorm and tremendous rain this arch became clogged with uprooted trees and various items torn loose upstream. Immediately this surge of water began backing up flooding all dwellings along this normally quiet stream. He stated his father with expensive vehicles and machinery half submerged in muddy water is remembered wading through the waist high floodwater with several live chickens in each hand. In typical old farmer fashion that continues today, the first to be saved during a disaster is not that of greatest monetary value but that which is alive. Ralph Jr. stated that following that flood he had witnessed as a boy he possessed a great respect and a genuine fear of floodwaters. He remembers his mother looking in through a window of their home to see her freshly baked cake in an aluminum pan floating by.

The family I most remember living in Fishing Creek during my lifetime was that of Cecil and Virginia Griest Jackson and children, James, Mary, Thomas and Donald. Cecil was the son of John Evans Jackson and Louisa M. Harris who were married in 1903 and had 10 children. They moved to Fishing Creek in 1913 and lived along the river in a small house no more than a few feet from the railroad tracks. Locals would later state that is was a miracle none of the Jackson family was ever killed or injured living in such close proximity to the powerful, steel wheeled engines and variety of railroad cars that regularly rumbled past vibrating their entire home. Occasionally cars would jump the track causing a massive pileup along this line, with a few plunging into the river.

John Jackson's children later stated, "We lived in the river and even our favorite hymn was, I got peace like a river." Later 4 of the Jackson daughters married 4 Flahart brothers. The Jackson children remember their father as soft-spoken and never raising his voice. He loved to whittle and supposedly drank, smoked and chewed everything available but always in moderation. His wife Louisa suffered much of her life with epilepsy and although much younger than her husband died 10 years before him. John Jackson at times spoke in parables and spoke this particular one often following his wife's death. Missing his wife he said, "How slender the thread needed to hang a man without a wife."

Following the marriage of Cecil and Virginia, he worked for neighboring farmer Joe Cutler and other local farmers before getting a job with the Pennsylvania Railroad as a trackman. In 1943 they moved from a nearby home in Fishing Creek to the home where they lived together for over 50 years, formerly the home of the Ralph DuBree family. Cecil always claimed they moved all their belongings to this house in a wheelbarrow. Cecil worked on the railroad for years with our Italian immigrant neighbor John Angeline who always humorously referred to him as Cease-ah-the-Jack.

There were numerous occasions when fellow Chestnut Level Church members and we locals helped the Jackson's relocate themselves and their belongings to higher ground while experiencing rising floodwaters. During one of these **Heading for Higher Ground** brief marathons, a neighbor was heard to utter under his breath, "Hopefully this time they won't go back." They always did! Cleaning up following a flood is even worse than cleaning up following a fire is my final thought. Cecil and Virginia are both deceased and only memories, as is all of Fishing Creek that they knew so well. All except the trains and the tracks on which they run that Cecil helped maintain for much of his life.

There was also located in Fishing Creek a well used boat ramp and boat storage facility that was originally, during my lifetime, run by Roy Smith then Meryl Murphy and finally Harry Fulmer. Roy Smith, son of local farmer Gerritt Smith, is remembered by the locals as a man who could tell stories, some true, some bordering on fiction and a few remembered as down right lies. When Roy would brag about the large quantity of items he handled and sold in his small country store, customers both black and white would refer to him wryly, as "Johnny Wanamaker."

This boat storage housed most of the entire fleet of the Drumore Navy. Those who migrated habitually to the vast waters of the Susquehanna, held behind the Conowingo Dam North to Holtwood, concentrated mainly on fishing and duck hunting. It was commonplace in the 40s and 50s to observe vehicles passing through Liberty Square heading for Fishing Creek on weekends towing a boat caressed affectionately by a trailer. We always assumed those not transporting boats had them stored at Fishing Creek anxiously anticipating their arrival. Those folks heading in the same direction driving vehicles not attached to anything were always thought to be attached to one another.

The conjunction of boats of all shapes and sizes from sleek and expensive to rough, cheap and leaking similar to those on board concentrated mainly on catching and removing fresh fish fillet from the river ripe with scales and tails. Other sportsmen, smaller in quantity but greatly perpetuating perseverance during foul weather, pursued the vast variety of ducks and Canada geese that were also abundant, especially in fall and early winter on the river. This sport required hand-held cannons (or shotguns as referred to by the hunters) to bring down these elusive, free flying waterfowl. Wooden carved decoys were used to lure the waterfowl near the patiently awaiting hunters camouflaged, cowering and covered in boats with river edge underbrush. Calls mimicking their quacks and honks were then, as now, used by these hunters coaxing them close with fowl language and water fowl conversations evidently totally misunderstood by these nearby high flyers.

Perhaps those with down feathers, web feet, and a clean bill of health, slowly approaching with fixed wings and landing gear lowered were anticipating a quiet lunch with friends instead of being peppered with lead and becoming lunch for our hunkered down hunters. As our local military force modernizes I suppose anti-aircraft guns and remote controlled drake decoy drones will one-day aid in this sport. I'm also anticipating a waters-edge, stadium-size screen showing thousands of ducks and geese in a video entitled, "Waterfowl At Play," will one day play a part in this sporting activity.

The Drumore Post Office, once located in Fishing Creek, is the only office in this Township still active. It is only open 4 hours a day as most of its mail is processed at Holtwood. First established in 1815, Drumore was open only 3 months when for some unknown reason, it was closed in favor of Mount Pleasant, now Chestnut Level. Phillip Housekeeper was postmaster at that time. Then, in June 1879, Drumore was reopened. For many years, it was housed in the Fishing Creek store. Former Postmasters were William Brown1879, Albert Cramer1915, J. Roy Smith1926, Gertrude Smith1944, Verna Mae Murphy 1955-1986 all located at Fishing Creek. Then in 1970 the Post Office and Verna Mae moved to Liberty Square where it remains today. Postmistresses at this location were Sally Hunter 1987-2007 and presently Patty Dissinger and Brenda Grumbling. Following an unsuccessful robbery attempt in the late spring of 2011 the Drumore Post Office was closed permanently. This ended the nearly 200 years of we locals possessing the convenience of our own local Post Office. Some refer to this as progress but it is doubtful our Drumore ancestors or present residents would agree.

The Liberty Square Post office was located directly beside the present Drumore Post Office in a store in the village of the same name. It was established in 1850 and closed in 1908. Former Postmasters were John Hatton 1850, Jacob Carrigan 1859, Edward Ambler, David Brown 1862, Harry Ambler 1899 and Edward McClenagan.

Other Post Offices located in Drumore Township were, White Horse Tavern, Mount Pleasant, later known as Chestnut Level, Furniss, Greene, Hensel, Hubers, Buck and Fern Glen making a total of 11 Post Offices located in Drumore over the years. The very first was located along 272 at the bottom of the incline halfway between Osceola and Oregon Hollow road in 1811, later known as Hake's Hill. One Postmaster who served here was a J. Showalter, who according to old maps owned this place around 1821. Old timers like me remember the house sat on the East side of the road and the barn and a concrete silo sat on the West side. During much of my lifetime, Clayton Kreider, then Ralph and Robert Kreider owned all the land surrounding the house and Stanley Kreider later owned all the land surrounding the barn. Those remembered that lived in the house were, Joe Eshleman and family, the Hake family, the Rufus Good family, Garland Eller family, Fred Long family and lastly Mary Roland and children. These buildings were all demolished late in the 20th century.

The first Postmaster at Mount Pleasant that became known as Chestnut Level when this Post Office was founded in 1815 was Mahlon Pusey, who also built the Chestnut Level Store in 1824.

My over-80 close friend and neighbor John Adams related this Fishing Creek story to me that I found most interesting and should be duly noted. Similar to other stories printed in this local conglomeration of by-gone memorabilia, for some unknown reason I have selfishly convinced myself that most of what I know of this area will someday die with me if not recorded.

John Adams's parents lived in Lancaster where his father worked at Armstrong. They had a boat they kept at Fishing Creek during the summer months and mentioned to local acquaintance Hughs Smith of their interest in acquiring a Southern end property. Smith later told them of an upcoming auction of a small farm that they later visited and observed. John's Dad went to the sale of the property, with Kersey Bradley being the auctioneer, but was out bid by a Meyers from Holtwood. A few minutes following the sale John

Adams's mother arrived and was very irate that her husband didn't purchase the farm. John's dad, evidently wanting to keep peace, approached Meyers and offered him $85.00 to renege on his winning bid. Meyers accepted and the Adams's were owners of this 10 acre farm with stone house and barn for $615.00. Adams later attended many of Bradley's auctions, becoming the nickel man (one who acquires any sale item that receives no bid, for a nickel) all the while eventually furnishing the empty house and filling the barn. This farm is located at the corner of Silver Springs and Furniss Road.

Being now close to Fishing Creek, the Adams's spent more time at their boat and became acquainted with a man named Ward Evans. Evans was born locally in Lancaster County, but when asked for the precise location always claimed Beggar Row. He knew the local area well and spoke often of McCall's Ferry and the Quade family who ran the Ferry and lived there. John's wife Loretta was a Quade and was born at McCall's Ferry. According to John, Ward Evans fit right in with the locals in all aspects of dress and mannerisms although most knew very little about him. Evans became friends with the Adams family, and would stop at their recently purchased farmhouse when in the area following a day of fishing on his own boat. Although acquainted with Evans they also knew little of his personal or professional life.

Serving in World War II, John ended up in Biarritz, France approximately 15 miles from the Spanish border, near the Bay of Biscay when the fighting ended. He was sent with his unit to the American University located there and one day while walking the local streets in this town he amazingly meets Ward Evans, on the street, and during this short conversation learns he is teaching chemistry at the University.

Retuning home sometime later John got a job offer that took him to Evanston, Illinois also home of Northwestern University. Out of the blue, Dr. Evans called, inviting the Adams to dinner and to a Northwestern-Illinois football game. It was during this time that John learned that Dr. Ward Evans was a professor and head of the chemistry department at Northwestern.

Earlier in this chapter Robert Neuhauser has given a vivid description of Dr. Ward Evans's association with Robert Oppenheimer, who helped develop the first Atomic Bomb. Evans because of his vast knowledge of explosives was called as a witness at several trials. Once during an exchange between himself and an arrogant Attorney concerning his age and experience, Evans, evidently miffed by the questions of his knowledge and being elderly, told the startled courtroom that he had indeed struggled against the Indians. Reprimanded by the Judge, Evans apologized, then related he was on the F&M football team when they played the Carlisle Indians. I believe Carlisle had a team member named Jim Thorpe.

Many years ago B. Cookman Dunkle wrote a brief history entitled, "Rafting on the Old Susquehanna." I wish to conclude this Fishing Creek chapter with his remembered words of life on this vast body of water that begins with a trickle in New York and culminates its journey into the headwaters of the immense Chesapeake Bay. This nearby river has always and in many ways still defines this area of which I write.

Perhaps it was his unusual name, "Cookman," that when mentioned even today causes me to picture his countenance, mannerisms and appearance. Maybe, I recall him as an old neighbor who was married to Alice Shoemaker, a relative of my Mother, also a Shoemaker. I remember his devotion to nearby Bethesda Methodist Church and his long association with Rawlinsville Camp Meeting, both still in existence and very active at this time.

Cookman was also a mail carrier out of Rawlinsville for a spell and although he drove a car, similar to others of his generation he never became completely accustomed to the clutch, brake, gears and other mechanical functions of dashboard controls. Chet Graver farmed Cookman's farm for many years and was of the next generation. This man and machine were very comfortable with one another during on and off road operation, as were most of this generation. In observing them as a child these folks operating car, truck or machinery appeared as one unit meshed and molded together maintaining a constant smooth flow of man and machine. Cookman and his vehicle, however, always appeared to me as 2 separate entities. Chet always claimed Cookman, at every stop on his mail route dug a hole at every mailbox. He evidently never acquired the art of releasing the clutch cautiously.

Chet and Mary Gravers' 4 children always had nicknames for one another and many others. They always referred appropriately to Cookman as, "The Duke," a perfect description of this old, white haired, gravel voiced gentleman. The Gravers lived with and cared for him following the untimely death of his wife in 1945. Cookman's 207-acre farm was one of the first properties purchased, November 8, 1962 for the Muddy Run Project. I don't know the purchase price but do know a 200-acre Southern Lancaster County farm today is expected to fetch at least 1 million at auction. This entire, old river hill farm now sleeps, forgotten by most, near the deepest section of Muddy Run Lake. Cookman is also gone, as are Chet and Mary Graver who lived, loved and raised 4 children while caring for Cookman and working their farm, a daily reminder to this old farmer of the inevitable consequences of this brief life. The following is a brief summary of Cookman's words published in 1953:

"In colonial days and up until the Civil War Era, fish from the Susquehanna constituted a large part of the local food supply. All-important roads in the area either led to the ferries across the river or to the many fisheries located on the islands or along the shore. Many of these roads are no longer in use, but their courses in many places can still be traced through the river hills by deep ruts cut in the rock by the passage of many cartwheels.

"While the river was not navigable in the usual sense of the word it was the scene of considerable activity for 2 or 3 months every spring when the river was usually higher than normal from melting snows and spring rains. Thousands of rafts of cut timber were floated down the river to Tidewater and market. The records also show that in addition no less than 3,000 arks and flat boats came down the river in the short space of 90 days, loaded with grain, other produce and many kinds of merchandise form the upper counties of Pennsylvania and New York.

"It is of this timber rafting that I write especially. During the year lumbermen cut the virgin timber in the mountains of the headwaters of the river. The vast quantities available in that era are now unimaginable. The logs were floated down the smaller streams to booms and held there until high water. The logs were generally cut in 16-foot lengths, never shorter, and sometimes longer, especially if they were destined for use as spars in shipbuilding. These great logs were pinned together with wooden pins to form flat rafts 16 feet wide and several logs long.

When the waters were sufficiently high these rafts were started down the river manned by a crew of 10 men. Each raft was equipped with 2 large oars for steering, one at each end and each oar manned by 4 men. A steer man and a pilot rounded out the crew. The current carried the raft along. It could not run during the night, as there were no lights. The river, therefore, was divided off in sections that could be traveled by the floating raft in 1 day. The raft was moored to the shore at night, and the next morning a new, different crew that was in readiness would take over and pilot it to the next stopping place. These overnight stopping places were really booming during the rafting season. With many rafts coming down the river daily and 10 men accompanying each raft I can't imagine the number walking the river's edge and visiting the local establishments.

"The regular stopping places, or changeovers, on the lower Susquehanna were Marietta, Washington Boro and Peach Bottom, the final run to Tidewater. It was hard, strenuous, dangerous work and required strong, husky men. The pay was 8 dollars a day for common oarsmen, top wages for those days but they certainly earned it. To realize some sense of the dangerous undertaking, glance at the rocks on either side of the Norman Wood Bridge as you cross it and visualize floating and steering these rafts on the wild, rushing, spring current of the raging river.

"Upon reaching their destination with most of these men being drinking men who felt the need for something stronger than water to keep up their spirits, so consequently to supply this need many hotels sprung up along the raft man's path. They walked this path that led North to where they had boarded this last raft that was trodden upon daily by all that participated in this occupation returning for the next log float South.

Murphy's Outboard Center–Fishing Creek 1950s.

"When departing the rafts at the conclusion of this daily excursion these thirsty hard working men rushed these accommodating, over whelemed landlords. If business was too brisk to handle everyone at Peach Bottom, they only had to walk a half-mile up the river on their homeward trek to reach "Whitakers Hotel" that also did a brisk business. Then only another ½ mile to another stopping place known for years as, "The Haunted Inn." Almost within sight was Mr. Sweigart's, "Fairview Inn" later known as "Bald Friar" and further up the river was, "Fite's Eddy" where Clark Bostic passed out the beverages. All those places have since disappeared with the building of the Conowingo Dam and the consequent rising of the railroad along the river.

Bald Friar–Hotel along the river visited by raftsmen before 1900.

"At Fite's Eddy with the original owner an ancestor of the Fites of Quarryville, the raftman's footpath left the river shore and the men had to climb the hill and cut across country not coming back to the rivers edge until they reached the village of Pequea. It was practically impossible to follow the river shore the whole way, as there were points where the hills descended in shear, steep rock, to the very water's edge. It seemed property owners did not object to these scores of men passing over their land and even built steps to aid them in crossing over fences.

"On leaving Fite's Eddy the raftman's path led up through the woods to the top of the hill near the residence of Colonel Neel, later Dave Wisslers. Today this plot of land lies at the Southeast end of the large earthen Muddy Run Dam. The path continued past Snavely's Mill, the Harner farm then another opportunity for refreshment at Frank Groff's bar near the present Holtwood ball diamond. Refreshment was evidently furnished all along the raft men's path at least to Pequea."

Fite's Eddy–Hotel along the river visited by raftsmen before 1900.

    As for now Fishing Creek, the tiny community is but a ghost town minus the town buildings and missing even the ghosts. The trains still pass nearby but no one waves to them as in the past although they continue to blow the train's whistle not from necessity but from habit. Formerly they picked up the awaiting mail, acquiring it without stopping using hooks that caught or released the mailbags. Many years ago we occasionally drove down to this area and it seemed we never had to wait very long before a train passed. Now running only at night, if one is heard where we live, the old folks would have said, "Must be gonna rain." This meant the breeze carrying that sound was coming from the South and was thought to also bring moisture.

    There is still something to be said for lying in bed on a warm summer night with southern exposed windows reared up, listening to nighttime creatures and in the distance to a far off rumbling, rolling train. The methodical rotating steel wheels provide the tempo for the low, single key sound of a hundred cars with this song interrupted only by the french horn blare of the engine whistle. A window air conditioner may cool a bedroom but I haven't yet found one that can reproduce that somber, soothing, distant sound that transports a cargo of welcome dreams.

    During the dead of winter this, "Polar Express" makes its way along the frozen ground and ice covered Susquehanna. Not sure if "Tom Hanks" is aboard but I would bet his namesake, and our man about town, "Tim Hanks" is probably nearby on a horse.

PART FIVE

STORIES "FROM" AND "ON" THE LEVEL

Echoes From The Past
The Academy

The following stories were written by me for our Church's monthly newsletter. They offer a tiny glimpse into the history of this 300-year-old congregation and stories from our present-day activities.

The Chestnut Level Academy, built in 1852 through the efforts of Rev. Lindley Rutter, was situated directly between our Church and our new Family Life Center. Paid for by the community, it served local Chestnut Level students who would commute and numerous others farther away of many denominations. The tuition was 75 cents a week. These students would live at the 3-story boarding house built after the Academy and later used as our Sunday School building.

With the coming of high schools around 1900, the Academy was no longer needed and was used for a few years as a Sunday school. Jim Moss, late father of Jean, remembered meeting as a Sunday School group in the old academy for opening exercises and listening to Irena Penny, a violinist, and J. Edgar Brown, who played the cornet, as they led in these exercises each week. I find it interesting that 100 years later Jean Moss, and Barb Reagan, granddaughter of J. Edgar Brown, are both members of our present day chancel choir, as was Barb's father, Edgar K. Brown, an occasional soloist. Both Jean's parents and grandparents were active members at Chestnut Level throughout their lives. The marvelous historical fabric of our nearly 300-year-old congregation continues inter—woven with new friends, families and those families who have worshipped here for more than a century. This fabric, as the fabric of our lives, is sewn tightly and beautifully and framed with love and respect for one another. It is displayed in each of our hearts for everyone to observe and dedicated to the one who made us all.

During the early 1920s, it was suggested that the Academy be torn down and the material used to build an extension to the Sunday School building.

Many members of the church, who with the generations before them had received their education at the Academy, could not bear to see the dear old building demolished. A congregational meeting was called to discuss the matter. Needless to say there was much discussion for and against the demolition of the Academy. I'm sure the disagreements delivered by our red-faced, Scotch Irish ancestors were long, loud and heated at times. I recall a few of these folks from my youth, who seemed to relish nothing more than a good argument.

In our old church minutes they describe this angry discussion as the occurrence of "much wailing and gnashing of teeth." But the farsightedness of the younger members prevailed and we have the Sunday School building as it is today. If anyone who reads this is ever involved in a meeting, church or other, where there are many disagreements and arguments, it is my hope that you would use that old phrase, "much wailing and gnashing of teeth," in describing it.

The Old Farmer

Echoes From The Past
Bats in the Belfry

Prior to 1882, the year the bell tower was added to the Chestnut Level Church, during the pastorate of Rev. John M. Galbreath, the left end of the building, near the cemetery, was a summertime rendezvous for bats. According to records left by the Rev. Robert Clark, D.D. the air around the Church swarmed with the nocturnal creatures during every evening prayer service.

The curiosity of young Clark and other boys attending the Chestnut Level Academy led to an investigation to determine just how the bats roosted in the loft during daytime. They climbed a ladder, entered a trap door in the ceiling of the gallery giving access to the Church loft.

The first thing discovered was that not a single post supported the massive framework of the roof, representing great engineering skill by the builders. The other great surprise to the boys was the discovery that bats did not roost, they simply hung with heads downward, clutching fast to the timbers with their claws. During later trips to the loft each boy armed himself with a club and great numbers of bats were killed.

After the bell tower was installed the interior walls of the auditorium were frescoed or painted. It was found that this material would not adhere to the ceiling due to being impregnated with an oily substance caused from the long residence of bats overhead. Furring strips were nailed to the ceiling, which were lathed and plastered to overcome this condition. Following the erection of the bell tower all openings were sealed, putting an end to the bats.

The pranks of inquisitive boys did not harm this sacred edifice but they did kill the unclean mammals that were defiling the house of God. In retrospect of all who have attended our Church regularly during the past nearly 250 years, these creatures may have been the only ones that were not searching for the light.

I would hope that this information, well over a century past Church history concerning bats, causes none of our present congregation to glance heavenward throughout Sunday morning services, especially during the sermon! I shall be observing each of you from another "loft" now used by the choir. Most choir members will be seen sitting upright and not hanging by our claws upside down. This position may be altered only by strained attempts to reach notes unattainable from limited voice range or on instruction from our choir director, EricWelchans.

The Old Farmer

Echoes From The Past
Church Furniture

As we approach the 300th anniversary of our congregation in 2011, the following is a brief history of the furniture and pews located in our sanctuary. They were purchased in April of 1914 from Dittmar Furniture Company, designers and manufacturers of church seating and pulpit furniture located at the corner of Day and Light Streets, Williamsport, Pa. The first correspondence between our Church and Dittmar occurred December 26, 1913 and was addressed locally to fellow Church committee member Thomas Ankrim. The remaining correspondence occurred January thru April 1914 and was addressed to Church committee chairman Irwin Cutler. Cutler built the house directly beside our new Family Life Center, known to my generation as the home of Bob & Kay Powl.

It is stated in correspondence that our Church committee is not all pleased with the comfort of the sample pews. The furniture company "response"—we wish that it were possible for you to place one of our seats right beside any other seating on the market and try them out. They recommended the committee visit Bethany Pres. Church in Lancaster, where they recently installed seating. Bethany's congregation informed them through a letter that they were well pleased with the comfort of the pews. We Presbyterians have the long-standing reputation of seldom agreeing 100 percent on anything. This continues in my lifetime but is surely waning and growing less vigorous with each generation, is my observation. A testament to that belief is the way our congregation has accepted subtle changes in our worship service and the construction of our new Family Life facility.

The committee originally preferred circular pews but eventually chose straight seating. The pews and furniture were shipped by rail to Peach Bottom on April 11, 1914. They were loaded and hauled to Chestnut Level on horse drawn wagons. All of the cargo was made of solid oak and anyone who has ever helped move an occasional pew or the pulpit furniture will attest to its weight.

The furniture company sent men to set up the pews and asked that the floor be unobstructed so they could begin work early in the week. That would allow them to return home before Sunday. All meals for these workmen were to be provided by the Church. The total cost of pews, pulpit set, and 4-dozen chairs with quartered oak gloss finish, delivery to Peach Bottom and installation was $1,525.00. I can't help but wonder, as I write this, if 100 years from now the cost of our new building will seem as frugal as the present Church furniture.

The Old Farmer

Echoes From The Past
The Old Sunday School

In the early years our Sunday School was not held during the months of Jan., Feb. and March. During the years 1938-39 the session voted to begin having Sunday School in these winter months. For many years before this change of having Sunday School year round, the men of the Church, including my grandfather Smith, had sat in their cars during Sunday School time. Grandpop, who enjoyed nothing more than enthusiastic, unending conversation with his fellowman, was known to go from car to car for this Sunday morning visitation. I'm not sure of the content of this man-to-man communication but I'm told he was known to say that not all the Sunday morning sermons he encountered occurred inside the Church.

With the addition of the auditorium and the basement below it they, like our new building, were to be used by the community. They certainly have served this purpose way beyond expectations is my feeling.

A men's Bible class taught by Rev. Carruthers was organized and met in the dining room. The slogan "Be Square all week and Round on Sunday" was made into a sign and presented to the class by one of its members, Lem Boyce, known for his humor, cleverness and acting ability. He played the lead in "A Mock Trial," a memorable performance staged by the men's class, directed by Rev. Carruthers and performed on the stage of the new addition. Much to my satisfaction, the committee tells me that this old sign will soon join the exodus of memorabilia from the old to the new building. Someone recently confided to me that they knew their childhood was over when they fully understood the words on that sign.

Having written "Sounds from the Past" in my book, I've been told by a few fellow worshipers that they also have listened to the startled sound of a rooster crowing, the mournful cry of a sheep, the whinny of a horse or the beller of a cow in the distance on a Chestnut Level Sunday morning. Being an old farmer I thought perhaps I was alone in observing these Sunday morning solos also performed by those in praise to their maker. With the influx of the Amish and the clippity clop outside our Church windows these sounds will surely survive from our past well into our future in downtown Chestnut Level.

As a farmer I also would hope that each of you who observe and later use our new building in various ways would take the time to enjoy the scenic view from the back of the Family Life Center. The beautiful, well-kept family farm of fellow Church members Bill and Lena Aaron is certainly Southern Lancaster County at its finest and gratefully appreciated by me and hopefully all of you. This personal life-size landscape mural belongs to each of us and has no mortgage.

The Old Farmer

Echoes From The Past
Racing Results from Chestnut Level

My current neighbor, Don Martin, and former neighbor, Darlene Gaus Gilbert, each gave me a tiny article that recently appeared in the Lancaster Newspaper that I had overlooked. I suppose my interest in our local history prompted their thinking of me—and I'm grateful.

100 years ago August 10,1910

Horse Racing: The first matinee horse race of the season was held at the Speedwell Track on the farm of Mr. G. Ed Brown at Chestnut Level. Brown and his neighbors had built a half-mile track in a desirable location for picnickers and lovers of good horses to try their speed. The meet was well attended. The Witmers, McCauleys, Glackins, Smiths, Joneses, Seldombridges and others were present with their horses. Many ladies and their escorts were on hand to enjoy the sport.

I believe this track would have been located directly behind the Brown home owned today by Dr. Wayne Kreider, a local large animal veterinarian, and his wife, Carla. I would assume the first turn on the track would have been very near, if not upon, the present land occupied by the Chestnut Level Family Life Center. The backstretch would have been visibly situated on one of the lengthy fields below and west of the Family Life Center. The clubhouse turn was probably behind the large garage built by Mart Sechrist, near Ed Brown's barn, with the finish line behind the home of Scott and Alice Rohrer. G. Ed Brown was the grandfather of Barb Regan, wife of Quarryville dentist Dr. Tom.

I'm not sure how occasional horse races, held 100-years ago, within the lengthy, far reaching shadows cast by Chestnut Level Presbyterian Church were accepted but evidently they were well attended. Apparently having a good time and enjoying life by ladies and gentlemen was no more a sin a century ago in Chestnut Level than it is today.

However, I'm reminded of a few women from my childhood and Quaker roots that just might not wish to reside within the following thoughts of Robert Risk, quoting nearly 100-years past from a book entitled "The Bad Results of Good Habits and other Lapses."

He states, "It is a curious fact that I have never felt quite at home with good people. I should have been a foreign missionary, for I have so much in common with the heathen. But I know I speak to a small band of kindred spirits when I say that there has always seemed to me to be an unnatural and strained atmosphere among the gatherings of professedly good people. In order to be convinced of this fact, one only has to visit a ladies sewing circle of any Church."

I'm sure my grand and great grandmother Smith were part of this afore-mentioned Church circle, as are family members today. But I recall my grandmother and her sisters joking and making fun of one another and enjoying nothing more than unrestrained laughter among themselves. Laughter, especially at one's self, will corrode self-rightousness. However, I should mention these 3 ladies were the granddaughters of Rev. Lindley Rutter, Minister at Chestnut Level for 40 years, and were expected to appear reserved and God-fearing publicly. Nevertheless, grandfather Smith would have been across the street at Ed Brown's horse races during circle meeting, the first to arrive and the last to depart.

The local persistent Ladies Circle, however, must have won out because this Church organization continues to flourish and the Speedwell racetrack is long gone and forgotten. These local fillies continue to win, place and show even today in downtown Chestnut Level as each enters and runs the exhausting race of this life to the finish line and then to her final triumphant glory. Those wonderful ladies that I recall have each stood in the winners' circle before walking in green pastures beside still waters.

The Old Farmer

Echoes From The Past
Christmas Eve

Several folks within our congregation have shared a similar sentiment to mine in that it just isn't Christmas without attending Christmas Eve services. This was not always the case as no services were held at Chestnut Level before the early 1960s. I'm not sure when the first service occurred and would appreciate anyone who knows of the year or has a bulletin from that service to contact any of us from the Archives committee. I would be surprised if Mary Ankrum, Pauline Stoner and Dick and Lois Dunham did not play significant roles in this original service. Ben and Donna Miller were married in this Church on Christmas Eve 1961, with no service held before that time.

In talking with Donna Miller, a 50-year fellow Church member, she thought the change happened in 1964 but wasn't sure. She remembers the first Christmas Eve service was a big deal, especially for her. She had her hair done by a local beautician, Helen Styer, for the big event only to realize-not long before the service-that it looked absolutely horrible, causing her to stay at home. Evidently in the 1960s there were few things more important to a young lady than her hair! Helen, was also a long time member of this church and choir.

Many of the past Christmas Eve services found Ruthie and I seated somewhere on the steps at the rear of the sanctuary leading to the old choir loft and, higher up, to the bell tower. As our 7 P.M. service became more popular and well attended we, along with fellow Church family members Roger and Peggy Brown and a few others, always gave our seats to those latecomers in the crowded sanctuary. The Browns and Smiths initiated our own tradition as in recent years we always go directly to our seats on the stairway to heaven and sit together.

Having attended most Christmas Eve services held at Chestnut Level and experienced the peace and serenity along with the joyous singing of the age-old Christmas carols, I thought I had completely perceived all the heart-warming emotions of this special time. The last few years, however, being perched on the staircase at the back of the Church has added an entirely new dimension to that experience. Gazing down on fellow Church family members from above, with most faces obscure as a candle flickers from each hand, is similar to gazing at the starry, transparent sky on a moonless night. This tiny light, a brief occurrence of hope held by each individual, glows resembling all others, as does the light that shines within each of us.

The familiar refrain of Silent Night reverberates throughout the natural acoustical wonder of this old stone church, completely anointing every nook and cranny as it has for over 200 years. The feeling that overwhelms me as I observe and experience all of this below is: Could this be but a tiny glimpse of what God observes this Holy Night?

The commercialization and anticipation surrounding Christmas, which when I was a boy began for me a few days before December 25th, now appears 2 months prior to Christmas. Some appear to look forward to all the hustle and bustle of those 8 weeks of anticipation while others seem to dread it. All welcome that time on Christmas Eve when this concentrated confusion hopefully concludes as we silently offer a grateful sigh of relief and once again realize in our hearts why we celebrate Christmas.

Christmas brings us memories, of good times from the past
The light that glows in children's eyes, the joy when old folks laugh
The love we hope remains for all, beyond this Christmas Day
That started with a newborn child, who in a manger lay
The aroma and taste of scrumptious food, occurs throughout our home
While conversation runs amok, as little children roam
Lord teach us to savor every moment, of every precious day
And as we journey through this world, help us to find our way
For this time with friends and family, remembered through the years
Each Christmas is recalled again, then one day through our tears
For every earthly thing we've known, shall pass I do believe
But "Silent Night" remains eternal, to sing on Christmas Eve.

The Old Farmer

Echoes From The Present
Family Life Center

All of us that are a part of this congregation continually give thanks for our new building and all that now occurs daily within its walls. I think that as each of us appreciate all those wonderful times that played out in our old Sunday School for generations we should also be thankful that a tragedy that could have happened the last few years in the life of that wonderful old building never occurred. Those who worked regularly in the old kitchen, with unpredictable ovens those last few years of its life, all concur that a silent prayer of relief was offered following those meals. Although the kitchen was cleaned and maintained as best as humanly possible, I've often thought if the board of health had ever inspected those facilities during a meal served to the community, that function would be remembered as "The Last Supper." As one who lives in a 200—year-old farmhouse, I have experienced first hand a fire in our home and it is not used daily by the public as was the old Sunday School.

As I recall a dream, then a vision of this congregation to build a new 3 million dollar Family Life Center, I am in awe as to how this has been approached and accomplished and now become a reality. Our building committee, our finance committee and all who directly or indirectly contributed to and continue to financially support this project should harbor a great deal of joy and satisfaction upon its completion in approximately just 1 year.

More gratifying to me than the construction of our new building is the way our congregation responded to and supported this tremendous undertaking during a time of recent, unexpected, economic downturn. I hesitate to list some of the fundraisers dreamed up by fellow Church members because I will surely forget several and there remains some that have not yet surfaced or taken place or even been thought of. I will attempt, at a later date, to list all fundraisers, as I believe these extraordinary efforts by so many folks should be documented for our Church Archives. As for now I'll just say everything from Christmas at the Level to the production and preparation of "Presbyterian pickles" has taken place.

The question I wish to pose to everyone who reads this is: would any of the activities have occurred that seemed to bond us together and strengthen our Church family occurred had we dismissed building the Family Life Center? Following God's direction, we old folks, somewhat set in our ways, have joined our enthusiastic young people and the vast majority of those in between and come together for a common cause. There is no stopping us and what we can accomplish together. Our much needed building is wonderful and I'm sure will serve us well for generations. But my personal recollection of this time will not be the construction of the building but the entire congregation working together as one. To me this is every bit as important as the Family Life Center, perhaps more!

I have heard so many folks state both within our congregation and outside it, that we certainly are blessed with an abundance of talented people. Would we have totally realized and appreciated this had the opportunity not arisen for this God given talent to rise-up and shine within all of these wonderful folks associated with Chestnut Level Church?

In the Bible we read of miracles performed by Jesus including turning water into wine, while some non-believers scoff and question this as an exaggerated story or myth. What would you call this if I told you a couple ladies and a handful of craftsmen, all members of our congregation turned pieces of broken, discarded, stained glass into a fundraiser totaling $12,000.00 dollars? Miracles occur everyday in our lives, my friends, and several have appeared before, during and following the construction of our new building.

> A lots been accomplished, since our ground breaking day
> And that very first spade of sod
> To our dedication, the last day of May
> And we give all the glory to God
> With the building complete, the construction now finished
> We expect no fanfare or fuss
> Because each of us knows, we were all part of something
> That was so much greater than us.

The Old Farmer

Echoes From The Present
The Wedding Day—Razing

Following the completion of our Family Life Center, a certain amount of time was allotted for the demolition of the old Sunday School. Members of the trustees and other Church members began removing doors, light fixtures, wainscoting, exit light signs, etc. to be sold at our recent auction and to be used by our craftsmen to construct items to be sold later. Following this, a demolition crew was to remove the building. A next-door Amish man, Sam Stoltzfus, who lives at the former Mellinger home, asked if he could remove a few items. He was granted permission and in the following days several other nearby Amish were also given permission to salvage some building material.

I was there during the beginning of this process one morning to meet John Styer, a former member and wood-worker who wished to acquire a couple pieces of lumber to make something to later donate to the Church for sale. Sitting quietly in the Church parking lot, directly across from the Sunday School, I was startled by the abrasive sound of a chain saw. Not sure at first where this sound originated, I visually searched the grounds surrounding the old Sunday School building. As my eyes rose, I was amazed to see an Amish man perched on the roofless rafters of the building, 3 stories in the air, cutting through beams. Totally startled, I was astounded as no more than 15 feet from him-and at a similar height-was, I presumed, his wife. She was using a digging iron, prying nailed rafters free from beams. Having been around the Amish the last several years, I have observed their barn raising and building removal, but this close—up vision of this man and wife working at this height was totally unexpected.

A few days later, as more Amish arrived in horse-drawn-wagons, a large amount of lumber was removed daily. Observing this I couldn't help but imagine that these plain dressed, bearded Amish farmers, removing this building piece by piece may have appeared very similar to the men who constructed this

Sunday School 160 years ago. I'm sure each horse and wagon, parked randomly with the nags' heads tied to trees and anything else substantial, would have looked the same as in the past.

I was there one evening after sunset with pounding still heard in the bleak building. My observation revealed an Amish fellow working in pitch-black darkness, wearing a hard-hat equipped with a light resembling headgear worn by a miner. In talking with those from the Church responsible for the removal of the building, their comment was, "Every piece of material removed by the Amish is one less to be removed by the demolition crew and lowers our cost."

During this ongoing Amish barn raising in reverse, 2 weddings were scheduled at our Church across the street. The marriage of Brenda Trimble was scheduled for Friday, April 17th and the wedding of Sara Cullen April 18th. The Trimble wedding, one of the largest bridal parties ever assembled in Chestnut Level Church, was not affected as none of the Amish worked during this service. Sara Cullen's wedding the next afternoon found Amish in abundance, in, around, and on top of, the old Sunday School building.

This Saturday bride wished to dress in her wedding gown in our new Family Life Center located beside the building being razed. An hour before the wedding she, along with her bridesmaids, made their way to the Family Life Center through wagons, lumber, Amish, sawdust, and tail-switching horses patiently waiting, pondering retirement. My wife, Ruthie, and sister, Lane, wedding coordinators at our Church responsible for 2 weddings in 2 days, related much of this information to me. Everything at the Trimble wedding had gone off without a "HITCH," (sorry about that pun; I've got Amish on my mind). The next day, our 2 wedding coordinators were horrified by apparently having to usher a breathtakingly beautiful bridal party through a construction zone, among a demolition crew, past a building that could collapse, across beams, nails and sawdust, around horses and wagons, with roaring chain saws drowning out every audible sound in Chestnut Level, to an awaiting Church containing parents, friends, preacher and groom.

Many Amish children of all ages had accompanied their fathers to this demolition derby and watched wide-eyed as a shiny fire engine drove into the Church parking lot. By this time many of the younger fellows had formed a line along the Sunday School side of Chestnut Level Road and wondered what could possibly be next. And did fire engines appear at all Chestnut Level weddings?

Approximately 10 minutes before our wedding party was to cross this Amish mine field, as our 2 coordinators silently prayed for a miracle, Cindy Derr arrived to begin cooking a dinner to be held later that evening in this place. Quickly assessing the situation, Cindy went outside and approached our Amish neighbor, Sam, explaining our bridal circumstances. Chain saws stopped immediately, horses and wagons were relocated, lumber was moved and brooms of every description swept a spotless path all the way to the Church walkway. The bridal party, unaware of much of this activity, emerged from the Family Life Center with Ruthie behind the beautiful bride carrying the train of the wedding dress and Lane assisting the bridesmaids. The only sound heard during the journey of this bride and accompanying entourage was that of an occasional robin. The first bride to ever dress in the new Family Life Center was Sara Cullen.

The Amish men had completely disappeared, although I have a feeling all inquiring eyes missed none of the bridal party. The young folks still lined up near Chestnut Level Road expecting a fire, stood steadfast. Although the Amish returned to work, everything remained quiet for half an hour. As the wedding party eventually emerged from the Church, the Amish activity increased. The children, still located nearby to observe the activity, were beside themselves as bride and groom crawled onto the fire engine and were driven away. The groom was a member of Lafayette Fire Company. This scene prodded one small Amish boy to ask if all newly-weds married at our Church leave in a fire truck. I'm told the answer given to him was, "It's a Presbyterian thing."

The following week the Amish continued their demolition of our naked, sad—looking building. When the demolition crew was later contacted, upon observation with nothing left but a shell, they realized it wouldn't take much to finish the job and they were not needed. Burnell Andrews provided a crew to dismantle what was left and remove it. The Amish intervention surely saved our Church much money.

The auditorium of the old Sunday School was built from salvaged material from the Chestnut Level Academy. Some of this material may now be recycled and used for the 3rd time in its 160-year history on local Amish farms. Hope a few who read this may someday recall and repeat any or all of this story to a younger generation. This is but a "WHISKER" of our legacy preserved for our future.

The Old Farmer

Echoes From The Present
So Who's in Charge?

Recently our congregation voted on whether to have summer Sunday worship services in the air-conditioned new Family Life Center or in the Church. In typical Presbyterian fashion, the vote was split practically 50-50. In talking with older folks of this congregation who worshipped in our old sanctuary 75-80 years ago, none could recall ever having church services canceled because of summer heat. A few remembered the canceling of services because of the bitter cold of winter and, of course, snowstorms but never because of hot weather.

There remain many present day church attendees who would say, "It's too bad if we can't stand one hour in a church service with the only thing remembered being the unbearable heat of the day." Evidently for some, all singing, praying and inspirational words are totally diminished by the temperature within those 230-year-old native stone walls.

Recently during a brief speech at the second kick-off of our Capital Campaign, Bruce Dunham spoke as inspirationally as he did at our first kick-off at Willow Valley 3 years ago. When a few chided him before this recent speech about his sun-drenched tan from his summer on his boat in the Bahamas, he referred humorously to his bronze appearance as "suffering for the Lord." Perhaps this is what a few of us in our present day congregation feel that our own discomfort should be a part of worship as it was with our ancestors. There are others that remain steadfast to their opinion that worship should always be held in our old sanctuary. A few would concur that it's just not the same in a building that resembles a modern day school. I briefly have experienced this feeling in recently built sanctuaries I have attended. A few have stated that even the music sounds different in our new building than in the ancient church where evidently the acoustics are wonderful. Could it be we are spoiled?

With the vote for summer church services equally divided, the session decided to have services remain in the old church through July and in the new Family Life Center through August, simply attempting to appease everyone. The reality all of us need to remember is that 75 years ago air conditioning played absolutely no part in the lives of our parents and grandparents. You never miss anything you've never experienced. Today, most folks have access to an air conditioner, with many surrounded in their homes by central air. Many folks work in offices with AC, attend schools with AC and drive vehicles equipped with AC. Even many of my fellow farmers spend long summer days in cool cabs on tractors and combines. Would it be any wonder folks would complain sitting in sweltering heat when most all other aspects of their lives finds them warmed in the winter and cooled in the summer? The other fact to consider is that even a few years ago we had no choice on this campus; now we do. We also are cooling the new building every Sunday for the other activities, so why not use it for church services. Economically it would make sense to utilize what each of us is contributing towards. I also realize there are folks with health issues and breathing difficulties who simply can't tolerate excess heat and humidity.

I greatly respect the thoughts on both sides of this unfamiliar dilemma and offer no opinion of my own. We just can't pick up the necessary items for Sunday church services and move them depending on the temperature every Sunday morning. Last year we designated the usual time of the most intense heat before hand and moved to the AC. As I recall, every Sunday during that time frame the weather was cool. It was almost as if a higher power was saying, "So, you think you're in charge, go for it." Some of our activities must surely cause our creator to chuckle. Just keep in mind-if half of us are uncomfortable in our surroundings when its hot, the other half are pleased. Cool weather will reunite us all!

The Old Farmer

Echoes From The Present
Stitchers in Stitches

Our 300th anniversary committee, chaired by Cindy Derr, is in the process of creating a quilt, signed by most current Church members, to be hung permanently in the Family Life Center. Muggs Bledsoe, Cindy and Ruthie Smith purchased the material for the quilt and, after the signing, patches were sewn together by Muggs, Joanne DuBree, Libby Miller, Sandy Wissler, Cindy, Ruthie, Emma King, Ada Stoltzfus and Fanny King. The actual quilting was completed in August 2010.

Although several of our Presbyterian ladies are quilters, Cindy reasoned that including a couple of our local Amish ladies, all experienced, speedy, precise quilters would add much to this task from the past. The young Amish girls of today, in uninterrupted succession, learn to quilt and remain steadfast doing this throughout their lives. Continuing this old tradition maintains this quick finger with thread practice of perfection within the female Amish community. I recall our local Kings Daughters organization quilting regularly 60 years ago, then donating these beautiful finished creations to the needy. It seems to the old farmer that this art form among our ladies is declining.

From the beginning the Amish women and our Presbyterian gals got along famously. The Amish ladies, considered by most to be reserved, stoic and stern, evidently possess another side kept hidden from we English. Alone with giggly, full of fun Presbyterian dames they were merry, witty and comical. Cindy later stated she wished she had included others from our Church to enjoy this great fellowship. Evidently, at a quilting bee, seating is limited.

The Amish were fascinated with Mrs. Bledsoe's first name, "Muggs." "Surely your Mother wouldn't have given you a first name like that," Ada, in her Amish accent, blurted out. "Oh yes," Muggs replied, "I never knew why I was given this nick-name or that my given name was Betty Lou until I was 3 or 4 years old." Gales of laughter muffled by hands covering their mouths flowed uncontrolled from the Amish gals. This "in house" echoing laughter reoccurred a short time later when Muggs referred to her sister, Sandy, as "Pee Wee." Immediately, one of the blushing Amish ladies uttered abruptly, "What would be a Pee Wee?" That brought our English ladies to hysterics.

Shortly after this episode, Ruthie, in speaking to Joanne, referred to her as Jo, which caused another, surprised Amish glance and smile as Jo referred to Cindy as Cin. This back and forth nickname banter fascinated the Amish. Evidently, a few Amish men have nicknames but never the women. Later, Muggs, in addressing Joanne referred to her as woman. The Amish gals, startled with blank looks between one another, then at Muggs, by this time are completely bewildered. You know the feeling one experiences when surrounded by Amish folks as they converse with one another in their personal language? Well, on this particular day these Amish ladies, who speak fluently their language and ours, appear to have entered the world of Presbyterian women who apparently converse in a tongue completely foreign to them.

Muggs explained that when she forgets someone's name, as most of us sometimes do, she simply calls a lady "Woman" and a man "boyfriend." Her mother, an Eshleman, supposedly did the same thing, as did others of the Eshleman clan. Bob Powl, a cousin of Muggs, is remembered by me as referring to all forgotten names of folks as "Bertha DuBree," a long deceased older neighbor lady of his. I have witnessed him face to face with feed customers male and female, salesmen, ministers, relatives, undertakers and Amish men referring to each as "Ol Bertha DuBree." He somehow always got away with it, as does Muggs.

While quilting, Muggs stated she was late getting to bed the night before because of watching an extra inning Phillies game on TV. She also said that she envies the Amish girls and their simple life style and believes she would enjoy living within their ancient, primitive ways. Fanny perked right up exclaiming, "You couldn't watch the Phillies if you were Amish." Muggs, never at a loss for words, countered, "Oh Fanny, I'd be a closet Amish woman and keep the TV hidden in a closet."

When these same Amish ladies, along with others, made Ruthie a quilt years ago they insisted she contribute a couple of stitches. During the first stitch she stuck her finger with the needle, releasing blood on the white quilt. Ada recalled this incident and instructed Ruthie to only thread the needles on this day. Ruthie also served the ladies lunch and provided Amish transportation. The age of the Amish ladies ranged from 24 to 60. They thoroughly enjoyed this time of fellowship, as did all who attended, and hope to come to the Family Life Center and observe the quilt after it's hung. They also greatly enjoyed the lunch Cindy prepared and weren't the least bit bashful in asking for seconds, which was the ultimate compliment to the one that prepared it. They enjoyed looking at Cin's flowers, and the Chestnut Level cookbooks presented to them were the most appropriate and appreciated gifts that could be given.

I would hope all who read this presently and in the future would recall those who signed this quilt and also the Presbyterian and Amish ladies who worked together in creating it. The ways, means and mannerisms of the present stitched together with those from the past produced something special that all should be proud of. Each name was inscribed with remembrance and reflection, each thread was sewn with passion and hope and each stitch was quilted amidst laughter and love.

The Old Farmer

Echoes From The Present
The Dormant Stone

Recently I was asked by friends and fellow session members Barb Miller and Vonnie McLaughlin to bring a fieldstone to a Sunday morning church service. Being a farmer residing in these rolling river hills, rocks and stones have always been a part of farming in this place. Many years ago when the soil was tilled more intensely than today, stones needed to be picked and discarded regularly. I've become well acquainted with rocks and stones during my life.

Every year the spring plowing brought numerous rocks to the surface to be removed before planting. Fields were gleaned of these stones and if the soil needed harrowing one more time before the planters began their precise duty, many times more rocks appeared following this land leveling activity. It was as if they were being coaxed to the surface as creatures of the sea for a breath of air. Sooner or later the will of the farmer was broken as each realized, you will never remove them all.

50 years ago and beyond the most respected and admired farmers in this area were the ones that regularly picked and removed rocks from their fields. While I don't consider myself in the category of admired and respected, lets just say I've picked my share of stones and this necessary task had to by accomplished before the seed of the intended crop tasted the awaiting soil. My old neighbor, Dave Wissler Sr. always stated he never minded picking stones unless he was on behind with his work.

Today farming practices have changed dramatically. The soil is disturbed less and in some cases not at all as planters have been developed that handle this chore of placing seeds directly into the preceding harvested crop. Herbicides have been developed to suppress weeds and grasses that years past were another reason for the constant tilling of the soil.

I am presently one of only a handful of farmers now associated with Chestnut Level Church that in the past 50 years has relegated me from the vast majority to an endangered species. This I suppose is the reason for my invite to provide a fieldstone today.

Vonnie and Barb, both gifted teachers for decades in the Solanco School system had agreed to deliver the children's message in church, this first of many 300th anniversary celebrations for this congregation. Clothed in period garb these 2 gifted educators mesmerized the small children seated at their feet. Observed by me from a balcony seat in the back row of the choir, I could observe and scrutinize the facial expressions of this church's future. The children watched and listened intently, sat quietly and because of the way it was presented, seemed to understand all that was introduced to them. This was the 300-year history of this congregation and church displayed through pictures, words and deeds from our past. Our 2 teachers that captivated the children and the congregation beautifully crafted all this into a wonderful illustrative, descriptive story.

With nearly a foot of January snow covering fencerows where stones are dumped following their gleaning from cultivated fields I realized, the Saturday before church, I could have some difficulty with my sole, stone search. I remembered the barn bridge behind the barn that was held in place on either side by a wall of fieldstones. Luckily I found one that was partially loose that would serve the purpose. It was approximately 2 feet in length, 1 and ½ feet in width and weighing about 40 pounds.

I brushed most of the snow from this unassuming rock that would be part of the children's message Sunday morning. The snow stuck to the icy pores of the stone like plaster. I located a large bucket, filled it half-full of warm water, and gave this center piece to be, a warm Presbyterian baptism followed by a scrubbin' brush bath, removing all snow, dirt and mortar.

Working within a time limit the rock now needed to be dried. My wife was not at home during the resurgence, submergence and cleaning of the rock. I will admit to all of you secretly, the Maytag clothes dryer was briefly considered as an option for the drying process. I envisioned the sound made by the rock inside the rotating Maytag to be similar to Tom Smithson's rhythmic drums during an enthusiastic praise song at church. It was just a fleeting thought with the emphasis on fleeting so no need to repeat my thoughts to my spouse.

We have a small electric heater running most of the time in our kitchen during the winter, so following the placing of a few empty Musser's grocery bags in front of the heat, this local "Rock of Ages" migrated to our kitchen. As I placed the stone in front of the heater I realized one edge was flat enough that it actually stood upright by itself. One side was dried and then turned, to dry the other. It was almost as if it knew it was headed for stardom and an upcoming attraction in church. The following morning it was placed on a mat in the center of the communion table facing the congregation, where the children's message would take place.

The reason for the stone and the story was that the walls of this old church, built during the Revolutionary War, were made entirely of similar, larger, fieldstones. Lying dormant for centuries this simple fieldstone stood proudly in our church as a remembrance and symbol of our congregations 300th anniversary.

I can't help thinking how many of us lay dormant that if washed clean and encouraged could stand on our own and shine? It is possible, my friends, in every life. Perhaps the lyrics from a favorite gospel song from the past apply to this simple story: "I'm just an ol' chunk of coal, but I'm gonna' be a diamond someday." Happy 300th birthday to everyone associated with our humble, grateful congregation.

The Old Farmer

Echoes From The Present
A Fair to Remember

The Solanco Fair, that had its roots here at Chestnut Level, remains true to its initial purpose of being an agricultural fair. No Ferris wheel or rides will be found which probably is a good thing and in these times almost makes it unique. With the Amish and Mennonite folks gradually acquiring the available farms in the Solanco area and very few of them participating in this community activity I can't help but wonder the eventual fate of this AG celebration. I wish these plain sect folks would consider participating at the fair with their English neighbors as they do within the local volunteer fire companies.

So many of we English have left the farm during my lifetime, I realize this fair, as the State Farm Show in Harrisburg is no longer about the farmer but centers on the consumer. Perhaps this is the way it should be because they are the most important ingredients of that which is grown, harvested and sold down on the farm.

I have observed local, small children completely fascinated with farm animals they have seen close up and personal. To touch the silky smooth, hairy hide of a steer or dairy cow, pat the buzzed forehead of a sheep or to look directly into the eyes of a fully-grown pig from a stroller can never be replicated. As a child I recall being nose to nose with a resident pig and looking directly into its eyes wondering what it might be thinking and if this hog, while looking into my eyes was wondering the same thing about me. Sometime, if you have the opportunity get yourself into a position to closely observe the eyes of a child as this occurs. This always fascinates young children even more than a new toy on Christmas morning as it does the one who sees them. The difference between then and now is that fifty to sixty years ago most of us locally, grew up near or on a farm. I sometimes wonder what percentage of folks attending the fair today live on a farm? Change is inevitable for this locality and those of us who have been here for generations or have recently relocated to this rural area realize that it is not so rural anymore. I would hope all may adapt to our dwindling farm life and that the fair patrons don't feel pressured to adapt to non-AG community changes at our fair.

Several folks from our Church worked in the milkshake tent and also provided food at the tractor pulls Thursday night. Rain cancelled the tractor pull following a couple hours of activity which meant these adults and youth had to repack all the remaining food, return it to the refrigerators and counters in our new kitchen then transport it the next day back to the fair. This required a lot of extra work for those involved, including Ben and Donna Miller, Peggy Brown, Pat Hoffman, Dave Miller, members of our Church staff and several of our youth.

At one time I counted over 2-dozen Chestnut Level folks in the milkshake tent, all busy as bees as milkshakes flowed through a Presbyterian assembly line to awaiting customers. Bruce and Shelia Dunham always appear this time of year to attend the fair and help at the chicken and waffle supper at Chestnut Level Church. Bruce, the most enthusiastic milkshake maker of all time is remembered by everyone involved in this activity from teeny-boppers to those near eighty. A few claim even today they are still removing milkshake ingredients from arms, hair, neck and from behind ears. Denise McCardell deserves the credit for arranging and making this happen in an orderly fashion enjoyed by all involved.

Preparing for the chicken and waffle supper, Bruce lifts and lugs the heavy pots of cooked chicken, pours the hot broth through strainers into buckets and also lifts the cooked apples for making applesauce. We have become accustomed to both he and Shelia helping with this annual event. We appreciate and look forward to their appearance, help, singing and laughter that revitalizes all who participate in this annual, long standing, Chestnut Level event. For those working in the kitchen with Bruce and Shelia it just would not be the same without them. It warms the hearts of all to have Bruce continually returning home with his wife working and worshipping within the congregation where he was born. They also worked joyfully at the tractor pull food stand. While observing Bruce I am reminded that he remains just as enthused with life as with his faith. I suppose one mirrors and promotes the other.

The Old Farmer

PART SIX

PARADISE LOST

Thoughts and Musings

It is both satisfying and rewarding to observe a ring-neck pheasant almost daily in my yard, cautiously inspecting the many old outbuildings that encompass our home. The fact that it remains wary of the bird feeders outside our kitchen window and the seed beneath them reassures me that being extra cautious, similar to his long ago ancestors, may insure his survival from the nighttime predators that patrol this same area. I will be disappointed, but not surprised, if the view outside my window some morning, slightly above a raised cup of coffee, includes an assembly of colorful feathers. Having observed a variety of tie-dyed shades of orange in a pile of pheasant plumage in the past, I am well aware that a bird and its feathers don't always stick together. The instinct to avoid all predators-from a resident fox crouching in tall grass, licking his lips, to a late-for-work neighbor lady who chooses her life over his as they each simultaneously navigate asphalt-cannot be instilled in a pen-raised pheasant.

While writing at my kitchen table, the head of my Amish neighbor, with beard and straw hat attached, passes a window in my overhead garage door. The abrasive rattling of steel wheels coming up my farm driveway alerts me to his presence, causing my head to swivel, observing his. Moving to a larger window that provides a panoramic view reaffirms my first impression, that he is standing on a flatbed wagon pulled by 2 horses that also were invisible at first glance and now meander up the lane toward the tobacco shed. For a brief moment I entertained a wry smile, reassured that his body was still intact and attached to his whiskers.

Several blue jays in nearby trees behind the house evidently suffer from very low self-esteem, as their shrill screams seem only to warrant attention from one another and me. The finch, chickadees, cardinals and sparrows below them foraging for seeds on the ground evidently find no justification for their abrasive sounds and completely ignore them. I have on occasion observed this trait in a few of us when meeting a person who seemingly has done it all, knows it all and continually strives to remind the rest of us of our shortcomings. I've often wondered what they may have missed or been denied in childhood, that we take for granted, that causes this constant nurtured need as an adult for attention. Most folks as the birds on the ground eventually avoid and ignore this one who thinks so very highly of them self.

2 doves solemnly sunning themselves side by side halfway up an evergreen tree near the blue jay choir endure their tune much like 2 family members at a relative's funeral listening to an off-key soloist. These 2 mates avoid turning their heads but make disgusted, periodic eye contact with one another until the "singing of the blues" subsides.

The mature evergreens residing behind and in front of our old farmhouse as a windbreak are slowly separating from one another. Planted 40 years ago by former owners Clarence and Mary Murry, they have served their purpose well but daylight between them and the landscape behind them is enlarging every year. But procrastination, practiced many times throughout my life when referring to various personal and farming decisions, always follows thoughts of their imminent removal. "Maybe next year?" Although change is inevitable and sometimes unavoidable, it must be tempered and given a full measure of thought before removing a tree. There is no null and void or forgiveness button on a chain saw.

The recently installed satellite TV dish, camouflaged within the shrubbery in front of the farmhouse, seems out of place, if only in my mind. Encompassed by a 200-year old house and out buildings from the same era, this dishpan set upon by a mule, fastened to a stick will have to endure decades of ridicule before being completely accepted by all that surround it. I imagine the conversation between the smokehouse, the icehouse and the outhouse to be something along the lines of, "This ain't the first thing to come along that we'll outlive." They're probably right! The buildings, the board fences and the resident farmer have an attachment, a respect and appear similar to one another in that all are well weathered. The satellite dish not only provides a clear TV picture but also resurrects the likes of Gene Autry, Red Skelton, Jackie Gleason, Arthur Godfrey and numerous sporting events from 50 years ago. With rabbit ears, it was always snowing at most all sporting events I ever watched on my TV. I never understood how snow could fall during an entire game with no accumulation visible at its end! We now pay $30.00 a month to watch TV shows, TV personalities, and sports events from 50 years past that during that time were free. Around Liberty Square, we refer to this as progress.

With all that I have witnessed in a full life of living and what I've learned from parents, grandparents and ancestors, I can't help but wonder, have we made any progress in the area of getting along with one another? My grandparents went from horse and wagon to a man standing on the moon. My own life has been a witness to things thought to be merely science fiction to becoming a reality. As an old farmer, I've observed great strides and progress that has been accomplished in all fields, whether scientific or those of maturing corn by imaginative, intelligent men and women. Yet folks die everyday in the midst of conflict and strife. The resourceful human mind has been developed and trained to reach and strive for the betterment of mankind, yet the human spirit has evidently never abandoned the cave.

The scary fact is that our intellectual minds have developed to the point that it is actually possible to now destroy our entire world. I suppose this fact would be found under the heading of World Progress.

I'm not sure if the apparent steady decline of one's faith and religious beliefs is directly related to this calloused notion. Some would even conclude and concur that organized religion could be the cause of most world conflicts.

It would appear to me that there are many who assume that intelligence and success begets self-reliance. A prosperous man, an assemblage of successful folks and a nation considered a world power evidently have little need of faith beyond themselves. Faith and religious beliefs are apparently only for the poor, weak and those incapable of comprehensive, perceptive and resourceful thinking on any subject. I always assumed that to be a generous description of me.

Whether we wish to believe it or dismiss it, the Bible does provide the formula for getting along with your neighbor living down the street or the one residing on a sandy desert halfway around the world. Those of us who have personally witnessed the Nickle Mines Amish shooting and experienced the Amish forgiveness first hand have learned much that can be beneficial to others and ourselves. My mother always offered the following words of wisdom, "Any argument or contention among family members or folks in general can easily be diffused if one of the parties involved simply backs down." Sadly, being humble, as in the case of the Amish children at Nickel Mines, doesn't always resolve every conflict or desperate situation.

Please don't dismiss the ancient Holy Bible as a history of stories of times long past not related to or relevant within our lives and our present world without reading it. You may be amazed at the similarities we share with those from centuries past and the simple formula for leading an abundant life through all our difficulties and triumphs. You will not discover the chemical formula for building nuclear long-range missile warheads in the Bible, just the simple recipe for living an abundant God-fearing life. Don't pass through this temporary, brief time allotted to each of us and disregard it. Guard and extend your faith if you're fortunate enough to possess it. Consider acquiring and accepting a small dose if you've never tasted it.

This more than 60-year-old local story was told to me by classmate and friend, Denny Hess, concerning his father, Ed, and my old neighbor, Bob Burkins. Many years ago Ed Hess owned and operated a small spraying business, particularly spraying dairy barns for flies. Like many of his generation living in this area, Ed enjoyed rabbit hunting and good beagle dogs, as did my good friend Bob Burkins.

Bartering in those days was still in fashion, so Hess and Burkins struck the following deal: Ed would spray Bob's dairy barn in exchange for an expensive, well bred beagle pup. All went according to plan as Ed arrived to spray the deserted milking stable for flies. He asked Burkins about a large Guernsey bull in a back pen. Burkins replied, "That old bull's been through a lot in his life, a little fly spray won't phase him."

The exchange of spraying for a beagle pup occurred following Ed's work that day, with both parties well pleased and motivated by the fact that each acquired from the other exactly what he desired, all without the exchange of any currency.

Sometime later, Hess encountered Burkins in Quarryville and wished to reaffirm his job of killing flies. Burkins stated enthusiastically to Hess that he must have killed every fly from his farm to Liberty Square. "How's the old bull?" Hess asked proudly, "Oh, hell, Ed, he's dead too," Burkins replied. I'm told the deflated Ed then paid Bob in cash for his beagle pup. Perhaps from this old account of this local incident one can surmise why bartering, along with Bob Burkins, flies and Guernsey bull, is for the most part in this area now deceased.

When asked by someone how I'm doin' the optimist in me replies, "doin' great." Moments later the pessimist in me whispers in my ear, "your day ain't over."

Don't regret or dwell on the mistakes you have made during your life. It is these mistakes you've made that allow you to forgive and overlook the mistakes of others.

A thistle seed is transported by material similar to that of a dandelion. This gray, light, natural fluff floats across the landscape late summer resembling a tiny hot-air balloon. This rudderless ship is totally dependant on the whims and impulses of the breeze that carries it similar to some of us. This past summer at our early church service my eyes caught the late arrival of 2 thistle seed transporters, evidently a couple, entering together through a tilted, unscreened, stained glass window. Once inside the sanctuary they each went their separate ways. One slowly headed near the ceiling, then directly toward the pulpit. It hung unnoticed by all of the congregation and the sermon-speaking minister whose voice and exhaled breath may have provided the thrust to raise this seed heavenward while inspiring his faithful flock. Upon sermon's end, before the singing of the final hymn our tiny, thistle seed, space ship slowly dropped from its Presbyterian orbit and disappeared beneath a church pew.

The other seed, evidently a true Presbyterian, cautiously hung near the back of the church. As the congregation began singing "Amazing Grace" the jet stream inside the church changed dramatically causing this thistle seed transporter to move erratically to its maximum ceiling altitude. Suddenly, riding on "Amazing Grace," this tiny, fuzzy capsule found its way to the only window without an oscillating fan and floated unceremoniously out it.

I later wondered if either seed, the one trampled into the carpet, then probably removed by a vacuum cleaner, or the one outside perhaps still floating aimlessly will ever come in contact with soil and germinate. I'm reminded of a line from that particular, appropriate sermon on this day: A seed, as each of us, must first die in order to live again.

Anyone who enjoys and looks forward to goose hunting season has surely never owned a farm near Muddy Run Lake during that set—aside season for the war on web-footed Canadians. Friends are both gained and lost daily depending entirely on their granted permission to hunt my land. This does however allow a newfound perspective on true friendship.

An elderly relative speaking years ago of a male friend with a terminal illness and expected, yet prolonged, death. He just can't seem to be through with himself.

The late Jim Groff of Quarryville dealt in scrap metal when I was a boy. My friend, Bob Holzhauer, related he approached Groff when Bob was also a young lad over 50 years ago with Groff dirty, fully engaged and engrossed in his far from fancy or appealing career. When asked by young Holzhauer why Groff worked so hard at this discarded scrap metal business, Groff replied sternly, "Boy, you can't spend yourself rich." Many years later Jim Groff died a respected and supposedly wealthy man.

With several chestnut trees planted years ago locally by an old neighbor, Horace Long, falling or walking on these chestnut burrs in fall or early winter can prove painful. We refer to this as Liberty Square acupuncture.

My neighbor, Kip Adams, son of John participates in a unique hobby of building a carefully balanced pile of unworked rocks and river-hill stones, called an Inukshuk(in-ook-shook). They were originally symbols of survival built by the Inuit, a nomadic people of the frozen, unforgiving climate of northern Canada 3000 years ago. They were built to guide travelers, assist with hunts, warn of danger or indicate buried caches of food. Strong winds sometimes destroys Kip's stone balancing hobby, but most times they are visible across from the Adam's farmhouse, located along Silver Springs road near Furniss Road. Occasionally we give directions to our farm starting at; 272 south right onto Silver Springs then left at the Inukshuk!

As I'm slouched and halfway dozing in the passenger seat as Ruthie enters Good's, store a van loaded with plain, proper Amish ladies pulls into the space directly beside me. Upon the departure of these docile dames, the older driver immediately reaches under his seat and pulls out a copy of Playboy Magazine. He is so engrossed in this publication he never notices me as he turns the magazine that revolves sideways and upside down. Ruthie's return startles him as he simultaneously notices me seated beside him. The Playboy drops and disappears as the Amish taxi driver also slowly slouches out of sight. I suppose his location may have proceeded downward to where the rubber meets the road or perhaps in Amish terms, where the steel meets the stone.

Thoughts from the late Jack Shuman at age 84—I've learned more about life in this past year than I did in all my previous years when I knew it all. Age is only a number and my number is unlisted.

Thoughts from 90-year-old Suzi Farmer, a friend of the late Sally Gibson; A few years ago if there was something we didn't agree with family, church, school or any aspect of life in general we were told: "Go with the flo." Although we still have some difficulty accepting changes, the new phrase for it is: "Adjust we must."

Our local Willow Valley restaurant was one of the first in our immediate area to provide a smorgasbord breakfast many years ago. I visited an elderly lady from our church, who was obviously near the end of her life in a local retirement home. During the course of our conversation, I inquired about her life to which she replied—"I have few regrets but I would love to go to Willow Valley just one more time for breakfast." In Lancaster County, where most all religions flourish, over-eating may be life threatening but at this point in time it is not considered a sin.

Are you old enough to remember riding in or driving a car on 272 north, and when you entered the tunnel at Smithville your car radio went silent until you drove out the other end?

Most people at some point in their life realize they can never go home again. The few who never contemplate this are the ones who never left. In this fast-paced, ever changing world I suppose we should pity them both.

The senses of sight, sound and smell are in constant communication with the one who loves the land and works the farm. They encourage, sustain and reward every moment they are awake.

The total content of your accomplishments on any given day are directly proportionate to how well you slept the night before. Slumber begets success.

I've always thought that working in the fields on Sunday is like hunting on posted property. You can do it but not with any satisfaction or without feeling guilty.

Bob Kauffman—"My vacation is my vocation!"

Henry Huffnagle Sr.—"It is only a sin to swear if you're angry."

Seated beside Jay Chryst at a Lancaster Barnstormer's game one evening we were conversing and missed a great defensive play on the field. Jay, a businessman, who started the very successful "Jay Group", offered this comparison of the unseen catch to life. "There are people who make things happen, there are people who watch things happen and there are the rest of us who say what happened." Knowing the business history of Jay Chryst, I'm sure he will be remembered in the first of these 3 categories listed.

Jim Sperry—former President of Fulton Bank; "Most bad loans are made during good times."

I don't know enough to have an opinion concerning politics, although this reasoning hasn't deterred others from running for office.

Story related to me by a relative concerning an elderly acquaintance in June 2009. You may recall during this time an Air France plane went down in the Atlantic on a flight from South America to France with no survivors. This elderly lady, well into her 90s, unable to eat or drink, on morphine and supposedly close to death had been watching the TV coverage of this airplane crash. She mistakenly assumed her son was on this downed airliner and insisted he had died. Sometime later on this same day her son appeared by her beside. Thinking she had died and was in heaven, her immediate comment to her son was, "Am I here with you or are you here with me?"

This line was uttered to Thurston Hassler and his brothers involved in the local grocery store business (Ferguson and Hassler) by their father over 50 years ago; "You can't take it with you so put your money back in the business, where it belongs." A blue print for success.

Ever notice that shrub of a tree that is misshaped, looking out of place, residing at the edge of woodland filled with mighty oak, poplar and birch? Perhaps even residing in a briar infested fencerow that come mid-October is the most brilliant and colorful of all. Over shadowed and over looked for 50 weeks out of the year, it finally absorbs some praise and attention for those 2 short weeks of its otherwise drab life. This brief time of appreciation is evidently sufficient to encourage this wooded, small-limbed arbor to live another year. Never postpone giving someone praise or a compliment, especially one who rarely receives it.

Years ago many neighbors near our farm would periodically search our fields for arrowheads and Indian artifacts. They also have on occasion driven our fence jumpin' livestock from their well-manicured lawns. Times have changed and many who live beside us now comb our land for something they've also driven from their yards, Golf balls!

I was recently told this story by my favorite sister, who has come to the conclusion that if we are lucky we will die a dignified death still conscious of our life's interests. It seems Lane and Kenny attended a recent seminar held at Willow Valley's Palm Court sponsored by their financial advisor. She stated that although they are both collecting Social Security, at this particular function they felt as if they could have been the children of most who attended. During conversation at their table of 8 elderly folks, who appeared to all be well over 80, an elderly gentleman spoke of visiting a lifelong friend the previous day. His acquaintance, a patient at Hospice, was surrounded by his family and rapidly approaching the end of his life. A family member confided to the visiting friend that this was not a good day to visit. As the gentleman turned to walk away, the bedfast patient caught his friend's eye and uttered a few undistinguishable words and with his hand urged him to come forward. The visitor slowly approached his dear friend as the family parted, providing a path to his bedside. The dying man took his friend's hand, weakly pulled him close to his face and in a quiet, raspy voice whispered these words. "Did the Phillies win last night?"

An unbelievable family story remembered by all our family and our church family. My sister Lane and her daughter, Kim, were both diagnosed with breast cancer on the same day, month and year at the exact same time by 2 different doctors. Both have since emerged from this ordeal unscathed and are able to console and truly understand others who face a similar diagnosis.

While conversing with Dr. Tom Regan Jr., a friend and local Quarryville dentist, he mentioned that occasionally he runs late taking scheduled appointments of patients due to the unexpected complications of preceding patients. During his apology to the waiting folks, he claims that most stop him mid-sentence saying they're glad for those few moments to relax from their own hectic schedule.

This leads me to believe that many of us who run the never-ending rat race of life need to slow down. When we've reached the point in our hectic lives, much of it self-imposed, and during our daily routine we look forward to contemplating a root canal to interrupt these feverish activities, something is wrong. For the sake of our own well-being and sanity it becomes important to take a step back, take time to smell the roses, compliment someone who rarely receives one, speak to folks older than yourself, share and appreciate all that surrounds you every day. A rich rewarding life will not be measured in frequent flyer miles, what you've seen or where you've been, but in those lives you have touched, altered and improved.

I've always known for the first 65 years of my life, the doughnut would eventually cause me distress. With today's insurance my mental anguish, worry and financial ruin is now directly related to the invisible vacuum of the doughnut "hole."

Armageddon

As one who appreciates our local history and has contemplated and written of our past, I sometimes retain a vision of how Southern Lancaster County may change and appear by the end of this 21st century. The following lines are but an assessment and perhaps a forecast of these random thoughts to contemplate today and for any who will live at the end of this century and into the next to consider in this beloved land of my ancestors.

Today, this day in 2111 is the day my friends. The time has come that was envisioned by this one living here in 2011 when farming as I knew it in this fertile area would one day cease forever. As predicted a century earlier, cities and suburban sprawl have finally converged and locally cornered our last available open land located just south of The Buck. As Baltimore has expanded to the north, Philadelphia's encroachment continued unchecked to the west and suburban sprawl diagnosed yet unrestrained as a spreading cancer betwixt and between them have finally captured and acquired all remaining open land. The once smaller inland towns of Lancaster, York and Harrisburg have intertwined into one large metropolis ever expanding southward intersected only by crowded, crumbling highways and the stagnant Susquehanna River.

One hundred years ago agriculture was blamed and severely reprimanded as the principle cause of polluting this once aquatic source of life for the Indians and our early settlers. But as the farms slowly disappeared into houses, buildings, shopping centers and roads this once mighty waterway is now lifeless and slowly strangles the Chesapeake Bay. Recent floods in 2011 that washed raw sewage from these cities and towns were but a preview of things to come later. I'm thinking the Chesapeake Bay will one day be known as the storm sewer of the Susquehanna Valley. The realization that farms and farmers were not the reason a century ago for that rivers decline came too late. Through better environmental practices the farms actually later served as a buffer and improved water quality. But I'm sure at a later date, I will observe the photo of a dairy cow standing in a stream on a humid day with the caption reading: Farmers disregard saving the Chesapeake Bay.

This acquisition of land was accomplished using similar methods and tactics that the white man ascertained in exploiting the Indians. Threats, broken promises and force were used in conjunction with the most lethal and persuasive approach of all to eliminate, remove and relocate the farmer: excessive taxation. The confident, trusted laws of farmland preservation for agriculture, instigated by local Lancaster County farmer Amos Funk during the latter 20th century, have long since been broken, ignored and forgotten. Considered out-of-date and unenforceable, this once right to farm is no more recalled than prohibition.

Just as a golden spike was driven, securing the final rail at the completion of the transcontinental railroad, this symbolic green fiber glass one, thrust proudly and unwavering into the center of our last remaining, cultivated field will likewise penetrate the decaying hearts of every former farmer of this rich, fertile soil. The politicians, the developers and the suburban transplants all enthusiastically rejoice. They smile through congratulatory remarks at this celebration of the culmination and success of this 21st century quest.

Standing somewhere at the outer edge of this jubilant, festive circle is a farmer appearing old, gray and bent gazing across his now dormant fields one final time. There is no one engrossed in the merriment that knows, contemplates or even comprehends what he observes this day. None can appreciate or grasp his feeling of futility as this once independent, proud stranger to most, with calloused hands and shattered spirit turns away. He changes position to conceal embarrassed tears from sad eyes that no longer sparkle or dance. These streaks of salty moisture, coaxed by gravity down leathery cheeks are as drawn to mother earth as their humble source. They are shed on his fertile field and passing lifestyle. Soon, if not immediately, he will be forgotten.

A longing gaze toward the far corner of his fields end and the beginning of his former neighbor's land rekindles memories of 2 of similar age, thoughts and vocation. The long ago remaining and still visible, unfarmed strip of brush between their farms that served as their boundary was a witness and counsel to numerous, sweated-brow, fence-row conversations over the years. Although thoroughly appreciated and enjoyed at the time they now will remain absent forever and are already regretfully missed. Perhaps he hears the 19th century soft, peaceful, muffled sound of a horse-drawn-plow inserted and cautiously drawing a straight furrow, encasing and concealing the remnants of last years crop under this season's fresh, dark dirt. In the distance he may hear and visualize the purr or putt-putt of a 1950s tractor as it labors across this virgin soil resurrected by an ancestor from a forest to a farm.

To this old farmer it's more than a damn shame but a mortal sin to cover this rich, fertile, fragrant soil—once known as the Garden Spot of the world for being the most productive non-irrigated soil ever formed, ever farmed—with concrete and asphalt. Now this productive, food producing gift of God will only nurture, and grow to maturity roads, houses, buildings and places for recreation and amusement to entertain oneself. I suppose there may remain a few crowded open spaces to curb the presence and pressure of depression and subsequent insanity, a direct effect of surrounding one's spirit and soul with concrete and a sea of humanity.

At this occurring time in 2111 only ½ of our present work force are employed with the others receiving subsidies of entitlement. Unlike 100 years ago when food accounted for less than 10% of a worker's income it now requires 50% of an employee's wages. Some food is still grown in this country but most is imported and expensive.

Unlike the after-math of 9-11—close to a century ago—many countries do now possess weapons of mass destruction. We no longer serve as the world's policeman but concentrate on defending our borders and our own country. Those serving in the military that formerly served our nation stationed around the world now serve as police at home. Unrest and revolt, much of it caused by food shortages, is an everyday occurrence. More inhabitants of this world die today of starvation than in 2011. Available water for irrigation of crops, which greatly diminished decades ago, is now pumped from the oceans through miles of giant pipelines. The process of removing the salt from this water has allowed this to occur. This tremendous removal of ocean water has helped negate the rising of these waters from global warming.

Folks travel worldwide much less than 100 years ago due to economic, political and social unrest. Due to the food shortage and their decreasing numbers, farmers worldwide have been greatly elevated in importance and stature during the 21st century. This began when our national debt rose to unsustainable levels and Ag subsidies were eliminated. Retiring farmers were not replaced by the next generation of those illiterate to Ag ways and ingenuity and food prices rose dramatically. I've always believed Ag subsidies were created, not for the farmer, but for the consumer. Cheap food and a full belly diffuse many revolutions and revolts.

Cheap food also led to the obesity crisis that shortened the lives and depleted and suffocated the health care system at the beginning of the 21st century. Fortunately a pill was developed that curbs one's appetite for food and drugs that is mandatory for anyone over weight or addicted. The sale or growing of tobacco in this country is illegal and a federal offense. Due to the population explosion and most senior citizens living to the age of 100, families in this country are limited to 2 children.

Many of the services provided by the government and other agencies at the beginning of this past century that were taken for granted are no longer sustainable. Unfortunately, while taking control of our lives and regulating them to an extreme also financially, the government diminished dramatically. The power and funds or lack of them gradually returned to the individual states and local government. Following many decades of advanced communication technology a vast majority of English speaking citizens of this world are revitalizing an art form from decades past. It is referred to as conversations between one another and has really been catching on.

Unfortunately politics and the remnants of religion continue to divide us as many nations continue to possess nuclear warheads and regularly play the childish game of chicken between one another. Sadly many churches both old and new, large and small containing walls that once reverberated within the singing of joyous hymns, praise songs and the preaching of God's gospel by eloquent, inspiring ministers, now sit empty and crumbling. Remarkably, the symbolic observance of birth, marriage and death remains but God is rarely mentioned in any of these ceremonies. There remain small groups of religious believers in God who regularly meet publicly and privately unchallenged. But they are considered unorthodox by most at the beginning of this 22nd century similar to the Amish at the onset of the 21st.

As to exactly when or why religion in this nation diminished dramatically I cannot answer. It appeared as simply the slow progression and culmination of liberal thinking to the belief that we are completely in charge of our lives and destiny. Words mentioned in day-to-day conversation a century past like faith, prayer, charity, hope and genuine concern for our fellow man are now foreign to most. A century and a half ago in the 1960s, the young folks were referred to as hippies. These inhabitants from our ancient history were also referred to as the me generation. If alive today, they would be astounded and discouraged by what the me generation has progressed to and become. Although there is a remote resemblance today to those of Woodstock yesterday, these are the broken ones without jobs and hope that the government and those working provide for their humble existence and bare necessities of life.

Those considered radical 150 years ago protested with full bellies. It's difficult today—in 2111—to grumble and growl when the sound from your stomach dominates that from your mouth. Fighting and unrest, as in Bible times, continues in the Middle East. In 2011 words spoken of defending freedom and promoting democracy, the death of thousands of our soldiers, those of other nations including civilians and billions of dollars spent now in 2111, fall on deaf ears. Every one now realizes it was all about oil.

Religious holidays from the past are no longer celebrated. Stories of Jesus and Santa Claus are thought of in similar connotations. Although most everyone recalls hearing stories from the Bible of the world ending in flames most believe God plays no part in this eventual destruction. With the advances of technology most believe man will take care of this global holocaust very well without any intervention from an unseen and presently unknown God. Perhaps at this present time in our history in 2111 the final question to ponder: Will it be God or the absence of the belief and faith in God that leads to the total annihilation of this world? Perhaps it may be God and the resurgence and revival of faith in God that saves and spares this world and in the end, mankind.

Acknowledgements

1. The Entire Musser Family
2. Stu Mylin
3. Debbie Byers Wenger
4. Joetta Wolgemuth
5. Frank Reese
6. John Allen Hambleton
7. Merle & Millie Reedy
8. Shorty & Elizabeth Herr Family
9. Jim & Gordon Herr
10. Denny Hess
11. Dick McMinn
12. Bob Sturgill
13. Betsy Bonholtzer
14. Dick & Doris Lefever
15. Jack Stoner
16. Saralee Bradley Tollinger
17. Joe Sinclair
18. The Late Mart Eshleman
19. Robert Neuhauser
20. Verna Mae Murphy
21. Dick Rohrer
22. Harry Fulmer
23. John Adams
24. Julie Markley
25. Lorraine Hess Herr
26. Kurt Wagner
27. Ken Denlinger
28. Bill Russell

Edwards Brothers, Inc.
Thorofare, NJ USA
December 2, 2011